THEATER
IN THE
AMERICAS

A Series from
Southern
Illinois
University
Press
SCOTT
MAGELSSEN
Series Editor

Bertie Ferdman

Off Sites

Contemporary Performance beyond Site-Specific

Southern Illinois University Press / Carbondale

Southern Illinois University Press
www.siupress.com

Printed in the United States of America

21 20 19 18 4 3 2 1

Cover illustration: building used for Dominic Huber's *Casa / Prime Time*, as part of the festival Ciudades Paralelas (Parallel Cities) in Buenos Aires, 2010. *Courtesy of Lola Arias.*

Library of Congress Cataloging-in-Publication Data
Names: Ferdman, Bertie author.
Title: Off sites : contemporary performance beyond site-specific / Bertie Ferdman.
Description: Carbondale : Southern Illinois University Press, 2018. | Series: Theater in the Americas | Includes bibliographical references and index.
Identifiers: LCCN 2017050729 | ISBN 9780809334704 (paperback) | ISBN 9780809334711 (ebook)
Subjects: LCSH: Site-specific theater—United States. | Site-specific theater—Latin America. | BISAC: PERFORMING ARTS / Theater / History & Criticism. | PERFORMING ARTS / Theater / General.
Classification: LCC PN2081.S58 F47 2018 | DDC 792.02/2—dc23
LC record available at https://lccn.loc.gov/2017050729

Printed on recycled paper. ♻

Contents

Illustrations

Acknowledgments

I am grateful for all the artists who took the time to speak with me, read excerpts of the manuscript, exchanged emails, or allowed me to include images of their work. Thanks to Gülgün Kayim, Nicolás Goldberg, Erika Latta, David Levine, Marsha Ginsberg, Ant Hampton, Noémie Lafrance, Lola Arias, Gabriele Schafer, Nick Fracaro, Jeff Stark, Michael Rohd, Aaron Landsman, Karin Holmström, Mary Ellen Strom, Juliana Francis-Kelly, Anne Hamburger, Adam Soch, Jim Findlay, Christina Campanella, Okwui Okpokwasili, New York City Players, Gob Squad Arts Collective, LAPD, Henriëtte Brouwers, Dominic Huber, Margaret Morton, and Brian Rose.

This book has developed over the course of many years, and I am thankful for the feedback I have received from peer scholars through multiple ASTR Working Groups (Time, Sixties, Public Sphere), as well as IFTR's Architecture Working group, in particular, Andrew Filmer and Juliet Rufford for welcoming me and providing feedback on early versions of what eventually became chapter 4. I am especially grateful for the generous exchange with friends and colleagues who read portions of the manuscript and discussed particular chapters with me: Peter Eckersall, Jovana Stokic, Daphnie Sicre, and Jill Samuels.

Thank you to Frank Hentschker and the Martin E. Segal Theatre Center for providing a space to bring artists and hold public forums and symposia that featured many of the artists I discuss in this book. A special thank you to Mariellen Sanford, for her editorial prowess, guidance, and invaluable feedback. I am also indebted to Scott Magelssen, who saw the potential for a book in a meager twenty pages, and encouraged me to propose a book for this series. I am thankful for his continued generosity, encouragement, and feedback throughout the manuscript's various iterations.

Thank you as well to all my colleagues at Borough of Manhattan Community College (BMCC) for their support throughout the years. I was privileged to have received numerous PSC-CUNY grants and BMCC's Provost Funds to support my research, as well as a Faculty Publication Fellowship, which allowed a lighter load in order to be able to balance teaching with completion of the manuscript. I would also like to acknowledge Kristine Priddy, acquisitions editor at Southern Illinois University Press, who put together the manuscript, for her patience and dedication throughout this process as well as the anonymous peer reviewer who provided me with insightful ways to improve the clarity of the book.

Portions of chapter 1 appeared in HowlRound, and an earlier version of the essay appeared in *Theater* ("New Journey through Other Spaces: Contemporary Performance beyond Site-Specific," *Theater* 43, no. 2 [2013]: 5–25). I would like to thank *Theater*'s editor Tom Sellar for his editorial guidance and his support of my work and encouragement to develop the material into a book. Portions of chapter 4 appeared in *TDR* ("Sleeping Our Way to Consciousness: Jim Findlay's *Dream of the Red Chamber*," *TDR* 59, no. 2 [Summer 2015]: 151–57). Portions of chapter 5 appeared in an earlier version in *PAJ* ("Off the Grid: New York City Landmark Performance," *PAJ: Journal of Performance and Art* 37, no. 2 [May 2015]: 13–29); with thanks to Bonnie Marranca for commissioning the essay.

This book could not have been written without the unconditional love and support I have from my friends and family. A personal thank you to my mother, Debora Ferdman, who provided countless hours of childcare, love, and support, and a passion for the arts. Merci a mon partenaire quotidian et de la vie, Julien, pour ton indispensable encouragement, et amour, toujours, y por supuesto, a mis luces y adoradas Talia y Paloma.

Off Sites

1. Off Sites
A New Journey through Other Spaces

> It is only in a place and at a time where we do not expect anything to happen that something we will unquestionably believe in can happen.
>
> This is the reason the theatre, which has been completely sterilized and neutralized by centuries-old practices, is the least appropriate site for drama to be materialized.
>
> —Tadeusz Kantor, *A Journey through Other Spaces: Essays and Manifestos*, 1942–44

> I always go back to the hotel, in a way.
>
> —Sophie Calle, "How Suite It Is: Sophie Calle Makes an Artwork Out of a Hotel Room," 2011

Considering Site Specificity

A few years ago, in 2013, I attended *The Quiet Volume*, a performance that took place on the third floor of New York University's Elmer Holmes Bobst Library. Co-created by Ant Hampton and Tim Etchells, *The Quiet Volume* was part of Hampton's Autoteatro series. The series comprised performances that were *automatically* structured: they were "self-generating," triggered by a specific set of instructions given via personal audio equipment, printed text, or visual cues that indicated what to do or say and when to say it. There were no actors other than the participants themselves. These performances could take place pretty much anywhere: from a café to a street corner to a park bench to a deserted beach. For *The Quiet Volume*, these instructions had to be read, an action commonly associated with libraries.

Upon my arrival at Bobst I was paired with the only other audience member, a colleague who sat down next to me. The two facilitators gave us iPods with earbuds, cued to begin simultaneously. On the long table in front of us were three novels and a yellow notebook. Throughout *The Quiet Volume*, a comforting voice guided us through several instructions.

Among these, we were told to read passages from the novels in front of us, which included José Saramago's *Blindness*, Agota Kristof's *The Notebook*, *The Proof*, *The Third Lie* (the trilogy), and Kazuo Ishiguro's *When We Were Orphans*; to consider a setting for them; and to choose an image from Gabriele Basilico's photobook *Cityscapes*. At some moments, the voice was silent, substituted by sounds that theatricalized what we were reading: footsteps, a baby crying, people talking, a church bell. I was startled at one point by a woman, who I thought was speaking directly to me from my left side. I took my headphone off and turned around, only to realize it was the sound recording. At another point the voice asked us abruptly to stop reading and to remember the last word we had just read (mine was *disaster*). Then we were told to imagine that word on the blank notebook paper in front of us, point to it, and show it to our fellow audience member.

Using liveness—our live presence—as a vehicle through which to examine the act of reading, *The Quiet Volume* was more about the nature of theatre than about reading per se. Reading, like performance, is active and participatory, an experience of total immersion. As you read, you abandon yourself to the words, yet you are fully aware that you are reading. In a

The Quiet Volume, September 2010. *Photo taken at "Jacob-und-Wilhelm-Grimm-Zentrum / UB der HU Berlin" in the frame of Parallel Cities, curated by Lola Arias and Stefan Kaegi, coproduced by HAU. Courtesy of Ant Hampton.*

sense, you are fully in control. You are here and there simultaneously. You are present, yet absent at the same time, as the gentle voice reminds you. As I became the actor performing the tasks—reading, listening, turning the page, pointing a finger—the contemplative act of reading became live. I was both a passive spectator (enjoying the ride) and an active enabler (creating

The Quiet Volume, September 2010. *Photo taken at "Jacob-und-Wilhelm-Grimm-Zentrum / UB der HU Berlin" in the frame of Parallel Cities, curated by Lola Arias and Stefan Kaegi, coproduced by HAU. Courtesy of Ant Hampton.*

the ride). *The Quiet Volume* was an experience that mediated presentation (what is really there) with representation (what is imagined to be there): a sort of intimate and solitary experience taking place in public—where nothing happens, really, except in our own minds. Yes, the performance, which was produced by a theatre, took place inside a library, away from a theatrical building. And it clearly engaged with an act commonly associated with libraries, generally speaking. But what was most compelling was the negotiation between the various sites of presence: the real, the imaginary, the here and now, our memory. *The Quiet Volume* exemplifies a search for new theatre forms that can take place in a space that is easily transformable and not expensive to operate.

Over the past decade there has been a surge in the use of nontheatre spaces for performance: from empty garages and automobiles, to underground tunnels, cafes, lakes, empty pools, private apartments, boats, and abandoned warehouses—the list is practically endless. Some of the most memorable theatre performances I've experienced are those where I did not go to a theatre. Instead, I walked through Central Park and discovered the newly renovated public restrooms next to the fountain. Or I was led by a cowboy in a rickshaw through the streets of Fort Greene, Brooklyn, from a funeral parlor to a barely lit park in the freezing cold. In yet another performance I dined on wine and cheese at a fancy loft in Greenwich Village, and on a different night (part of the same performance), had beer and pretzels at a home in Bensonhurst, Brooklyn. As with *The Quiet Volume*, the creators behind many of these theatrical performances were trying to get away from conventional theatregoing in order to challenge its very confines. As Mike Pearson, founder of the British company Brith Gof, who has written on performance in nontraditional locations, describes this trend:

> Experimental theatre has always sought other venues. This is not solely for expediency but to challenge the notion that the auditorium is a neutral vessel of representation, and see it rather as the spatial machine of a dominant discourse which distances spectators from spectacle and literally "keeps them in their place" in the dark, sitting in rows, discouraging eye contact and interaction.[1]

Space, and, more specifically, space in theatre and its relationship to its audience, is at the core of this challenge to traditional theatregoing. More than half a century after director, painter, and avant-garde luminary Tadeusz Kantor proclaimed the most powerful theatrical spaces to be those outside the institutionalized theatre auditorium, performing artists have generated countless ways of appropriating, reimagining, recreating, staging, recontextualizing, and occupying found spaces, be they physical spaces or imagined, for performance and performance-based events.

"Site specific" is the common and generic term that by now lumps together such a diverse range of approaches—both experimental and traditional—that it has become overused, thus robbing the term "site-specific performance" of any meaning or use in categorizing a specific and important genre. "Site specific" has become usurped by mainstream marketing: a promotional catchword and trendy signifier for innovation and pseudo-alternative experiences that promise to jolt audiences, to shake them up, so to speak, in "new" or "found" spaces. I am critical of the way the term has become co-opted by neoliberal cultural economies, has become a cliché, and is unable to adequately speak to the diversity of practices that incorporate site and site-based practices. Some of the variations I have encountered by artists to describe their work—perhaps to avoid this conundrum—include, but are not limited to, immersive theatre, interactive theatre, live installation, ambulatory performance, promenade performance, itinerant performance, site-generic performance, urban space intervention, urban sound walk, smartphone play, environmental construction, simulated reality, and time-based public mixed-media event. The term *site specific*, at least in theatrical practice, has become meaningless due to the sheer amount and variety of work that identifies with it, which is perhaps the reason artists have begun to look for different names for it. Site specificity has become so common, so banal, that we no longer necessarily label it as such. And yet approaches to site-specific performance abound with endless possibilities for reinvigorating theatre and performance and pushing at disciplinary boundaries; it would be unfortunate to dismiss the form for being too vast. On the contrary, this amassment of new forms calls for a more open and diverse approach to site-specific and site-based practices.

Indeed, as Joanne Tompkins writes in her introduction to the collection of essays she coedited with Anna Birch, *Performing Site-Specific Theatre*, "The specific nature of this increasingly popular genre is not as easy to isolate as many other forms of performance for several reasons, the most significant being the propensity for the boundaries of both 'site' and 'performance' to slip."[2] Citing Nick Kaye, whose book *Site-Specific Art: Performance, Place, Documentation* is notable among the wealth of literature devoted to site-based practices in art,[3] Tompkins explains how "this slippage is inherent to the form: 'site-specificity arises precisely in uncertainties over the borders and limits of work and site.'" If these slippages, as Tompkins asserts, are a "central, significant trope of site-specific work,"[4] then they are also what give the form its potential to break boundaries, defy categorization, and give new meaning to what theatre is and can be.

External Shifts: Technology, Globalism, and Climate Change

My first encounter with the term *site specific* was as a student in the early 1990s, when Anne Hamburger, then creative producer of En Garde Arts, the New York City–based company she founded in 1985, came to speak to my theatre program at Yale. At the time, En Garde Arts was the American frontrunner in this kind of performance, producing plays whose meaning was reinforced through their staging at numerous unusual, suggestive locations, including the Chelsea Hotel, the then-abandoned Victory Theatre, the streets of the Meatpacking District, and in an abandoned car showroom. Hamburger spoke to us about the challenges of producing this kind of work and its merits in terms of accessibility and expanding theatre's audiences, which was, in retrospect, not unlike Joseph Papp's visionary dream for free Shakespeare in Central Park.

While location-driven issues and access are still factors in site-specific practices today (and producing in alternative locations remains a huge financial and logistical challenge), circumstances have changed since the heyday of En Garde Arts, making site-specific performance then and now markedly different. A first major shift concerns technology. Exponential advances have been made in artificial intelligence, digital media, and communication distribution. Sites today can be virtual and group events can take place remotely, resulting in major changes in the way artists conceptualize situation-based performances, interactions between spectators and performers, private experiences in public places, and even "presence" and "liveness" in general.

Technological advances have greatly shifted our perception of space and time, in ways artists decades ago could not have envisioned. Take, for example, Richard Schechner's famous interview with Allan Kaprow published in 1968 in *TDR*, titled "Extensions in Time and Space," where they discuss the notion of Happenings and Marshall McLuhan's ideas on information deluge. Kaprow states,

> Our space nowadays is no space. It used to be that space was those places that you couldn't get into, that were too far away. Now we can get anywhere. In the past we had a closed, relatively focused space. Today we feel a lot freer and we can celebrate extended space. I think this new feeling needs to be recognized by the traditional theatre, which still treats space in the old way. Why not move the locales of plays around, do each scene on location and have the audience follow?[5]

What is particularly striking is how, if taken out of context, Kaprow's declaration from fifty years ago could very well describe our "nowadays": *It used to be that space was those places that you couldn't get into, that were too far away.* While Kaprow may have been referring to advances in transportation that made travel easier (although not necessarily more financially accessible), and even referencing the possibility of space travel (the walk on the moon was less than a year away), someone declaring this today would most likely be referencing the technological advances that would define this "extended space" as virtual and/or digital. *Now we can get anywhere.* Today, we can be on a bus in Barcelona, while talking to our grandmother in Chile, while a surveillance camera films us in real time with the footage going to someone in Washington, DC. We are in three spaces at once. Whether *we feel a lot freer* or not as a result of this extended notion of space is relative. Given the myriad advances in technology, doing *each scene on location* and having *the audience follow*, as Kaprow suggested, might mean an actor performing (or a person simply *being*) from her living room projected live via camera to an audience of a hundred or more, except the audience is not actually present (together in one physical location) with the performer. Audiences already "follow" thousands of "scenes" promoted via Twitter and Instagram and Facebook on a daily basis.

A second major shift since the 1980s is the expansion of world trade and the advent of our neoliberal economy and cultural globalization. Neoliberal globalization, as the *Guardian*'s Gary Younge succinctly puts it, "allows (and promotes) capital to roam the world in search of labor that is cheap and regulations that are weak. Multinational companies and big businesses have more power than national governments."[6] The rise of income inequality and the disproportionate distribution of wealth across the world, where less than 1 percent of the population owns more than half of the world's riches, is just one effect of a widespread neoliberal ideology spread by globalization.[7] As corporations outsource their labor to countries where labor is cheaper, businesses set up shop all over the world, and retailers market their products worldwide, perceptions of physical space (or geographic location) and social activity have become more and more disjointed. In New York City, for example, to capitalize on the anxiety emerging from this disjointedness, the word "local" now has itself been primed as both a branding tool to attract consumers willing to spend more for what seems "unique" as well as a form of activating community engagement in neighborhood urban planning decisions. The spread of globalization in cities in particular has thus altered our sense and perception of what in fact *is* local, affecting how current artists approach site work in, say, distinct historical places versus generic urban landscapes like a subway station or a busy street corner. The growth of the international theatre festival circuit, which provides important financial livelihoods for artists, is also part of a larger system of global consumption that affects how live art travels and is consumed. Because it is more and more common for site-based performances to tour—seemingly a problematic even contradictory endeavor—artists are increasingly "localizing" content, integrating local factors (such as performers, geographic entities, and cultural references) into the fabric of the work. Simon Dove, co-curator of the Crossing the Line festival, commented on how "adopting a 'specific site' helps both the artists and the public to become much more aware of the way a context shapes the way we engage with or perceive a work of art."[8] Promoted by Dove as a challenge to globalization, contemporary theatrical site-specific practices have moved away from merely performing in "alternative locations" to "localizing" performance, providing audiences with a raised awareness of how their surroundings actually affect the way they live.

Neoliberal economies have also greatly shifted views of private and public space, in particular as spaces considered public increasingly reflect private-public partnerships in the interest of capital. There is an increased awareness of the privatization of public space, as well as an awareness of post-9/11 surveillance, which affect the perception of how "public" these spaces really are. Places like Central Park or the Meatpacking District, for example, are no longer neutral ground, as perhaps they might have been perceived decades ago, but now represent spaces that are regulated and managed and owned in various ways.

A third major development is in the growing awareness of pressing ecological issues such as climate change, threats against biodiversity, and the earth's diminishing supply of natural resources. While environmentalism was certainly a concern in the 1970s, in particular as a direct reaction to the energy crisis, the stakes are much higher now. Scientists predict that unless countries reduce their greenhouse-gas emissions and adopt cleaner energy systems, temperatures and sea levels will continue to rise, which will lead to a devastating ecological and humanitarian crisis. Over the last two decades, (despite the Trump administration's withdrawal in June 2017 from the Paris Agreement,[9] which will isolate the United States and weaken efforts to diminish global warming), the awareness of "sustainable" living practices and environmental consciousness has greatly increased. For site-based theatrical practices, this means that some artists resist large-scale productions not only because the cost of touring them would be too high, but also because it is not ecologically sustainable. "Big touring companies seem to be out of date," Stefan Kaegi points out in "Works Sited."[10] Some artists are implementing site-based practices that place an emphasis on sustainable production models, including fair labor practices, ethical funding strategies, and energy-saving resources. In addition, there is a growing and important movement in the Anthropocene toward ecocritical and indigenous perspectives in the arts that relates to land and place in relation to coexistence.[11] Some artists are thus increasingly concerned with political and social efficacy, as well as with process over product, producing experiences that engage a critical awareness, through context, of the immediate environment (be it physical, political, cultural, or economic).

The historical shifts in these three areas—technology, the global economy, and ecological crises—since the 1980s have greatly influenced how current theatre artists play with site-oriented approaches—blending disciplines, defying categorization, and creating work that in process determines its (new) form. These life-altering changes demand a new way of thinking about making art, including what has been generically referred to as site-specific performance. Contemporary approaches to site specificity now question theatrical form by blurring the traditional fictional-versus-real distinction of experience and suspension of disbelief; mapping new practices for audience/actor landscapes; fabricating sites from physically bound, conceptually constructed, or virtual spaces; staging live situations in real/nonreal and often mediated encounters; extending preconceived notions of time and space. The outdated theatrical engagement of the term will no longer suffice for its many contemporary variations. Instead, as Kantor himself insisted more than four decades ago, we need "to move beyond theatre in order to make good theatre" and thus integrate an interdisciplinary framework to accurately describe the interplay among different trajectories of site specificity prevalent in contemporary practice.

A Brief Genealogy (Part 1): A Visual Arts Trajectory

The term *site specific* originates in the visual arts and is grounded in minimalist art practices of the 1960s, in particular in its influence on sculpture and artists' desire to extend their work beyond a flat spatiality. Artists such as Donald Judd, Frank Stella, Beverly Pepper, Jo Baer, Dan Flavin, Mary Obering, Sol Lewitt, Eva Hesse, and Robert Morris reacted against the modernist tendencies of Abstract Expressionism to create art that centered on perception, the viewer in relation to the art object, and consequently often invoked three-dimensionality in spatial terms. Critical debates regarding minimalist art centered on the importance of the *encounter* (of the body) with the art object, which at the time tended to define the work more than the object itself. In *Art and Objecthood* (1968), Michael Fried famously critiqued minimalist art for precisely this reason, arguing how "the experience of literalist (minimal) art is of an object *in a situation*—one that, virtually by definition, includes the beholder," and therefore is not an autonomous work of art.[12] It was exactly what Fried predicted and abhorred, the intrusion of "theatre" into "art," that was at play in site-specific art practice from its earliest inception. In *Site-Specific Art*, Kaye asserts that the minimalist object, precisely because of its theatricality (in the Friedian sense), suggested "site" as a transitive as opposed to a fixed entity. Based on these debates in minimalism, in particular referring to art critic Douglas Crimp's argument tying the origins of site specificity to the "conditions of reception" in the minimalist object, Kaye proposes a site specificity linked "to the incursion of performance into visual art and architecture,"[13] where artists began to work with the *spectator's perception*, or awareness, as integral to the work.

In practice, "site specificity" initially referred to artwork creatively tailored for a specific location—the architecture or geography of the space, as with Land Art, otherwise known as Earthworks, most famously exemplified by Robert Smithson's *Spiral Jetty* (1970). Before the term site specific came into use, and concurrent with the advent of minimalist practices in the early 1960s, visual artists who were beginning to move toward live action performance also began to make the formal characteristics of place explicit in their work. Kaprow developed "Happenings" (which Michael Kirby would define as "the new theatre,"[14] a direct derivative of both theatre and visual arts) out of what he called "environments," which were the visual art answer to making a painting in space. Joan Jonas established the use of live performance in video and installation art. Equally important was

Carolee Schneemann, who radicalized painting with the use of her body in space, which she termed "kinetic painting."[15] In *Performance Art*, RoseLee Goldberg discusses at length how artists such as Yves Klein, Ken Dewey, and Claes Oldenburg, among others, constantly reimagined site contexts that were integral to their work.[16] Moira Roth and Rebecca Schneider have also written at length on feminist performance and the role women artists played in pushing the boundaries of performance art.[17] These early "liveness" experiments in visual art practice not only reflected the desire to break with the institutional spaces of art but also staged ways to intervene in real life.[18]

Eventually, the term caught up with practice in what became its heyday in the early 1980s. Then, in 1989, after a public hearing and an appeal, Richard Serra's site-specific sculpture *Tilted Arc* was moved from its original location in Federal Plaza in New York City, eight years after it was installed, due to complaints about obstructed passage.[19] By this time, public art commissions were on the rise as cities competed in the world market. The rise in commissions urged artists to include the public in the process, sometimes engaging the community and making local cultural interventions, as with Suzanne Lacy's new genre public art.[20] During this period, the artist Robert Irwin published *Being and Circumstance* (1985) "to help sort out some of the confusion of ambitions and practices," as he put it, "in terms of how we generally process (recognize, understand)" variations of site practice, in particular in public art commissions. He delineated four categories: "site dominant," which is work that itself creates a site, as a monument does; "site adjusted," work that changes, or adjusts, to where it is; "site specific," a work created for a specific site; "site conditioned/determined," where the *idea* or *concept* of a work is site specific, but can eventually be moved, transported.[21]

"Site-specificity used to imply something grounded," writes art historian Miwon Kwon, referring to this time period. The way Kwon describes site specificity is in sync, in general terms, with the way Irwin maps out its parameters and the site-specific theatre of the same era: site was an actual, physical, geographic location, a tangible reality (as opposed to the virtual, conceptual, discursive, situational, and/or interactive space it would later become) that, as Irwin phrases it, "sets the parameters and is, in part, the reason for" the work. In her chapter on the genealogy of site specificity, Kwon traces how the term, which originally highlighted the physical space out of a need to rebuke the boundaries of the conventional gallery space (which also meant resisting forces of a capitalist market economy), eventually moved away from "something grounded" when artists began to use space in other ways than just physically; to something transient, when artists began to question the very uses of that space—socially, economically and politically.[22]

Site specificity in visual art practice thus began to change, characterized primarily by impermanence, quite akin to what performance scholars might refer to as ephemerality or, more plainly, liveness. Interestingly, Kwon stays away from any (overt) theatrical terminology or influence, nor does she consider what Kaye asserts is the incursion of performance in site-specific art's very ontology (from its inception), despite the fact that, as Shannon Jackson points out, "terms like 'context-specific' and especially 'audience-specific,'" when used to describe visual art experiments, are "reproducing and perhaps reinventing theatrical art traditions."[23] As site-specific experiments in the visual arts moved to welcome conditions of transience, to use Kwon's term, in particular as a move against the commodification of art,[24] site specificity in theatre also began to embrace context-driven situations that questioned, rather than affirmed, site. These histories, though parallel, were removed from one another.

A Brief Genealogy (Part 2): A Short History of Site-Specific Performance

Although the term "site specific" originated in the visual arts, aspects of site-specific *theatre* have been around for a long time, preceding its terminology. Long before modernism, theatre directors experimented with using real sites ("rooms destroyed by war, abandoned railway stations," as Kantor would write)[25] to stage pre-existing texts as well as devise new performances. In the twentieth century, Salzburg Festival founder Max Reinhardt's "localization" of *Merchant of Venice*, described in a *Time* review dated 1934, placed Shakespeare's play in an actual street in Venice (stemming from a search for an extreme realist setting for the drama as called for by Victor Hugo in his 1827 treatise[26]). Marvin Carlson explains how in the twentieth century, artists have more consciously experimented with "pursuing theatrical activity in non-theatrical spaces," citing such open air spectacles such as Evreinov's 1920 recreation of the storming of the Winter Palace on the actual site of that 1917 event.[27] Kantor also staged performances in nontheatre spaces to dissociate theatre from its high-art affiliations.[28] Becoming disenfranchised by the avant-garde's increasing institutionalization, in 1955 Kantor and a group of visual artists formed a new theatre, Cricot 2, calling for a "real place" to make theatre happen, "a 'poor' place that was on the margin of the life's practice."[29] David Wiles has argued in *A Short History of Western Performance Space* that Kantor is one of the most prominent voices from within the theatrical spectrum to speak to and continuously vouch for site specificity (without using that terminology) in staging drama.[30] A decade later, in the United States, there emerged a number of well-known street-theatre companies with explicit political agendas, including the Bread and Puppet Theater, the San Francisco Mime Troupe, and El Teatro Campesino, all of whom performed outdoors, on location. However their work was not always necessarily site-specific.

Political street theatre, environmental theatre, invisible theatre, ambulatory theatre, Happenings, the early twentieth-century avant-garde, and popular festive traditions such as parades, carnivals, and processions are only some of the myriad theatrical influences on site-specific practices. Influenced by Allan Kaprow's Happenings and Jerzy Grotowski's productions,[31] Richard Schechner introduced the term "environmental theatre" into the critical performance lexicon in the 1960s and 1970s as a way to designate stages that broke realism's "fourth wall," getting out of a proscenium stage format by placing spectators inside the action to interact with performers.[32] The Living Theatre's *Paradise Now* (1968) and The Performance Group's *Dionysus in '69* (1968) epitomized the use of audience engagement in environmental theatre practice, where participation was meant to incite spectators to move toward political action, inviting audiences to join the performers out of the theatre and into the streets. Schechner's writings on environmental theatre challenged aesthetic form and sought precisely to change the theatre-going experience so that the actor's playing space was not necessarily separate from the spectator's viewing space. It drew from the aesthetics of earlier avant-garde practitioners as well as on more popular festive traditions where the boundaries between actor and spectator and between art and life were tested.[33] In addition, Robert Wilson's *Ka Mountain* in 1972 at the Shiraz Art Festival, Ariane Mnouchkine's work with the *Théâtre du Soleil*, as well as the early theatrical experiments of Peter Brook, in particular his journey to Africa in the early 1970s with his theatre troupe, his stage adaptation of Farid Uddi Attar's *Conference of the Birds* in 1979, and his ten-hour staging of the Indian epic *The Mahabharata* in Avignon in 1985, although later problematized for their cultural appropriation, were also highly influential in the search to question theatrical space, make theatre "accessible," and redefine location-based theatre.[34]

Around the mid-1980s, certain theatre groups, among them Brith Gof in Wales and En Garde Arts in New York City, both of whom devised performances for abandoned or derelict spaces as a way to transform otherwise forgotten locales, began to use "site specific" to describe their own particular performance practices and their relationship to the local environment,[35] whereas before, the term "environmental theatre" was more common. Initially, as Mike Pearson of Brith Gof describes in his book *Site-Specific Performance* (2010), site specificity referred to a particular mode of working where performance was generated "for special locations and occasions" and was "inseparable from its site," similar to visual artworks like *Tilted Arc* that were categorized as site specific. The practice now concerned itself not just with the physical attributes of a given location (its visible architecture) but also with the history, cultural identities, and the social relationships present on site.[36]

There are a number of notable examples from the early 1990s. En Garde Arts' *Another Person Is a Foreign Country* (1991), written by Charles Mee and directed by Anne Bogart, was set in the abandoned courtyard of the Towers Nursing Home in New York City, where widespread patient abuse was said to have taken place. It incorporated historical elements not only in the performance text but also in its casting.[37] Meredith Monk's *American Archeology* (1994), a large-scale, two-part piece that took place on Roosevelt Island also used the island's history to inform the performance's content, its casting, and the audience's journey through the island's architectures.[38] According to Jennifer Dunning, the performance had forty extras, including children, office workers, and senior citizens, as well as doctors from Bird S. Coler Hospital and Goldwater Memorial Hospital, both of which were located on the island at the time (Goldwater closed in 2013).[39]

"If site-specific performance of the 1980s and 1990s was concerned with taking audiences to locations to which access was under usual circumstances restricted," explains Pearson in describing how his own approaches changed, "more recent practices have rendered familiar places unfamiliar, or taken unfamiliar locations to the audience."[40] In this sense, the expansion of site-specific practices in theatre has embraced its roots in the visual arts as situation-based and context-driven. As Fiona Wilkie, who has written extensively on site-based practices and mobility, articulates regarding this development, "A shift in form can be noted from performance that *inhabits* a place to performance that *moves through* spaces; from a concern with the political and cultural meanings of particular locations to a focus on broader questions of what *site* as a category might mean."[41]

In addition, many contemporary site-based theatre artists emphasize civic engagement and community participation as a main concern in their practice. "In the contemporary theater and performance worlds," explains Michael Rohd, founding artistic director of Sojourn Theatre, "there is more and more site-based work that is driven by an interest in experience and participation."[42] Rohd's work with Sojourn includes *How to End Poverty in 90 Minutes* (2015), a participatory theatre event that engaged audiences with community experts to help decide, over the course of the performance's ninety-minute duration, how to spend a thousand dollars in cash from ticket sales;[43] and *On the Table* (2009–10), a "site-based journey show" that was staged in "a church, an elk barn, buses, and a riverside parking lot," with two audiences in two cities in Oregon—Portland and Molalla. Rohd detailed how the relationship between "site" and social practice evolved for *On the Table*:

> We want to create a performance-based event where we are building the space for encounters between urban and rural community members. . . . We have to find a way to bring them together in a site that is actually neither of theirs, but a new site. And what is that site? What does it signify? What does it allow to happen?[44]

As with its trajectory in the visual arts, Rohd's search for a "new site," moves away from site as a fixed geographical or physical location—and sees it, instead, as a set of dramaturgical questions and choices that relate to how they are choosing *to site* the piece.

Another notable example of this shift from site as a geographical location to a more context-driven approach was Peruvian theatre collective Yuyachkani's resurrection of the protagonist, Alfonso Cánepa, from their one-man show *Adiós Ayacucho*, two decades later on the steps of Lima's Government Palace. Originally written and performed in 1990, the play begins with Cánepa, an indigenous farmer depicted as a comical and greater-than-life character, explaining to the audience how he has been murdered, mutilated, and left to rot by Peru's military regime. In the play, Cánepa decides to travel to Lima to search for his remains and, more symbolically, his dignity. He reads from a letter he plans to take to the president to denounce these war crimes. Yuyachkani wrote the piece to denounce Peru's "Dirty War," which left more than thirty thousand dead and eighty thousand people displaced in Peru from 1980 until 2000. As theatre scholar Francine A'ness explains, "The vast majority of the victims were not only from the mountainous region of Ayacucho but were either indigenous (and Quechua- or Aymara-speaking) or poor peasants

Act 1 “Molalla in a Barn on an Elk Ranch” from *On the Table*, 2010. *Sojourn Theatre. Courtesy of Michael Rohd.*

Act 1 “Portland in an Old Church” from *On the Table*, 2010. *Sojourn Theatre. Courtesy of Michael Rohd.*

of mix-raced descent."[45] In June of 2002, at the Government Palace in Lima where crowds had gathered to witness the beginning of Peru's Truth and Reconciliation Commission, the actor Augusto Casafranca resurrected Cánepa. As A'ness describes, "Casafranca climbed up onto the palace steps and, speaking into a microphone as Cánepa, began to recite the letter that, within the context of the play *Adiós Ayacucho*, he had intended for a previous president of Peru."[46] The letter details not only his plight but also symbolically represents the plight of thousands of massacred Peruvians who demand to be remembered:

> Dear President: I, Alfonso Cánepa, the undersigned, citizen of Peru, domiciled in Quinua, occupation farmer, directs himself to you, the highest political representative of the Republic, to express the following: On the 15th of July I was arrested by the civil guard of my village. Placed incommunicado, I was tortured, burned, mutilated, and killed. I was declared disappeared. . . . As you well know, all national and international laws, as well as special declarations for Human Rights, recognize not only the inalienable human right to life, but to a dignified death with complete and proper burial. The most fundamental respect for human life presupposes a more basic obligation and one that exists as part of the military code of honor of any war: the dead, sir, are not to be mutilated. A corpse is the minimum entity in death; to dismember and scatter its parts, as occurs today in Peru, is a violation of natural and social laws. The country's anthropologists and intellectuals have determined that violence originates in the System and the State that you represent. I tell you this as one of your victims, one who has nothing to lose, and I speak from personal experience. I want my bones, I want my body, complete and whole, even in death. In the end, I doubt that you will ever read this.[47]

By resurrecting a fictional character who asks for justice and reparations on the very steps where Peru's Truth and Reconciliation Commission takes place, Yuyachkani's performance shifts the emphasis of site from a geographical location to its sociopolitical and historical context, resurrecting the ideals of Cánepa to bear on this stage.

Moving *beyond* Site-Specific

Many of the practices involved in contemporary site-based performance have in fact moved away from a concern with location to a concern with interaction and mediating situations *through* sites, what performance scholars

Cathy Turner and Stephen Hodge aptly characterize as a "movement *between* situation and displacement, ground and groundlessness,"[48] and art critic Claire Doherty calls "situated practices,"[49] (coincidentally reminiscent of Hans-Thies Lehmann's notion of the postdramatic as "in fact a theatre of *situation*").[50] Similarly, Kwon identifies a transformation in site specificity from a "physical location (grounded, fixed, actual)—to a discursive vector (ungrounded, fluid, virtual),"[51] suggesting a "relational specificity" whereby artworks straddle "a terrain between mobilization and specificity."[52]

By contextualizing site-specific practice within both visual art and performing arts discourses, we begin to see how the term "site specific" has evolved from indicating an experimental staging practice to an engaged situational event, across the arts. Of course, as Shannon Jackson points out, how we measure such advances depends on the medium-specific angle we use to engage with the work.[53] (Going to see Marina Abramović's *The Artist Is Present* in a theatre auditorium, for instance, would generate a different expectation and therefore a different experience of the piece than seeing it in a museum context.) Given the cross-disciplinary legacy of site-specific performance, theatre and visual art scholars apply different critical criteria to their interpretations of works categorized as site specific. In his article on the group Skewed Visions, for example, Branislav Jakovljevic quotes Nick Kaye's notion of site specificity as transforming "the very site it seeks to expose." Jakovljevic adds that although "this may be the case with many site-specific artworks and performances," it is different in theatre: "When it comes to theatre staged in found or readymade environments, this transformation often works the other way around, and the specificity and concreteness of the site translates into an excess of naturalism within theatrical performance."[54] As Jackson has often pointed out, what might be innovative for visual artists might be a *been there done that* thing for theatre people. I'm attempting to bridge these conversations and engage with site specificity in contemporary performance practice as a marriage between both visual art and theatre discourses, positioning theatre, as Kantor professed, in the domain of ART (capitalized here as he wrote it).[55]

In *The Quiet Volume*, "site specific" appears nowhere in the marketing materials, nor do the artists use the term to describe the work. However, it is evident that it takes place at a specific location that is determined by the content of the piece. It is participatory, immersive, solitary, eventful, stationary, and mobile all at once. *The Quiet Volume* was commissioned as part of *Ciudades Paralelas*, an itinerant festival curated by Stefan Kaegi of Rimini Protokoll and Argentine director Lola Arias. They invited artists to create works for a city's functional spaces—a shopping mall, a factory, a library, a hotel, a train station, etc.—examples of what French anthropologist Marc Augé has famously called "non-places."[56] The city is the setting for these installations, which theatricalize everyday spaces for the urban dweller. *The Quiet Volume* was thus created with a specific type of site in mind, and has since toured internationally. As Arias explains,

> The pieces were genuinely portable, in the sense that the only thing we would be transporting were concepts. The concept for each piece would be fully developed, and each piece would be restaged in the context of each city with different performers, different spaces, and so on. The only person traveling was the artist and his or her idea, recontextualized at every site.[57]

Both Etchells and Hampton are artists who have individually engaged with creating live art in alternative theatrical locations and public spaces in the past, but what has become most prominent in their work, along with the work of numerous other performing artists devising theatre today, are the approaches they have developed to establish new modes of performance that move *beyond* the "site specific," but which nevertheless incorporate (cross-disciplinary) strategies that are related *to* site. *The Quiet Volume* existed in the very form (theatre) that it simultaneously sought to deconstruct, and this is a tension that runs throughout many of the performances I write about in this book. On the one hand, I observe in these artists a desire to move away from the theatre building/black box/theatre auditorium/gallery space for various reasons (political, aesthetic, financial), and thus a need to find new forms that accommodate their work. On the other, there is simultaneously a desire to move away from theatre as a medium, and the first step is to find a new space that is not associated with theatre. The question then becomes: Do new forms of theatre generate new spaces? Or, conversely, do new spaces generate new forms of theatre? The performances in this book demonstrate how contemporary approaches to site specificity address both simultaneously.

For some examples of projects that exemplify this move *beyond* the limitations of what might otherwise be categorized as "site specific," let us go back, as Sophie Calle would say, to the hotel.

Hotel #1

In January 2003, the InterCityHotel in Hamburg is the site of Gob Squad's *Room Service (Help Me Make It through the Night)*. Lasting from ten o'clock in the evening until four o'clock in the morning, this durational performance, billed as such by the Berlin-based performance collective, invites the audience to lie down on beanbags and sleeping bags in the hotel's lobby to watch, via live steaming video feed, four performers "try to be themselves" in their individual identical hotel rooms: "None of them can sleep, instead they kill time in cold baths or by finding comfort in the solace of the hotel mini bar. Each is being watched by a surveillance camera, sharing their moments of fear and boredom as they sit out a long and sleepless night."[58] As the night progresses and their boredom peaks, the performers try to connect with the audience through phone calls, in some cases inviting them to their private rooms (while everyone watches) "in a plea to remain with them and help them make it through the night."[59] Spectators are therefore free to choose their own level of participation: they can continue to watch comfortably from their beanbags, or leave, go get a drink, come back, perhaps answer a phone call, or even visit with one of the performers. As with many of Gob Squad's performances, the actor-audience divide continuously shifts, with the audience sometimes guiding the action. Each performance depends greatly on the level of interaction the audience generates—the focal

Video still of *Room Service (Help Me Make It through the Night). Gob Squad Arts Collective.*

point here being the fabricated yet "in the moment" situations tailored so specifically by Gob Squad for the present audience. The "specific" nature of the event is on multiple levels, more than just the hotel location site.

Hotel #2

In January 2003, while Gob Squad's *Room Service* played at a hotel in Hamburg, playwright-director Richard Maxwell's company New York City Players premiered *Showcase* in Manhattan's New York Hilton Hotel and Towers, Room 2705. *Showcase* is a play written to be performed in any hotel room. The main character is Jim (played by Jim Fletcher), a lonely businessman who prepares to attend an important conference. He is surprised to find his own shadow there with him and debates with his shadow self in an attempt to reconcile his struggles with the world beyond the hotel walls. A limited number of audience members witness this Jim character for each performance—as many as can fit on the other queen-size bed opposite his. As we enter the room, we wait in the dark. Nobody dares move a muscle. Suddenly Jim, a naked man who gets up from under the covers, turns on the light, and begins a conversation with his shadow. The event is fully scripted and fictional, except of course for the bodies barely two feet away and the audible murmurs and chatter of the real businesspeople who walk the hotel's hallways.

Jim Fletcher in Richard Maxwell's *Showcase. New York City Players.*

Hotel #3

Room Service and *Showcase* are theatrical events staged in fully operational hotels, but Dominic Huber's *Hotel Savoy* (2010) led spectators one at a time into a fabricated and surreal interactive hotel experience. Each participant is the (seemingly) sole guest of this once-occupied and apparently haunted building. Presented in the "unseen spaces of 1014 5th Avenue" in New York City, where I saw it, "visitors . . . encounter past employees: an elevator operator, a young maid, the hotel barber, the concierge, and a barmaid."[60] Entering the space was overwhelming. I was led from a small and dark lobby to a grand staircase entrance where an elevator operator accompanied me to "my room" and then left me there to handle this particularly tiny space with a broken television. Before I could decide whether or not to take the exit (after sneaking a peak at the slippers carefully placed under the bed), the phone rang and a voice instructed me to open the door. Soon the hotel maid arrived, confessing a personal story about escape and resentment. Throughout my stay in the hotel, I met a series of rather incongruous characters on my ambulatory journey, including a teenage Harajuku-style Japanese girl who played cards and made me tea. In the kitchen I saw various actual newspaper clippings, including one of a man who leapt to his death from the very window I happened to be looking out. Part art installation and part immersive theatre experience, *Hotel Savoy*

Dominic Huber's *Hotel Savoy. Photo by Paula Reissig.*

combined the building's environmental features with some of its historical events to create an off-kilter world, an alternative time/space dimension where nothing is quite what it seems.

Hotel #4

At the 2012 Singapore Arts Festival, audiences witnessed yet another hotel-inspired production. *Hotel Maids*, at the Ibis Singapore Novena hotel, was Lola Arias's contribution to Ciudades Paralelas (Parallel Cities), the itinerant festival of urban space interventions that also featured *The Quiet Volume*. For *Hotel Maids*, Arias created an installation inside a hotel, using

Lola Arias's *Hotel Maids*, Buenos Aires, 2010. *Photo by Mikko Gaestel. Courtesy of Lola Arias.*

five rooms, each displaying the inner life of one of the room-service personnel who clean it. For each hotel, Arias created a local installation, working with the actual staff responsible for cleaning the rooms the audience visited. Spectators are led in one at a time every ten minutes (the exhibit is open for eight hours at a stretch). Once inside they are free to discover the work at their own pace, moving from room to room, as in a gallery space. As the Ciudades Paralelas website describes it, "Each visitor adopts the role of a chambermaid responsible for five rooms per hour. But instead of cleaning, the audience spends the hour walking through the five rooms, where they discover portraits of the cleaning staff: films, original voice recordings and photographs that bring to light something of the invisible spirits who clean up after others."[61] Arias's project occupied real space with the otherwise ignored labor that enabled it. It was a dramaturgy of site, where the site was neither fabricated (as in *Hotel Savoy*) nor manipulated (as in *Room Service*) nor displayed (as in *Showcase*).

Clearly, *Room Service*, *Showcase*, *Hotel Savoy*, and *Hotel Maids* have little in common, other than the fact that they all take place inside a hotel. The landscapes, approaches, logistics, and artistic influences of these "hotels" are each very different, making this locational similarity all but irrelevant. Instead of generic hotels we get tailor-made experiences, with varying degrees of interactivity and participation, at specially manipulated sites. The performances seem to highlight the "nonplace" of these hotel sites, which are both intimate and impersonal. These four hotel performance projects, taken together, exemplify the range of strategies through which "site-specific" art practices have infiltrated contemporary performance practice.

Going "Off" Site

The "site" of a performance today is not only its location but also its construction (the way it has been redesigned and repurposed), its historical legacies, its temporal framework, and its unintended destinations (in terms of audience engagement and intervention). To respond to the increasing volume and variety of site-based performance practices, this book explores recent tendencies to address a new generation of artists whose work testifies to a growing practice actively engaged with site and challenging the disciplinary frameworks conventionally used to delimit "site." Rather than thinking about "site specific" as a genre of performance, or a subset of practices that can be easily compartmentalized, I'd like to think about it as "an idea where the arts merge,"[62] as Turner and Hodge suggest, themselves following in Kwon's footsteps, who approached the term "site specific" as a "problem-idea."[63] How are artists and performances engaging with site? What sites do contemporary theatre practices engender? How does live performance negotiate such sites?

"Off site" is the terminology I use to think about such strategies—those that may take place outside traditional theatre buildings, but that more importantly engage with the experience of space, place, and/or situation as an integral component to the very fabric, structure, and content of the work. The term "off site" is a common phrase to characterize something that is happening in a location that is other than the location from which it originates: "I'm going to complete the job off site," or "I'm working off site today." It signals a connection between spaces, in this case perhaps the office (on site) and wherever "off site" may be (home, another office, even the beach, depending on the task). "Off site" thus acknowledges the inherent contradictory essence of working *off site*: rather than *on* and therefore *with* the site, a performance can *belong* to a site while simultaneously working in reaction to it or against it. And off site is different from site specific: an off-site is not so much about the specific space where it *is*, as much as it is about where and when it *is not*.

The term suggests both a relationship with and an independence from a site. The engagement is as much about dis-locating (the time and space it is removed from) as it is about context (where and when something/someone is presented or represented). The term also references a frustration or fatigue with the site ("I am *off* it," as in "done with it"), as well as utilizes the term's literal meaning ("it takes place *off site*," indicating that it is somewhere *else*, not *here* but *there*). I think of the experiences of immigrants (like my own family) and the millions of refugees for whom identity is completely linked to this on/off conundrum, always in relation to both where they are and where they are not. "Site" is therefore never a whole. It is always incomplete. It is off-kilter. It is *off*. This "off-sited-ness" is carried everywhere; it is imagined; it is real; it is embodied It is often invoked but not necessarily materially present. *Off site* is both the term I use to denote a space of site specificity in performance but more importantly, it is also the approach I take to analyzing and discussing the specific other-than-physical "locations" of performance. "Off sites" are thus the spaces *off* of the site where performance exists.

I use the word "contemporary" not necessarily to categorize performance of the twenty-first century per se, but to identify projects and practices that deal with the contemporary moment in which they were made/

created/produced—in this book, since the 1980s primarily. I see the "contemporary" as a term that is itself defined by its historical antecedents, in particular as artists attempt to break away from aesthetic forms and disciplinary norms and forge new, unprecedented ones. It is art that grapples with the questions of its time and place, what art historian and critic Terry Smith describes as art "shaped most profoundly by its situation within contemporaneity."[64] Smith distinguishes between the standard use of the word—"it's hip, go-with-the-flow connotations, its default recognition of whatever is happening, up-to-date, simultaneous, or contemporaneous"—and the "depths of meaning contained within the concept itself: *contempus* came into use, and remains in use, because it points to a multiplicity of relationships between being and time."[65] Because we are living in a moment when adventure-oriented, thrill-seeking site-specific installations, urban soundwalks, immersive environments, and participatory experiences have become the hype, I find Smith's distinctions pertinent.

While a handful of studies consider the wide array of methodologies used in the creation of this kind of work, and provide valuable theoretical contributions to how we might begin to understand the notion of "space" and "site" in performance,[66] the emphasis for the most part has been on European artists, with particular emphasis on the United Kingdom.[67] And while there is a significant amount of literature on site-specific performance practices from visual arts perspectives,[68] there is relatively little on the intersections between disciplinary legacies.[69] In this book I focus on the Americas, mostly the United States, and primarily New York City where I am based, with some case studies from Argentina. I look particularly at contemporary companies and artists experimenting with new forms of site-driven work, with the exception of chapter 5, where my emphasis is on a historiographical approach to considering urban site specificity. Given the nature of touring and the international festival circuit, the categories are not so neat anymore, in the sense that artists nowadays disseminate their projects globally and in fact create them to relocate, and the artists are themselves quite mobile. Lola Arias (the Argentina-based artist whose work I discuss in chapter 3) created Parallel Cities (the festival I discussed earlier) with Stefan Kaegi (the German founder of Rimini Protokoll). Faivovich & Goldberg (an art duo, also Argentina-based) developed their concept for *El Chaco en Kassel* (discussed in chapter 3) specifically with Kassel, Germany, in mind. In other words, although my focus is on artists based mostly in the Americas, they are part of an international set of influences and histories. It is important to keep these issues in mind, as travel is a significant component to art making today—especially in terms of the dislocation of artists' own sitedness and their increasingly global and collaborative production and touring practices. The interest in socially engaged projects and the shift toward participatory and durational events in both performance and visual arts has affected not only what artists make but how they make it. The process of production—including in that process community engagement, placemaking, audience participation, interactive technologies—is becoming an important part of the conversation in American theatre institutions as well as around contemporary curating in performance departments in museums and galleries.

The "off sites" I address throughout my chapters constitute spaces of interdisciplinary discourse—*disciplinary sites*; spaces of audience engagement—*spectator sites*; spaces of time travel—*temporal sites*; and historiographical spaces of urban mapping—*urban sites*. In the chapters that follow, I will thus move beyond the "site-specific" to these various "off sites," to identify and examine work that pushes at disciplinary boundaries (chapter 2), actively engages with the audience/spectator relationship (chapter 3), radicalizes notions of temporality (chapter 4), and re-contextualizes the urban landscape (chapter 5). While this book identifies and expands on these four *off* sites, there are many more yet to be covered and *dis*covered, in particular in relation to how new technologies—including cyberspace, robotics, virtual reality, drones, and artificial intelligence, to name a few—generate "off sites" in performance.

Many artists are constantly toying with disciplinary boundaries and definitions by "infiltrating" the spaces of "other" art forms, and playing with such labels. In chapter 2, "Situating Theatre," I address how artists are using site to move across institutionalized art spaces. I highlight the work of David Levine, whose pieces demonstrate a contemporary kind of site specificity wherein context, interaction, and viewing circumstances in relation to disciplinary legacies, rather than location per se, are more pertinent to the work. In chapter 3, "Artistic Intervention and the Unintended Audience," I discuss the possibility of various modes of audience engagement at unintended destinations, primarily through the work of Lola Arias and Faivovich & Goldberg. These works generated new relations among otherwise disconnected audiences. They allow for spaces of alternative spectator sites, what I call an off-site spectatorship, to inform the on-site work. In yet another extension of the bounds of site specificity, theatre artists use "site" as a context. The site of an artwork need not be material; it can perhaps be located in the virtual, temporal, or imagined engagement of the event. In chapter 4, "Moving Site, Moving Time," I address the creation of temporal sites, where the manipulation of space conjures what I term an "off time," a nonlinear temporality. The performances I detail in this chapter displace us not only actually (in the physical sense of relocation) but also temporally—the artwork and its spectator participants travel imaginatively through multiple time periods, while physically moving through the here and now. Chapter 5, "Landmark Performance," tackles the performance of the city itself, in particular within the blitz of gentrification and the increasing privatization of public space. Given the historical contexts of such productions, the performances I highlight map urban change. Their site specificity is implicated in the very "trans" of the urban environment—the moving across, beyond, and through—that they purportedly want to save. They are entrenched in the changes in their respective neighborhoods, bringing to the foreground issues around art and gentrification, performance and the city, in ways the artists themselves might not have conceived. In retrospect, they are *landmark* because they left their own traces in sites that either no longer exist or that have changed so much that they are barely recognizable.

Returning to Kantor's epigraph, it is notable that he anticipated the ways theatre artists today continue to look toward a future art practice that will challenge rather than conform to any discipline-bound definition of site and its multiple historical legacies. If theatre, as Kantor professed, was a place for seeing, then site and consequently these *off*-sites, continue to be a source of inspiration for expanding theatre's possibilities infinitely beyond the auditorium, and way beyond physical location.

2. Disciplinary Sites
Situating Theatre

I'm convinced that half your experience of spectacle is determined by institutional conventions of spectatorship. The only way to generate a fresh experience is to short-circuit those conventions. That short-circuiting matters even more than the actual piece you are presenting.

—David Levine, Paul David Young's *NewARTtheatre: Evolutions of the Performance Aesthetic*, 2014.

What if, for instance, the formal parameters of the form include the audience relation, casting such inter-subjective exchange, not as the extraneous context that surrounds it, but as the material of performance itself?

—Shannon Jackson, *Social Works: Performing Art, Supporting Publics*, 2011

The Search for Theatre

On a blistering summer morning in June 2015, I headed out to Central Park's north entrance at 110th Street to see David Levine's *Private Moment*. The artist took scenes from eight movies and restaged them in the exact locations where they were originally filmed. Live actors in costumes comparable to those in the films enacted, in continuous loops, iconic scenes from Woody Allen's *Bullets over Broadway* (1994), Wes Anderson's *Royal Tenenbaums* (2001), John Guare's *Six Degrees of Separation* (1993), Roger Kumble's *Cruel Intentions* (1999), William Goldman's *Marathon Man* (1976), Peter Berneis and Paul Osborn's *Portrait of Jennie* (1948), Neil Simon's *Out-of-Towners* (1970), and William Greaves's *Symbiopsychotaxiplasm: Take One* (1968). *Private Moment* was part of a larger free public exhibit called *Drifting in Daylight* that was presented by both Creative Time and the Central Park Conservancy to celebrate the thirty-fifth anniversary of the conservancy and simultaneously highlight the organization's work in the park's restoration.

As I entered the park, a Creative Time docent suggested I begin my *Private Moment* at the French garden in the Conservatory, since the actors there were in period costume and it would be "difficult to miss them." The *Marathon Man* scene, on the other hand, would be "less spectacular" and "hard to see," since it was a real marathon athlete running in loops dressed like Dustin Hoffmann's character from the movie. "You might mistake him for a real runner," he confessed. I took the brochure he offered, which featured sketches of each scene I would encounter, and complied with his directive (after all, why risk confusing art and life?). As I made my way to the garden where the scene from *Bullets over Broadway* was being enacted, I begrudgingly became part of a large crowd, an organized tour of *Drifting in Daylight*, and together we waited for the characters of David and Helen to appear in the circular path. The tour guides knew the timing of the actors' entrance into the garden. Mickey Solis (playing David) and Caroline Hewitt (playing Helen) appeared out of nowhere as dozens of audience members surrounded and followed them à la *Sleep No More* (the off-Broadway hit from the British company Punchdrunk), hovering a short breathing distance from the performers. The audience clapped as the actors exited the garden.

Attempting to get past the organized art tour crowds (one of them led by Anne Pasternak, then president and artistic director of Creative Time), I walked briskly through the park to *The Royal Tenenbaums* at the pool's north pathway. I loved the movie and was excited for this reenactment, especially since I knew I would recognize the scene. When I arrived I immediately saw a discrete yet visible Creative Time checkpoint with the exhibit's logo. A volunteer told me the actors would be coming around soon. So I waited, noticing other "real life" in the park in the meantime: a runner with his dog, a child running after a balloon, the waterfall. As actors Henry Packer and Nancy Ellen Shore appeared from afar in front of me, I immediately remembered Angelica Houston and Gene Hackman's portrayal of Royal and Etheline. I followed these new performers (who resembled the film actors as much as the roles they originated), this time by myself. As they reenacted the scene I eavesdropped on their conversation. I felt like I had somehow infiltrated a fiction amid my very real surroundings, reminiscent of the way Cecilia breaks the fourth wall in Woody Allen's *Purple Rose of Cairo*, except here it was the other way around—the movie had come to me. At the end of one loop, they broke character. They needed a bathroom break. "You noticed us," Shore commented, as if surprised that I could tell them apart from other "real" couples strolling in the park.

Content to have witnessed at least one film reenactment by myself, I decided to take the subway to catch more scenes at the southernmost end of the park, which was quite a few miles away. *Cruel Intentions* seemed to be the closest to the Fifty-Ninth Street eastern entrance, right at the foot of The Pond, so I decided on that one. Once I got out of the subway, I walked past the medley of tourists, sunbathing New Yorkers, and manure-trailing horse-drawn carriages, searching for what was by now the familiar Creative Time checkpoint, which I never found.[1] I had not seen the movie *Cruel Intentions*, which I now know is an iconic American teen flic from 1999. Other than the brochure's rough sketch of the characters and one red dot on the Google map image on my phone (which incidentally was running out of power) showing the location of the scene, I had no idea what exactly to look out for. I must have walked around . . . and around . . . for about an hour, paying close attention to everything and staring unnecessarily at everyone. I climbed a rock, crossed a bridge, and passed by the same lawn so many times back and forth that I became self-conscious and thought people might instead be staring at me. Frankly *any* of the hundreds of scenes unfolding live in front of me—aka *life* as it was being *lived*—would have been just as exciting to sit and watch.

Why was I still searching for "theatre"?

This question illustrates my frustration with the current cultural landscape. For the sake of pseudo-innovation, productive marketing strategies, institutional affiliations, and thrill-seeking audiences, artists and cultural producers are going out of their way to situate theatre in alternative locations that are literally hard to find. It also reveals my tireless conviction that artists will continue to take me to new places where in fact theatre can be situated. Indeed, this is a contradiction. Before I delve back into the *Cruel Intentions* scenario . . . a brief intermission.

The Art of Resituating

In *Social Works*, Shannon Jackson explains how "medium-specificity structures the perceptual apparatuses of different viewers who might disagree about what in fact they are seeing."[2] By "medium-specificity," Jackson is referring to the reference points and vocabularies people use to discuss "what traditions of interdisciplinary art works remain blind to us due to our own artistic itineraries."[3] She writes,

> If, for instance, we understand a relational art work to be a revision of sculpture, we encounter it differently than if we understand it to be a

revision of theatre or dance. Some may not understand the work to be a revision of anything. The inclusion of an artists' body in a gallery is formally innovative to some viewers; to others, it is just bad acting. To some, the dispersal of an art practice is an intriguing "de-materialization"; to others it is an assembly of blocked site lines. To some, a durational experiment is tediously slow; to others it is a meditation on the nature of human endurance.[4]

I remember feeling completely stunned at the end of Frances Stark's *Put a Song in Your Thing* (2011) at Abrons Art Center, a performance commissioned for the proscenium stage for the 2011 Performa biennial,[5] when the audience—mostly fans of Stark's work—gave an enthusiastic standing ovation for what I and my colleagues (all performing arts people) thought was one of the worst shows we had ever seen: self-indulgent, grand ideas that did not coalesce, poor sense of timing, overly long passages . . . and the criticisms went on. Kameron Steele, the show's director, explained to me that whereas for him the rehearsals were meant to repeat and "tighten" the flow and rhythm of the work to ensure dramaturgical soundness, for others in the team they were an opportunity for a conversation about ideas, a chance to talk about doing rather than an actual doing. He never saw Stark rehearse any of the monologues she was to deliver onstage because she wanted it to remain "authentic." How could they program lights, or sound, or base the timing of any of the tech around something that had not been rehearsed? What for him was the threat of sloppiness, for Stark was part of the work's integrity. In other words, the performance succeeded depending upon what disciplinary conventions you brought to the table.

In 2007 I sat on a New York Foundation of the Arts (NYFA) cross-disciplinary panel that awarded fifteen fellowships to artists. The panel's category had previously been called "multidisciplinary" and previous to that in 1986 was called "conceptual" with awardees including artists Mierle Laderman Ukeles (known for "maintenance" performances[6]) and Theodora Skipitares (known for her puppet and object theatre[7]). I was the only panelist who came from a performing arts background. Although some of the other panelists (all of whom were previous NYFA awardees) had incorporated performance and theatrical elements into their work, Clifford Owens among them, none considered their work to *be* theatre or to be directly related to it. However, many of the artists who applied under this cross-disciplinary rubric did identify as performing artists: ensembles of collectively devised work, puppeteers, directors, set designers, dancers, etc. The only other viable categories related to the performing arts were "playwriting/scriptwriting" and "choreography." So unless you were writing scripts or choreographing dance, you would apply to the performance category.

During the panel's week of deliberations, I saw the work of numerous acclaimed performing artists whose body of work I believed would get them to a final round, at the very least. Instead, I was amazed to find that what I found virtuosic "as theatre" (since that is what they were making), the other panelists did not find groundbreaking at all. No matter how innovative the use or combination of theatrical elements, as long as the end product was, in fact, "a show," the work in their eyes was not worthy of moving to the next round. This began a heated series of debates about what criteria and disciplinary frameworks we should use to judge the work. As long as theatre itself, as a medium, was not overtly questioned by the artwork, the artist would unlikely be selected. For the other panelists the work had to innovate as visual art, even if it was not situated within that framework. It became very clear then, as Jackson would eventually come to write years later, that "one critic's sense of groundbreaking innovation [was] another critic's Emperor's New Clothes."[8] Given the panelists' diverse disciplinary backgrounds, we could not agree on what work was most compelling. Why, we asked ourselves, had all performance projects been clumped together under one category when the pieces in question clearly came from (and spoke to) very different genealogies and discourses, which themselves valued a different set of skills, concepts, and craft?[9]

The work of David Levine, it turns out, spoke to all the panelists in the room, and he was one of the award recipients that year. Here was an artist equally invested in both theatre practice (rehearsing with actors, using scripts, collaborating with playwrights and dramaturgs, as well as designers) and visual art histories (of performance art, endurance art, body art, land art, happenings, and conceptual art), whose work troubled the criteria by which we judged it. Levine's work simultaneously embraced the blatant theatricality so abhorred by many art enthusiasts, what art critic Claire Bishop refers to as "a visible excess of staging and a particularly queasy relationship to mimesis,"[10] as well as the conceptually abstract tactics often dismissed by theatre makers.

His performances prior to *Private Moment*, including *Habit* (2011), *Bauerntheater* (2007), and *Actors at Work* (2006), all of which I was familiar with before attending the Central Park piece, exemplified Jackson's intersections of discourse. *Private Moment* asked the same question as Jackson, quoted earlier: "What if, for instance, the formal parameters of the form include the audience relation, casting such inter-subjective exchange, not as the extraneous context that surrounds it, but as the material of performance itself?" It questioned notions of authenticity and presentation rooted in both visual art and theatre, thus engaging with different disciplinary legacies to create a new space for theatre. Acutely aware of how "disciplinary divides are determined not by the artist's technique but by the presentational frame,"[11] Levine very consciously employed this cross-disciplinarity precisely by *situating* such tensions as the very premise—or *site*—of the work ("not as the extraneous context that surrounds it, but as the material of performance itself"). The site of theatre, more than merely an alternative physical location, was here rooted in disciplinary expectations and fields of knowledge. The piece was concerned to do away with the conventions of theatre-going and how we *perceive* theatre—almost like tricking us into thinking we are actually *not* watching what we are watching—so that it could become something else. Levine's form of site specificity, in *Private Moment* and much of his other work, is a very deliberate attempt to interweave and therefore question disciplinary histories that define, separate, and categorize theatre versus art histories. This conscious *situating* of theatre is a new form of site specificity, where the site is the disciplinary legacy and discourse in which, or in relation to which, the artist locates the work. More than an attempt to *situate* theatre "as" art, Levine's work challenges perceptions of why audiences, artists, scholars, and critics alike define work the way we do. It is a playful encounter with preconceptions, labels, and marketing ploys. After all, what better way to stage a concept than by theatricalizing it, without, god forbid, making a show?

Back to the Search

Almost at the point of giving up, I somehow caught a glimpse from afar of two performers who resembled the sketch from the Creative Time brochure. I recognized the wicker picnic basket, light-blue blanket, fruits, including papaya and particularly its seeds, and a large black straw hat. No one seemed to be watching these two actresses (Xandra Clark playing Cecile and Camara McLaughlin playing Kathryn) perform in the middle of the meadow. I discretely walked over to sit next to them—not so close that they would know I was watching them; I didn't want to disturb them, or worse, have them "perform" for me. I pretended I was a "regular" person at the park who happened to sit there, as opposed to . . . well, a *spectator*. Thankful for my sunglasses, I sat down and leaned back, far enough so it would look like I was basking in the sun and observing the pond yet bent over enough so I could eavesdrop on the scene. I asked myself whether there were other people around who were also pretending not to watch. Was I the only one trying desperately to blend in, acting as if I was not doing what I was doing? Was I the only spectator *performing* not watching?

With the meadow as its setting, the scene replicated the scene from the movie, word for word and gesture for gesture, complete with a champagne toast and French kissing, *the* French kissing, which I would later learn was the most memorable part of the movie, the one everyone talked about—"the kiss bad girl Sarah Michelle Gellar shared with shy Selma Blair was one of the first lesbian liplocks [some] had ever seen."[12] I must have watched it about ten times, nonstop. The two performers never broke character. As I got up to leave, they continued the scene, on an endless loop. I looked around to see if others knew it was a staged, albeit very real, kiss, repeated over and over and over again.

As I left the reenactment of *Cruel Intentions*, all I could think of—besides, admittedly, the cliché *what a real experience!*—was how committed these performers were to kissing, for real. They were hard at work. The durational component of endlessly repeating the action *in public*—a public that was probably 99 percent clueless and maybe 1 percent on the lookout—had forced me to see their performance as anything *but* staged. In an interview with Robert Ayers, right before the March 2010 premiere of her well-known six-hundred-hour performance *The Artist Is Present*, Marina Abramović delineates the difference between performance art and theatre:

> Theatre is fake: there is a black box, you pay for a ticket, and you sit in the dark and see somebody playing somebody else's life. The knife is not real, the blood is not real, and the emotions are not real. Performance is just the opposite: the knife is real, the blood is real, and the emotions are real. It's a very different concept. It's about true reality.[13]

One of Levine's concerns as an artist is this disciplinary ("medium-specific" to use Jackson's terminology) binary between authenticity (what is real) and representation (what is staged). Or to use Marina's metaphor: between real blood and fake blood. "My endless problem with visual arts performance," explains Levine, "is that it cleaves to this idea of authenticity that every other aspect of contemporary art got over twenty-five fucking years ago. And because it cleaves to this idea of authenticity, it refuses to engage in convincing or unproblematic fictions or in virtuosic technique."[14] In *Private Moment*, and the *Cruel Intentions* vignette in particular, the actors were not

Cruel Intentions, part of David Levine's *Private Moment*, Central Park, June 2015. *Presented by Creative Time and Central Park Conservancy in the frame of* Drifting in Daylight. *Photos by David Levine.*

only engaging with durational performance but were doing so virtuosically, as only trained performers could, paradoxically in the present moment yet "for the *nth* time," as Richard Schechner has written regarding restored behavior,[15] short-circuiting Michael Kirby's famous distinction between matrixed acting (traditional dramatic convention, playing a character) and nonmatrixed performance (carrying out a task, such as kissing, in a determined context).[16]

In his essay "Bad Art and Objecthood," Levine, who opens with an epigraph by Chris Burden from 1973 ("It seems that bad art is theatre. . . . Getting shot is for real. . . . There's no element of pretense or make-believe in it"), focuses on why it mattered whether Burden "*actually* got shot."[17] After all, couldn't Burden have faked us all out? The answer to this question has everything to do with the histories that define (and separate) disciplinary categories of art and theatre, binaries that are completely fluid as performance—the live, the ephemeral, the transcendent, the immaterial—continue to join the two conversations. One could say Levine's obsession with Burden, more than a simple tug of war between what is more authentic—getting shot for real or doing a good job of pretending to get shot—is an ardent obsession with deconstructing the apparatus that itself labels an activity as "authentic" or "inauthentic" and values it accordingly. Levine's fascination with "the institutional conventions of spectatorship" becomes his brand of site specificity: dependent upon the interdisciplinary legacy of the frame. Although some scenes from *Private Moment* might be difficult to find unless one stumbles upon them and recognizes them in relation to the original (as evidenced by my experience of searching for *Cruel Intentions*), Levine does not hide the fact that this is theatre, in its most conventional form. On the contrary, he uses the script, costumes, props, and gestures that are meant to replicate the film scene, as closely as possible to the original. Depending upon your encounter with the work—going to Central Park especially to see it as I did, or stumbling across a scene reenacted from a movie you recognize, or simply seeing a person running—*theatre* exists in varying degrees, in a continuous spectrum that ranges from "very theatre" to "no theatre at all."

By situating theatre as a thing, an object, a ready-made, we become aware of its dependence upon its conditions of reception, what art critic Douglas Crimp referred to as site specificity in minimalist art practice.[18] The binaries—fake blood/real blood—are over. What matters is how such *acts, events* (be they theatre, performance art, live art—however you name it) are framed, labeled, marketed. Essentially, how are they situated? In what ways does this intentional "situating" constitute a more nuanced, hybrid, and contemporary form of talking about (or attributing) site specificity? I am interested in how artists and cultural institutions situate work discursively amid the increasing crossover pollination of performance, and how this situating: (1) changes the way the work circulates and its reception (2) describes a form of discursive site specificity that lies *in motion* amongst disciplines, as opposed to a borrowing of one from another; and (3) creates a form of ambiguity about how that work should be received, since there is no medium specificity we can (specifically) rely on. The question is not, what is the site of theatre, nor what *are* the sites of theatre; but instead: How are artists, curators, cultural producers, etc. *siting theatre*? How can we "locate" theatre, as a field of practice, an institutional affiliation, *and* a discourse, site specifically?

Citing Theatre

Private Moment not only *sites* theatre, it also *cites* theatre. It very deliberately takes its title from the method acting exercise developed by Lee Strasberg, in which an actor performs a private activity in public. Influenced by Stanislavsky's concept of being "private in public" and his "emotional memory" actor training that directs actors to identify deeply with their characters so as to disappear into the role, Strasberg devised the "private moment" exercise to help performers transcend the difficulty of revealing "real feelings" in front of an audience.[19] "The actor must be willing to create that kind of separation from the pressure of the public," wrote Strasberg,[20] fully aware of the contradictory condition of being in a real situation while simultaneously knowing full well one is on a stage.[21] The looping in Levine's setup, coupled with the strict maintenance of the fourth wall (the actors never acknowledge noticing the spectators), allowed me to view the characters' private moment—the actors' reenactment of fictional scenes—as completely artificial, even though they were *really* kissing, *really* drinking (perhaps not actual champagne but still drinking), and *really* repeating those lines on a continuous loop for six hours a day. Others, for whom the frame of theatre did not exist at all in relation to the *Private Moment* scenes, did not even question the reality of what they were seeing—whether they were actually watching or just noticing. The performers were enduring performance, quite literally. I could see the actors working at make-believe; I could simultaneously see the characters they were enacting. In this sense, *Private Moment* was an allusion not only to Stanislavsky and method acting techniques but also to the Brechtian dialectic of acting and not acting at the same time, exposing the theatrical apparatus of representation for what it is, except in this case, unlike Brechtian actors who might address the audience, the fourth wall remained intact.

But *Private Moment* also falls neatly within the trajectory of performance art. In an article titled "An Actual Subversion," Levine discusses how certain pieces greatly influenced his thinking about "actors, performance and spectatorship."[22] In particular, Levine discusses

> Vito Acconci's *Following Piece*, in which the artist followed people on the streets of New York until they entered private space; Lynn Hershman Leeson's *Roberta Breitmore*, in which Leeson created, registered, and lived out a whole new identity in San Francisco; Tehching Hsieh's *Outdoor Piece*, in which the artist refused to go indoors for an entire year; and Adrian Piper's *The Mythic Being*, in which Piper disguised herself as a man and inserted this new persona into the streets of New York and Cambridge.[23]

The common thread in all these works, and what is key for Levine, is that they were purposely unremarked as a performance as they were being performed. "Each piece could have gone on forever," writes Levine, "a node of tactical insincerity operating in society unannounced,"[24] akin perhaps to Augusto Boal's Invisible Theatre, whose means might be similar but whose ends were entirely different. These performances were hiding in plain sight. What makes these works stand out was that they shifted the context of art *to* life. And yet, as Levine points out, the artists simultaneously *framed* this lived situation as art: both as it was occurring, if only from the perspective of the artist, and after the fact in the subsequent documentation for audiences and the art market. These works highlighted the conditions under which art was perceived, shaping the very sites of art. "Try to imagine what Hsieh's year-long *Outdoor Piece* would look like if sponsored by Creative Time," Levine challenges the reader. Phony, ridiculous, preposterous. It would have defeated its whole purpose. There is an insincere paradox here, since in order to circulate as art these "authentic" actions—which went unannounced in the everyday—not only had to be documented but also had to exist (and persist) within an institutional and critical framework *eventually*.

Levine's previous work, including *Actors at Work* (2006), *Bauerntheater* (2007), and *Habit* (2011), similar to *Private Moment*, resituates theatre outside its habitual frame, amid a range of disciplinary influences, dislocating theatre from its institutional and historic affiliations as these relate to conventional theatrical modes of spectatorship. As with *Private Moment*, all of these works emphasize the labor of acting as a real, aka "authentic," undertaking. As Levine explains, "You start thinking about acting as physical work and not just as a really easy means of representation."[25] In *Actors at Work*, for example, Levine commissioned actors to go to their day jobs and framed it cumulatively as the theatre piece. Simultaneously fascinated by the day labor of working actors in New York City, whose real paychecks come from miscellaneous jobs like babysitting, office desk jobs, bartending, and waitering; and with the legal loopholes of the American actor's labor union that recognizes a performance as an "equity showcase," Levine had the actors' employer listed on the Equity contract as "producer," and their "acting" wage was their work earnings for that day. In other words, their day-job wages were simply transposed, in theatrical terms, into their actor's salary. In this sense, the actors' workplace officially became a "theatre," and their work a "performance" for the duration of one day from 9:00 A.M. to 5:00 P.M.[26] Levine exhibited production stills of the "actors at work" at the Ohio Theatre in New York City, alongside copies of the official documents, which included programs, budget projections,

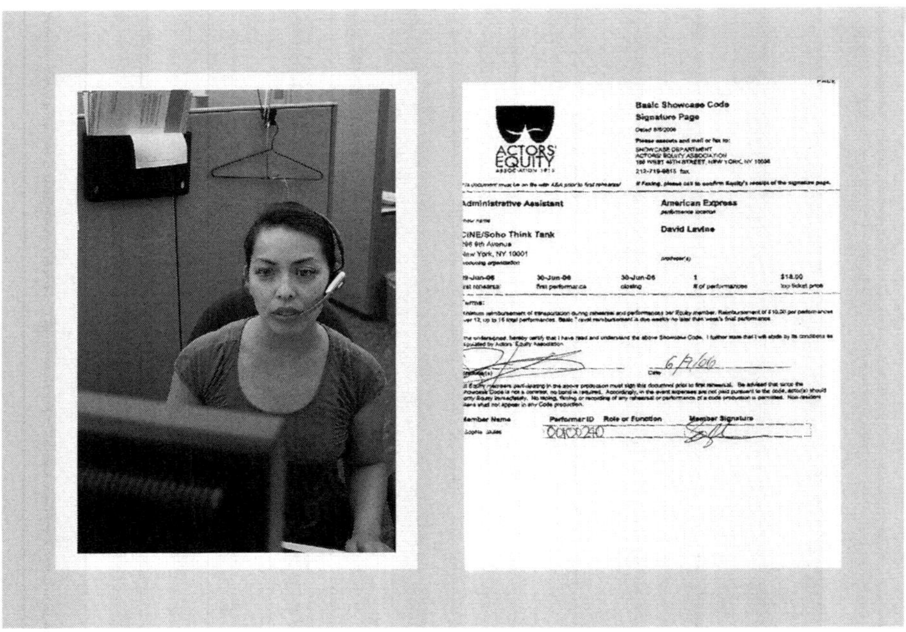

Sophia Skiles as "Administrative Assistant" in *Actors at Work*, 2005. *Courtesy of David Levine.*

contracts, and ground plans. Job titles became character descriptions, like "Babysitter," and "Freelance Editor"; "'audience capacity' was determined by workplace occupancy; 'costume budget' was derived from the cost of a set of work clothes (actor will provide); 'actor's compensation' was based on the employee's hourly wage, etc."[27]

Actors at Work placed the labor of theatre on display, essentially citing "theatre" as the specific site in question. In a similar vein, *Habit* and *Bauerntheater* turned to the actor's presence as the intentional object of labor. For *Bauerntheater* (literally "Farmer's Theatre"), Levine hired an actor to perform in character a real task, in order to short-circuit the distinction between the real-life action of the Happening and the make-believe world of theatre. David Barlow, an American actor who interpreted the role of Flint from Heiner Müller's 1961 play, *Die Umsiedlerin* ("The Resettler"), rehearsed for three weeks—the time allotted by Actor's Equity—in a studio in New York City, practicing how to plant a half a ton of potatoes, as close as possible to the way they had done it in East Germany (the DDR, or Deutsche Demokratische Republik). He then did this on location in Brandenburg, Germany, on two acres of land adjacent to the Biorama-Projekt Center, now a center for the study of the interrelationship of art, design, ecology,

David Barlow in *Bauerntheater*, 2007. *Photo by Joe Dilworth. Courtesy of David Levine.*

landscape studies, and tourism: for ten hours a day he essentially turned farming into an endurance performance, what Levine called a form of "DDR ecotourism."[28] Marvin Carlson, who saw the piece and wrote about it for *TDR*, detailed how Barlow first prepared the ground with a *Reihenzieher*, a large wooden rake used for making seed rows when neither tractors nor horses were available, in accordance with the script.[29] The audience, who were bused in from Berlin, watched Barlow work: both the acting work and the planting work. They could come and go as they pleased. By conceptualizing theatre, that is, framing the viewing circumstances in order to determine the experience, and theatricalizing performance/endurance art by having an actor really plant half a ton of potatoes while simultaneously faking (acting) it, Levine's *Bauerntheater* demonstrated a contemporary kind of site specificity, which resituated both the play (on location) *and* theatre (as a discipline and form of discourse).

For *Habit*, which was marketed for its iteration at MASSMoCA as "an installation/durational event/realist play that reorients the way we watch performance," Levine shifted the expectations audiences might have when they go see a show, as he had done with *Bauerntheater*.[30] This time he put the actors inside a four-walled, fully functioning house—with an operating fridge, stove, sink, and toilet, designed by Marsha Ginsberg—where they enacted a typical realist play (with "actor through-lines, and the way that dialogue rolls off the tongue, where the certain conflict lies, or the arc of the story"[31]). Written by Jason Grote, the script was performed in consecutive loops that ran for six hours a day (hence the need for food and plumbing).[32] I saw the piece at the Essex Street Market Building in the fall of 2012, when it came to New York as part of the Crossing the Line festival. Once you were inside the space, you could circulate outside the set (the house) and peer through curtains and windows to watch the actors work at pretending, what Amy Holzapfel describes as a "hyperbolic spectatorship,"[33] an experience shared by the audience of both *Private Moment* and *Bauerntheater*. We could walk in and out of the Essex Building (not the house) and observe the drama unfolding, as we pleased, just like during regular gallery hours (I took a lunch break with my friend and caught the end of the second loop when I came back). Admission, which was free, was during the day, all day. Like *Private Moment* and *Bauerntheater*, *Habit* was self-generating, with the actors adhering strictly to their lines, staying in character, never breaking the fourth wall (which in this case was literal), basing their actions outside the script solely on their necessities as performers (hunger, thirst, bathroom, rest, even boredom[34]). In its strictest sense,

Habit, Essex Street Market, September 2012. *Presented by Crossing the Line (FIAF Cultural Center) and PS122. Photo by David Levine.*

Habit, Essex Street Market, September 2012. *Presented by Crossing the Line (FIAF Cultural Center) and PS122. Photo, set, and costume design by Marsha Ginsberg.*

Habit was thus not really theatre, since it could exist without an audience, just like the performance art works by Vitto Acconci, Lynn Hershman Leeson, Tehching Hsieh, and Adrian Piper that Levine writes about in the quote earlier; but paradoxically, nor could it exist *without* theatre, since theatre was its very apparatus. Its intention was to create an object (art) but not a show (theatre). The show *was* the object; the object *was* the show. As Levine explains, referring to Michael Fried's critique of minimalist art as nonautonomous, "I finally managed to create this anti-Fried piece of theatre, which actually doesn't need you to complete it because it'll do its own thing no matter what."[35]

In his chapter "Naturalistic Theatre" in *The Art of Time*, Michael Kirby discusses a production from 1967 titled *A Study in Habitation* staged by Jerry Shultz at an off-off-Broadway theatre in New York. A group of people, who were not really a family, but were not really character acting either, lived together on a stage as if they *were* a family. Enclosed in a box set (like in *Habit*) they were surrounded by props to fulfill their human needs, as spectators paid admission to watch the nonstop twenty-four-hour performance as much as they wanted. Strikingly similar to Levine's *Habit*—almost half a century later—but also its exact antithesis, *A Study in Habitation* was, as Kirby writes, "an attempt to present 'fourth wall' naturalistic drama with all its voyeuristic implications in a way that would actually seem natural in our age."[36] However, *Habit* was meticulously scripted, designed, and somewhat rehearsed, whereas *A Study in Habitation* placed everyday actions inside the theatre, asking the audience to view them differently. While *Habit* situated theatre outside its conventional theatrical context, asking us to view it as something else ("If you transpose the convention into a gallery space can you then convince your audience they're seeing art?"[37]), *A Study in Habitation* situated nontheatrical activity (everyday uncrafted, unrehearsed actions) as theatre. *Habit* was both an object (in the visual art sense), and a show (in the theatre sense) all at once; theatre was both the emphasis *and* the object of our gaze.

Precisely by foregrounding theatre as crafted, critically showing the labor that goes into theatrical illusion and the artifice of inauthenticity, and making a spectacle of it, Levine situates theatre within the context and discourse of interdisciplinary art. His performances frame theatre as a discursive device, located site specifically at the intersection of interdisciplinary ontologies, where both craft (making fake blood look real, and pretending it is) and conceptualizing the craft (unveiling the theatrical apparatus) are simultaneous and conflated.

Interchanging Practices in Contemporary Art and Experimental Theatre

In her aptly titled article "Unhappy Days in the Art World? De-skilling Theatre, Re-skilling Performance," Bishop expands on the stakes, anxieties, and tensions surrounding the labeling of something as "authentic" versus "inauthentic." Whereas visual art discourse, she writes, has denounced "mimicry" and "representation," the performing arts camp has taken up a defense of craft and skill. As such, she historicizes how such categories came to be perceived:

> In the U.S. in the late 1950s, performance art emerged from the generative union of abstract painting and Cageian composition to mount a critique of traditional theatre. At its purest, this art spurned costumes, characters, narrative, rehearsals, and scripts in favor of everyday clothing, instructions, scores, and improvisatory chance. It took place in the actual space-time of the viewer, and these contingencies of location and audience were often factored into the work. The incontrovertible frisson of real life was the steering principle; no suspension of disbelief was necessary because everything was purportedly "real." This reality effect was perceived as a crucial counterpoint to theatre and spectacle, understood as commercial, traditional, and bourgeois. It resulted in visual art performance's long-standing "antitheatricality," a Platonic prejudice against mimesis and illusion. The solution was either to dissolve the space between viewer and performer, or conversely, to expose this division as essential to theatre's ontology (as Brecht had proposed in the 1920s).[38]

From an art history perspective then, performance art's coming into being already included a bias against any form of spectacle or artifice. This antitheatrical bias is predicated on "a visible excess of staging," and, as Bishop explains, engendered "a particularly queasy relationship to mimesis,"[39] in other words, an abhorrence of psychological realism—something that pretends to be real when it clearly isn't. However, as both Jackson and Levine have pointed out, artists represented by visual art institutions whose work circulates in the art-market economy incorporate the very "inauthentic" tactics they critique (such as acting, mimesis, illusion, and spectacle).[40]

Inversely, theatre artists are increasingly employing practices to counter established conventions of craft and making representation itself the object of inquiry. "The visual art world would be surprised," writes Andy Horwitz, "to be exposed to the work of Richard Maxwell, Philippe Quesne, Cuqui Jerez, Xavier LeRoy, Annie Dorsen and others who work extremely hard to create rigorous stagings of 'the real'—who use artifice to create an experience of the real that is almost indistinguishable from the 'real thing.'"[41] Sara Jane Bailes, in her book *Performance Theatre and the Poetics of Failure*, argues that experimental theatre companies such as Elevator Repair Service (ERS), Goat Island, and Forced Entertainment cite failure as the source of their aesthetic. They refuse "to make an event 'eventful,'"[42] thus opting to work against virtuosity, which is more akin to the "de-skilling" factor that Bishop argues is favored in visual art practices, even though there is great skill in "de-skilling" something for theatre. "Theatre, in its conventional sense," expresses Levine, "implies a degree of polish and repeatability (think of Donald Judd's industrial finishes), that performance art continues to avoid in favor of spontaneity and expression (think of Abstract Expressionism). If anything, theatre—think Nature Theatre of Oklahoma, Radiohole, or National Theatre of the United States of America—has been influenced by the aesthetics of performance art." De-skilling in this sense is nonetheless staged, performed, and repeated, on cue, no matter how "de-skilled" it appears.

Thus, on the one hand we have artists working within the contemporary art world (whose works circulate in the economy of galleries and museums) incorporating strands of mimesis and spectacle they otherwise seem to abhor (often precisely to break free from those preconceptions); and on the other, artists working within contemporary/experimental theatre who incorporate critiques of representation and counter artifice. There is an ongoing desire in contemporary art to de-emphasize the material object (participatory art, land art, performance art, relational aesthetics, collaborative art),[43] and a parallel desire in contemporary theatre to de-emphasize the show (from Grotowski's paratheatre to process-based work, the use of untrained performers, dramaturgies of the real, etc.).[44] Hans-Thies Lehmann's in-depth study famously grouped practices that challenge the conventions of script-based drama under the term "postdramatic theatre."[45] He coined the phrase in response to artists[46] whose work dispensed with traditional character acting, causal action, linear storytelling, and formal conventions between performer and audience members. Coming from a desire to unhinge dramaturgy from its connections to Aristotelian drama, Lehman's terminology stemmed from the German theatre studies tradition and the rise of European dance theatre.

Lehman's identification of experimental theatrical practices that questioned the form of performance just as much as its content, took into account a range of interdisciplinary influences. He was preceded by the critical theory of, among others, Michael Kirby, Richard Schechner, Marianne Van Kerkhoven (who coined the term "new dramaturgy" in 1994 to identify a trend in devised theatre[47]), and Andrzej Wirth,[48] as well as Bonnie Marranca and Elinor Fuchs, both of whom, as Bailes articulates, "identified a significant shift from script to image in experimental theatre practice since the 1960s, a stylistic and conceptual development that had become well established by the 1980s as a result of the gradual erosion of disciplinary divides between the arts, and the recombination of forms throughout the latter half of the twentieth century."[49] Marranca with *The Theatre of Images* (originally published in 1977) and Fuchs with *Death of Character* (the essay of the same title was published in 1983[50]) were both highly influenced by Gertrude Stein and Peter Handke, whose plays shifted the landscape of narrative playwriting to an emphasis on time and space in the present moment. Marranca and Fuchs wrote about the need to clarify the critical vocabulary used in reference to theatre that *itself* challenged the conventional use of language, acting styles that were presentational rather than representational, and the predominance of stage pictures.[51] "One can no longer re-present," wrote Fuchs in 1983, responding to experimental theatre artists Robert Wilson, Richard Foreman, and the Wooster Group, whose work at the time reflected "the collapse of traditional boundaries" and "an absorption with the theatre's own artifacts and techniques and styles."[52]

It is important to keep in mind here, as Marranca explains in her review of Mariellen Sandford's *Happenings and Other Acts* (published in 1995), which featured Kirby's influential text "The New Theatre" (originally written in 1965), that in the postwar period, the term "theatre" was in fact "used to describe 'events' or 'actions,' 'performance' not yet having become the catch-all phrase for live art."[53] This new form, "new theatre," was thus a precursor of what would eventually be referred to as either "postdramatic theatre," "live art," "visual art performance," or "contemporary performance," depending on how it was marketed, where it was performed, and who wrote about it. In her 1999 essay "Bodies of Action, Bodies of Thought: Performance and Its Critics," Marranca responds to Paul Schimmel's catalogue for the exhibit *Out of Actions: Between Performance and the Object, 1949–1979*, articulating the heightened attention that art institutions paid to performance art (as opposed to theatre) and anticipating by a decade the current onslaught of cross-disciplinary discourse on "the live" and how it already situated theatre within a certain hierarchy relative to performance history.[54] "There appears to be a full-scale, ongoing attempt to legitimize performance and establish its position within art history," she writes, adding (regarding Schimmel's emphasis on Kaprow's essay on Jackson Pollock) that "it should be noted that among visual artists and their critics, performance history is tactically linked to the history of painting and sculpture—art history—rather than to theatre history."[55] (Incidentally, *PAJ* changed its name in 1998 from *Performing Arts Journal* to *PAJ: Journal of Performance and Art*.[56])

Tracing the *Placing* of "Theatre" in Performance Histories

In the opening to the anthology *Performance and Place*, Leslie Hill describes the authors in the first section of the book as professionals whose role it is, "quite literally," she emphasizes, "to place [performance]—to place it in venues; to place it on the funding agenda; to place it in festivals; to place it in context with other works internationally."[57] As I've written elsewhere,[58] curators (as well as scholars and critics, and increasingly, artists—David Levine among them) are also responsible for "placing," and in this case *situating* theatre within a specific historical and interdisciplinary context. Roselee Goldberg, for example, is very particular about situating the performances she curates within a visual art paradigm, distancing the work from a theatre affiliation. I remember attending a 2014 panel on "Who Can Write about Performance Art," at Judson Memorial Church, not coincidentally the home of postmodern dance.[59] The panel centered on an important question regarding disciplinary discourses in relation to performance criticism: "How many histories do you need to know in order to write exciting criticism about art at the axis of dance and visual art, theatre and performance, and every iteration in between?"[60] When a panelist asked the audience how many people came from a theatre background, I was one of three people to raise their hands. Although there were many present from dance scholarship, there was no panelist whose background came from theatre history per se. Adrian Heathfield, whose books focus on the live and straddle between visual and contemporary performance practice (I will come back to him shortly), and Claire Bishop, who occasionally writes about theatre and dance, albeit from a visual arts perspective (which she acknowledged and spoke about) had arguably the most "theatre" in their published writings.[61] I was reminded, as I listened to the panelists, of Marranca's plea from her "Bodies of Thought" essay to integrate theatre research into that of performance and visual art "for the creation of a comprehensive, dynamic performance history."

Andy Horwitz discusses this binary between *visual art* performance and *contemporary* performance, two terms that have become prevalent in demarcating forms and histories of the live that, as with postdramatic theatre, distance themselves, from drama. He explains how these two distinct strands of performance practice circulate in very different economies. Visual art performance comes from "an object-making context" that either embraces or rejects that paradigm and circulates in galleries and museums. Contemporary performance, which stems from performing arts and includes theatre and dance, "actively acknowledges the essential ephemerality of the form," circulating in the economy of festivals such as Crossing the Line in New York City, TBA in Portland, On the Boards in Seattle, FuseBox in Austin, and PuSH in Vancouver, among many others.[62] Fittingly, and in a similar vein as Marranca's call for the inclusion of theatre's genealogy in performance discourse, Horwitz calls for a recontextualization of contemporary performance practice within the visual arts infrastructure, which "will *situate* performance predicated on experimental dance and theatre in the wider arts world" (my emphasis).[63]

Artists, curators, producers, critics, scholars—continue to situate theatre, no matter how interdisciplinary its practice, within certain very specific parameters, definitions, and contexts. While Goldberg's project has consistently worked to distinguish performance art and now "visual art performance" (the term Goldberg via Performa now uses to describe the work presented at that biannual event) from theatre, Lois Keidan, cofounder and director of Live Art Development Agency (LADA) in the United Kingdom and former curator at the Institute of Contemporary Arts (ICA) in London, established "live art" as its own category of interdisciplinary work that embraced both perform*ing* and perform*ance* art.[64] (Since the term "live art" originated in Great Britain it is more prevalent in Europe than in North America.[65]) Given the fact that prior to her tenure at ICA Keidan was responsible for funding interdisciplinary artists at the Arts Council of Great Britain, she is well aware of the process of optimally situating work to get it funded (unlike the NYFA process that clumped all performance projects together in one category).

As Beth Hoffmann has argued, although the label "live art" was deemed by Keidan to incorporate "processes and practices that might otherwise be excluded from more established curatorial, cultural and critical discourses,"[66] the term was positioned from the onset as separate from theatre.[67] "As a field of performance practice," writes Hoffmann, "live art has generally preferred a fine art to a theatre genealogy."[68] Again, we come back to how theatre is specifically sited in performance history. In her article "Radicalism and the Theatre in Genealogies of Live Art," Hoffmann historicizes how this disciplinary affiliation came to be, tracing the development of the term *live art* from its first use in print, which was, as she explains, "as early as 1979 by *Performance Magazine* to describe a broad area of work that included fringe theatre, performance art, rock gigs and political performance" through to 1987, the year "that the Arts Council of Great Britain published the paper 'Live Art Now,' by Gray Watson and Jeni Walwin, which marked the commencement of the use of the term 'live art' by the Arts Council." By 1991, she says, "live art" replaced "performance art" as the term of choice in funding discourse.[69] What Hoffmann points out is that while performance artists wanted to break free from the bounded genres of painting and sculpture, "performance art" had "itself become a rigid category to be resisted." In a volume titled *Live: Art and Performance*, which includes essays by Adrian Heathfield and Andrew Quick, Hoffmann unveils the common descriptors used to define live art, such as "in-betweenness," "the conditions of its 'liminal' form," and its "transcendence." Hoffmann points to the determining language that essentially situates theatre as outsider and out-of-touch:

> In this scenario, the well-made plot, characters, fourth-walls and other structural accoutrements of bourgeois realism denote the fixity, authoritarian practices of meaning-making and the reinforcement of social norms that constitute "the theatre," whereas bodies and everyday behavior and liveness of a visual art-based "performance" indicate the fluid, unpredictable, innovative and generative. Where the theatre [produces] a regime that prohibits any imaginative and critical intervention by spectators, denying them a role in the making of meaning, live art appears precisely as a disruption, not a deployment, of representational or rhetorical force; it stakes out no orders or regimes of representation of its own but rather comes into being when other regimes are undermined.[70]

Here, yet again, we see how discourses surrounding performance practice divorced themselves from theatre genealogies and, by doing so, reinforced the assumption that "theatre"—in its most conventional form—was something contemporary live art makers were aggressively working against. Like Marranca, Hoffmann maps the break between happenings/new theatre and plays/traditional drama that live art, as with visual art performance, seems to inhabit. Like Marranca, she argues against such a divide, proposing a continuum in its place.

Lost and Found: Theatre in Hiding

Times are changing, however, as artists and art critics are using theatre and its historical antecedents to influence their work and to write about it. Claire Bishop turns to theatre genealogy—primarily Bertolt Brecht, Augusto Boal, and the Russian Constructivist theatre—to trace the interdisciplinary histories in relation to participatory art practices today.[71] In *NewARTtheatre*, a series of "dialogues with contemporary visual artists who are appropriating theatre," Paul David Young tackles this contemporary trend. "The freedom of visual artists to turn to theatre is new," he declares. "While historically in the closed universe of art performance and visual art, theatre has most often been taboo, today many artists have come to terms with their use of theatre. Rather than shrinking from the opprobrium of being theatre artists, they run consciously to theatre in order to expand their artistic practice in terms of both means and ends."[72] Young interviews a number of artists including Pablo Helguera,[73] a New York-based artist working with installation and socially engaged art who stands out for his deliberate and straightforward use of theatre, even writing plays and staging them. For many years he organized panel discussions at the Museum of Modern Art as his day job (he is now their director of adult and academic programs), and soon began to wonder what it would be like to craft these panels—stage them with actors playing the roles of artists and art critics—without telling the audience it was a scripted event. He therefore stresses the importance of keeping the medium of theatre covert:

> I started composing symposia and panels with actors that were completely scripted but we did not tell the audience that it was a play or a panel. In fact, there were many panels that I organized that were really plays. So part of the test was to see if you could insert that fiction in reality and still maintain the tenuous line between what you think is real and something structured as an art piece.[74]

The audience could not know they were watching a rehearsed and scripted performance—knowing would render a very different experience of the work. Even though the event used traditional theatre's conventions—composed text (whether fictional or "theatre of the real"), rehearsal, character analysis, acting, staging, stagecraft, costumes, set, etc.—it wasn't thought of *as* theatre, since it was not situated as such, unlike Levine's pieces. "I wouldn't really tell people that it was happening because I realized that when you announce that you're going to do a play, the expectations are very different than for a lecture about art,"[75] explains Helguera, which is exactly the attention to framing that Levine also foregrounds in his work. Here was theatre front and center—one did not have to search for an hour in Central Park as I had to do to find *Private Moment*—and yet the point here was for the *theatre* to be unnoticeable. Even though the entire piece was predicated on illusion and employed the conventions of theatre, it wasn't theatre.

So, when does theatre stop being theatre?

If we go back to *Private Moment*, in particular the *Cruel Intentions* enactment, we could say that for audiences who did not know this was happening, theatre was also hiding in plain sight. But if you stood there long enough, it became obvious. The artifice was noticeable. Highly influenced by conceptual art and institutional critique practices, and yet committed to the craft and various skills of theatre (acting, dramaturgy, playwriting, design, etc.), Helguera's work, as with Levine's productions, emphasizes the relation of the art object to its reception. Whereas in this work Helguera was using theatre as a means to an end (for the panel to seem real it has to be staged site specifically in the museum), Levine situates theatre as the discursive site in question, setting it in relation to other art disciplines. Ultimately, Helguera, as with most of the artists in Young's book, sees the visual art world as the stage for his work, no matter how much he blatantly uses theatre and its conventions. However, by employing theatre, he continues to question the apparatus that deems an activity authentic or inauthentic, even if fully crafted, rehearsed, and repeated.

Leaving Theatre Behind . . . Only to Find It Again

In 1964 the French playwright, journalist, experimental director, and political activist Armand Gatti famously decided to stage his play *Durutti Column* in a factory. Disavowing theatre's location "as some kind of Utopian place,"[76] Gatti instead wanted to *take theatre out of the theatre*. "In order to create theatre," he professed, "it is necessary to leave it behind."[77] The play's main character, from the Spanish Civil War, had never set foot in a theatre, so to stage him there would have been taking him out of his element, as Gatti would later explain: "cutting him from his context, from the air he breathed, from all that made him what he was."[78] Instead, Gatti wanted audiences to experience Durutti in *his* terrain. He thus made a conscious political choice to dislocate "theatre" from its high-art and historically bourgeois associations. By having audiences witness this character *in another place*, "a place with a history . . . where you could still see traces of work," Gatti was altering theatre's elitist associations, and resituating theatre amid the realm of the real. In Gatti's production we have an example of what Michael Kirby described as "a theatre that rejects theatre buildings as 'artificial' and that uses the real places and 'theatrical equipment' of everyday life."[79] In its pursuit of authenticity then, theatre had to leave its institutional frame. Gatti didn't just stage resistance, he resisted the stage itself. The desire to "leave theatre behind," as a political gesture, was accomplished by challenging theatre's conventions, constructing the frame outside the physical theatre so that audiences could experience it differently.

Changing the physical location of theatre—in Gatti's case to a chemical factory, which had "known the labor of human beings day after day"[80]—altered the way audiences watched theatre. Although his methods were different, Gatti, with his dislocation, was not unlike other major theatrical luminaries who, for political ends, sought to challenge the illusion of the theatrical frame—in particular, Bertolt Brecht's focus on unveiling (and staging) the material conditions under which theatre was produced, and Augusto Boal's intent to hide the theatrical frame altogether in Invisible Theatre, precisely staging his events for unsuspecting "spect-actors" without disclosing it *as* theatre.[81] Regardless of where theatre was located—a factory, a theatre stage, or on the street—the emphasis was on the framing device, on the acknowledgement that meaning was derived from the institutional apparatus. This engagement with an artwork's conditions of reception, a perspective that challenged the idealism of modern art, which held that "the art object *in and of itself* was seen to have a fixed and transhistorical meaning," formed the crux of site specificity as a practice of institutional critique in visual art discourse.[82]

The space of the gallery or museum, the spaces in which art was framed, with their "stark white walls, artificial lighting (no windows), controlled climate, and pristine architectonics," as Miwon Kwon writes, were "perceived not solely in terms of basic dimensions and proportion but as an institutional disguise, a normative exhibition convention serving an ideological function."[83] We hear echoes of Gatti's rationale for staging *Durutti Column* in a factory, insisting that audiences experience his characters in a place that stood in sharp contrast to the theatre, with its red curtains and calculated artificiality. As if channeling Gatti's critique of the theatre-building-as-institution, Kwon continues: "The seemingly benign architectural features of a gallery/museum, in other words, were deemed to be coded mechanisms that *actively* disassociated the space of art from the outer world, furthering the institution's idealist imperative of rendering itself and its value 'objective,' 'disinterested,' and 'true.'"[84] We can reread the aforementioned statement substituting "gallery/museum" with "theatre" and consider the early desire for relocating theatre in the 1960s and 1970s not as a search for pure naturalism (as for example staging *Merchant of Venice* in Venice), or intercultural exchange (the spectacles of Peter Brook or Arianne Mnouchkine's Theatre du Soleil), or even experimental durational staging practices abroad (Robert Wilson's *Ka Mountain*), but as an indication that "theatre" was for such artists more than a physical container. The many new site-specific practices of experimental theatre were rooted in cultural, political, historical, social, and disciplinary affiliations. Gatti's desire to *leave theatre behind* situates theatre away from its conventional institutional affiliations, in a space where the content was not separate from the conditions under which the work was produced. From this perspective, the character of Durutti could not exist—even if enacted by a professional and credible actor—with a "theatre" as its framework.

Gatti's efforts to "take theatre out of the theatre" and Levine's *Private Moment* produce examples of site specificity that challenged how the audience watched the resultant event, altering traditional modes of spectatorship. For Levine, these included: the type of encounter with the audience and how much they could actually see or hear what is happening, the choice to have a box office or not, the price of a ticket, the way actors enter into the action, the performance's duration, the looping, and the start and end time of the production, the option for spectators to come and go—all of these are the modes of perception that are intentionally brought to the fore. Of course, while presenting a play in a factory fifty years ago implied an alteration of theatre's viewing conditions, nowadays "it doesn't matter how you tart it up," as Levine states. "You can do it environmentally, you can do it outside . . . as long as it is organized as theatre, *we watch it the same way*: you always carry the theatre in your head with you."[85]

Given that changing theatre's location nowadays does not necessarily dissociate it from its affiliations (as Levine says, *you always carry the theatre in your head with you*), and given the increasing cross-disciplinarity that is now occurring at the institutional level (museums increasingly presenting dance and theatre), *where* an event is staged involves a discursive set of parameters: a placement and conceptual context—a *situating*—that itself localizes the work's reception.

Disciplinary Sites

Acutely aware of some of the perceived advantages of relocating the performing arts into other institutional spaces that are potentially "even more determined and symbolically loaded," dramaturg Florian Malzacher advises that "site-specific work cannot just transfer the logic of a theatre venue into another spatial situation."[86] There are reasons why performing artists might find the white box appealing, including "trying to get into other markets" or "into discourses with seemingly higher prestige," explains Malzacher, who emphasizes how the "grids of perception and reflection" will change according to the "institutional, aesthetic, and architectural frame."[87] This act of positioning a work of theatre—situating it amid disciplinary legacies and their institutions—cannot be divorced from the works' content and reception. As Claire Bishop states, "This traffic of re-skilling between white cube and black box is more complicated than . . . simply switching the context for performance." She expands,

> The proscenium is a discourse (immersion), an architecture (the black box), and a structure of spectatorship (ticketed, with a beginning-to-end experience). The white cube, in turn, is also a discourse (of mythic transparency, assisted by the glare of full lighting), and a structure of experience (the autonomy of the viewer), giving rise to different modalities of performance: ongoing presence (like a sculpture) or the loop (as in video).[88]

Repositioning theatre to a new institutional space also requires an inquiry into the discourse and legacy that the new space brings to bear. When you are watching a performance in a museum, you not only "always carry the theatre in your head," you also always carry the "museum" as an institution in your head. Whereas artists have always experimented with form, collaborating across disciplines and breaking disciplinary boundaries, what is unique about the current moment is how this cross-disciplinarity has manifested itself at the institutional level. An increasing number of exhibitions in art galleries are not only embracing theatre and dance, but are using the live to attract more diversified audiences. Museums are opening performance departments and dealing with concepts otherwise familiar to theatre studies: ephemerality, the immaterial, the live, the embodied, and dramatic form. In tandem, theatres are embracing new ways of presenting work, such as staging durational works for an audience that can come and go as they please, or works that take over the entire building, or that perform for one audience member at a time.

This institutional resituating of performance brings with it institutional questions and problems: how to market, what to do with the audience/museum visitors, how to determine what the performing artists should be paid. The activist organization Working Artists and the Greater Economy (W.A.G.E.) in 2015 recommended a minimum of a hundred dollars a day for cultural institutions with annual operating expenses between five hundred thousand dollars and fifteen million dollars, which is unfortunately not always met.[89] Philip Bither, Walker Art Center's Senior Curator of Performing Arts, explains how museums often do not realize "how much it costs to run an active performing arts program," and admits that "colleagues are surprised when they mount live art in galleries that they have to pay people at all."[90] Besides artist fees, art institutions have had to deal with a whole slew of production-related labor issues and costs when theatre and performance is physically situated in their spaces, including casting, stage management, rehearsal, worker's comp, stage crew, backstage space, to name a few. The current trend toward interdisciplinary artwork has forced some artists to pay closer attention to where they situate their work—regardless of what elements and tools and skills they employ. Beyond the question of the basis for paying performing artists, this relocation of disciplinary practices has repercussions that imply how a work is advertised, critiqued, and marketed: from the handling of tickets (or no tickets) to guiding museum audiences who might not know how to deal with live art in their midst. Often, a work's interdisciplinarity is bound up with its resituation to an unanticipated disciplinary space—thereby engaging with multiple discourses at once, and entering into conversation with the legacies of multiple art worlds.

As artists and curators increasingly "relocate" theatre and the theatrical to diverse institutional spaces, the questions we ask of the work must equally engage with not just the disciplinary sites these spaces occupy, but how the relevant *citings* overlap. What histories? What legacies? What discourses? What frameworks? To use Richard Schechner's lexicon in describing the double negative of restored behavior,[91] my *Private Moment* was not theatre, but was also not not theatre. This resituating of theatre as an in-between space was the disciplinary site *Private Moment* occupied.

3. Spectator Sites

Artistic Intervention and the Unintended Audience

The spectators are always in the foreground. They are responsible for experiencing something that is not a show; it is an experience, a reflection, a thought, something more about life than fiction. What does that person *do* with that?

—Lola Arias, "The Work of Art Is a Parasite," *Theater*, 2014

Aesthetic experience has a political effect to the extent that the loss of destination it presupposes disrupts the way in which bodies fit their functions and destinations.

—Jacques Rancière, *The Emancipated Spectator*, 2009

Unintended Destinations

In March 2015, barely one year after the young, black, and unarmed Michael Brown was shot and killed in Ferguson, Missouri, by white police officer Darren Wilson, and only days after the Department of Justice cleared the officer of all charges, the conceptual avant-garde poet and self-described "uncreative writer" Kenneth Goldsmith read a poem he called *The Body of Michael Brown* at a conference at Brown University. The poem was an appropriation of the official autopsy report on Michael Brown as released by the county of St. Louis. Goldsmith, a tall, white, middle-aged American male artist with a long beard, stood in front of a large projected photo of Brown's body. In the image, recognizable after having been widely distributed in the media soon after his death, Brown posed wearing his green high school cap and gown, beaming with his diploma in hand. Wearing a black suit and a black sort-of kilt over it, Goldsmith took the stage and read the report verbatim, except for a few reordered passages and word changes ("I altered the text for poetic effect" he wrote on Facebook[1]). The performance was ostensibly an example of verbatim theatre, what Carol Martin describes as "the category of theatre of the real that uses verbatim quotation mostly from interviews, but sometimes also from documented public records such as inquiry and trial transcripts, public speeches, and private records such as diary entries, letters, and emails."[2] Goldsmith had used the autopsy report without contextualizing it, at least not beyond haphazardly using the frame of performance itself to draw attention to the report. The reading of *The Body of Michael Brown* lasted approximately thirty minutes and what remains of it is a transcript and the reconstruction of the varying voices that reacted after having seen it or heard of it, or like me, having written about it after reading articles about the performance by others who themselves did not attend the event. It is a kind of ripple effect ad infinitum, continuously adding on new spectators—onlookers, witnesses, commentators—mostly thanks to social media and the onslaught of online publications.

The reactions began immediately, with tweets from acclaimed poets coming out barely a few hours after the performance:

> Forget it bc Kenneth Goldsmith did a thing . . . made a thing . . . for a crowd . . . out of a black boy's dead body . . . he performed . . . and was paid well.[3]

> You know . . . it's WILD how many poets get a pass on the blatant racism / misogyny in their work because of poetry's relative obscurity.[4]

Less than one week later, Rin Johnson, an artist who attended Goldsmith's reading, wrote a piece for *Hyperallergic* titled "On Hearing a White Man Co-opt the Body of Michael Brown." In it, she describes her anger and discomfort: "As Goldsmith details the mutilation of Michael Brown's hands, I look down at my own. I want to raise one, to stop this, to slow things down, but I don't."[5] In addition to her own reaction, Johnson described what had occurred that evening as well as what followed. The private-turned-public reverberations of the reading had been reconstructed as a concluding event at the conference, where now thirty to forty people (new and returning spectators) gathered in an auditorium to continue the conversation. Johnson's article inspired a hail of comments, Facebook shares, and retweets. Months later, articles on the event continued to appear, including a *New Yorker* feature from October 2015.[6] The Poetry Foundation published a piece by poet CAConrad on its blog, titled "Kenneth Goldsmith Says He Is an Outlaw," for which he amassed over thirty poets' reactions to the event,[7] all adding to the voices that would now repurpose the death of Michael Brown and incite a meaningful conversation about the system that allows such racism to prevail—something the original performance had failed to do. As Fred Moten's contribution articulates, "I think you know you fucked up. But do you know why you fucked up? And do you know how you fucked up? Do you know that why you fucked up and how you fucked up are totally entangled?"[8]

While trying to make sense of this performance that I never saw, and that barely anyone saw—Goldsmith eventually barred Brown University from releasing any of the recorded footage—I read all manner of responses. The majority—tweets, commentaries, articles, blogs, Facebook threads, features, and all of the discussions they inspired—actually centered on trying to understand exactly "why and how you fucked up," as Moten put it. Goldsmith's ambiguous and "lazy" performance, as Johnson described it,[9] hid behind a veil of surface "activism" that made it harder to pin down as the more potent and dangerous breed of oppression that it actually was, reminiscent of the kind Ta-Nehisi Coates describes in *Between the World and Me.*[10] Its use of verbatim text was self-aggrandizing, reproducing the problematic racial politics it thought to critique. As I obsessed through all the literature and online forums surrounding Goldsmith's piece, I realized that I was now part of a larger group of spectators—an unintended audience if you will—involved in its off-site afterlife.

Kenneth Goldsmith's performance, or live reading of a poem he called *The Body of Michael Brown*, is just one of countless examples of a performance that lives on in public. For such a performance, in addition to a review in the arts section of the *New York Times*, we might read about it in their opinion pages or metro section, as a news item. We might read about it on our Facebook feed, or hear about it from friends and colleagues. A live event that occurs within a closed, private, institutional space in the name of art has the potential to incite controversy and go public, as was also the case with *My Name Is Rachel Corrie*, whose production and subsequent debate Carol Martin discussed extensively in her chapter "Occupying Public Space" in *Theatre of the Real.*[11]

The play premiered in London's Royal Court Theatre in 2005 and was scheduled for a run at New York Theatre Workshop, but was postponed (and eventually cancelled) due to "the sharply divided [public] opinions of Ms. Corrie" and in light of the intensification of the political situation in the Middle East after Israeli prime minister Ariel Sharon's stroke and Hamas's electoral victories.[12] Addressing how theatre that implements the real becomes "part of the circulation of ideas about our personal, social, and political lives,"[13] Martin illuminates the blurred boundaries between the stage and the "real" world, where the aesthetic realm contributes to "formulating what we understand as reality,"[14] extending "the public" of theatre to debates and disputes in real life. In addition to audiences who saw the performance, people who may not have physically attended might end up commenting on it, engaging in debates around its meaning, its worth, merit, moral compass, its ethics. In the case of artworks that incorporate documentary material, or that are influenced by real world events, these public forums also affect how we come to remember and think about the original event in question.[15]

Goldsmith's reading and *My Name Is Rachel Corrie* are examples of performances that went *off-site*. They leaked out into the public sphere, beyond their physically present attendees, forming alternative spectator sites that were not necessarily related to or envisioned as part of the actual, on-site event. These performances spawned new publics, generating "spectatorial" ripple effects ad infinitum, other forms of witnessing and reacting to a live event that lives on past its immediate present moment. The performances provoked a debate in public—like many art controversies—with other, often unintended, spectators.

In *The Theatrical Public Sphere*, Christopher Balme addresses the notion of political impact or artistic intervention, looking for how themes might travel beyond the private world of theatres to the public consciousness, and vice versa.[16] "Apart from exciting protests," he asks, "how can and has the theatre communicated with the public sphere?"[17] Using Jürgen Habermas's concept of the public sphere to explore twenty-first-century possibilities for performance to activate debate, consciousness, action, and/or content beyond its immediate constituents (especially given today's technological advances and social media boom),[18] Balme argues that the political effectiveness of theatre—"the truly political dimension"[19]—lies not in the "thematising of politically burning subject matters" (Balme, 7) but in its ability to transcend traditional modes of distribution and reception, returning to "questions of social and political imbrication which transcend any one particular occasion" (Balme, 14). Balme is interested in what he terms "a distributed aesthetics" where the boundaries of reception are "potentially unlimited" (Balme, 184). He writes, "If the interaction between spectator and performance via a performative feedback loop in the black box of a theatre space is itself outside the public sphere, then it is small wonder that artists have begun to change their strategies, at least those who still share the conviction that theatre has some kind of political or social efficacy" (Balme, 17). He therefore locates art's political efficacy in its (potential) distribution beyond the theatre, as an aspect of the aesthetic dimension of performance. If the theatrical public sphere does not end with its on-site audience, what other off-site reactions, and, by extension, off-site publics, does it engender? What kinds of spectating, audience engagement, audience makeup, will occur both in, but, also, beyond the theatre?

We might think about this "aesthetic distribution" as an *other* spectator site, another of performance's unintended or unknown destinations. One might also think of the aftermath of mass shootings and terrorist attacks, where the increasing rate and ease of image and video distribution, perhaps in an attempt to engage awareness or sympathy, rage or fear, as if we were there, leads to a wider range of so called "witnessing." We witness the event even if we were not there.[20] With the increasing access and affordability of digital recording, akin to Walter Benjamin's musings half a century ago on the loss of the "aura" after the advent of mechanical reproduction,[21] there are large numbers of audiences who watch a performance without being there. Nowadays, given the advent of such initiatives like Live at the Met and National Theatre Live, we have off-site audiences who watch on-site productions simultaneously around the world, thanks to live remote broadcast. In this chapter, however, I refer to an off-site spectatorship that exists independent of (or as an extension of) the work of art. It is the "non-art" audience, so to speak; the varying possibilities of the creation of an *other* spectator—an off-site spectator that is both impacted by and impacts the work itself.

In order to address this notion of an "off-site spectatorship," it might be helpful to think of it as a continuum. At one end, we have an audience who is not present (not even remotely) but who is nevertheless impacted by the artwork, as was the case with Goldsmith's live reading of a poem and *My Name Is Rachel Corrie*. One could even go as far as to say that this kind of influence is limitless, since one could never truly measure the impact a performance has on those who have never seen or experienced it. People who haven't seen Lin-Manuel Miranda's *Hamilton*, one could argue, might nevertheless view history differently, if only because of an infinite set of minute parameters that might include a teacher changing his/her lesson to focus on either the play or the man, or a discussion prompted by an article on Alexander Hamilton's life written as a reflection of the show, or the debate over changing the images on US currency and the fact that Hamilton will remain on the ten dollar bill, etc. In all of these cases, the off-site spectatorship does not necessarily come back to impact the artwork. These alternative spectator sites are not integrated back into the script or the performances.

At the other end of the spectrum, we have an audience that did not attend the performance, but that is impacted by its process, *and* that has an impact on the work itself. This off-site audience participates in the work even though they are technically "not present." As a way to explore such a continuum and how this off-site spectatorship might play out in relation to the work itself, I will discuss two works in particular: *El Chaco en Kassel* and *Mi Vida Después*. In what ways do these performances *materialize* a relationship that unites on- and off-site spectators? And how might such an interaction help us approach the porous divide that has always existed between art, on the one hand, and politics, on the other?

As part of their proposal for Documenta 13 (2012), artist duo Guillermo Faivovich and Nicolás Goldberg planned to transport El Chaco, the 37,000 kilogram meteorite, from its original crash site five thousand years ago in Argentina, to Kassel, Germany, for the duration of the art exhibition. They would create a mise-en-scène for the object and stage it in Friedrichsplatz, the main plaza, in front of the Fridericianum Museum.[22] This intercontinental and temporary relocation, which, as we will see, did not take place as planned, would have involved the single heaviest extraterrestrial object ever transported, and not only for the purposes of art but in general. It caused a public media frenzy and prompted the artists to cancel the meteor's scheduled trip. By embracing the public debates incited by their initiative, Faivovich & Goldberg changed the context of *El Chaco en Kassel* and raised questions about the very "object" of art. The final piece displayed not the meteorite but the debates surrounding the cosmic object—around issues of entitlement, ownership, privilege, and authenticity—on-site in Kassel. The meteor, in its journey as art, became the object through which a multiplicity of audiences, including a city council, emerged.

Mi Vida Después (2009), a play by Lola Arias written in collaboration with its original Argentine cast, all of whom were born at the height of the military dictatorship between 1976 and 1983, enabled the space of theatre to become the site of public witnessing. The participants told stories about their parents, some of whom had disappeared, others who had collaborated with the military government, and their lives. One of the performer's testimonies was accepted at trial, impacting Argentine law, generating an off-site spectatorship concurrent with the one on-site.

These two mise-en-scènes produced alternative spectator sites, creating and engaging with off-site audiences that impacted the on-site work. Both *Mi Vida Después* and *El Chaco en Kassel*, albeit in different ways, generated multiple publics who connected through national memory, heritage sites, and testimony. Both had legal ramifications. These works generated new relations among otherwise disconnected audiences. They allowed spaces for off-site spectatorship to inform the on-site work. The offsite spectators—the city council and attendants at the hearing (*El Chaco*), the judge's decision (*Mi Vida*), those who engaged in the surrounding political debate (both)—were perhaps not *of* the artworks but nevertheless belonged to them.

Before working through these two works in more detail, let's pause briefly to consider off-site spectators.

Spectating in Conversation

Artists' desire to intervene in the public sphere (Balme's "aesthetic distribution") runs parallel to critical discourse that engages with the role of the spectator, audience reception, modes of spectatorship, and audience makeup. Focusing on the political nature of spectating and of aesthetic experience, Jacques Rancière powerfully argues that all spectators—as individual subjects—are active participants, irrespective of the form of performance being witnessed. Rancière addresses what he perceives as a false dichotomy that has infiltrated aesthetic discourse whereby spectating is equated with passivity and participation with activity. He also refutes the separation of the aesthetic and the political realms, where the politics happens beyond the work of art. Seeking to dissolve such binaries ("Emancipation begins when we challenge the opposition between viewing and acting"[23]) and drawing heavily on pedagogy and the teacher/student metaphor to do so ("The spectator also acts, like the pupil or scholar. . . . They are thus both distant spectators and active interpreters of the spectacle offered to them"[24]), Rancière defends an aesthetics that sees the transmission of knowledge as fluid, where the artist and spectator (like the teacher/student) discover *together*, or as Rancière emphasizes, "apart but together."[25] The political in art therefore does not lie in the *desire* to emancipate the spectator,[26] but on the contrary, precisely in the willingness to explore aesthetic subjectivities that *rupture* artistic cause and political effect, what he terms "the distribution of the sensible." Rancière's vision of political efficacy is thus intricately related to the spectator's freedom of interpretation as integral to the aesthetic experience. That free interpretation engenders "not rhetorical persuasion about what must be done. Nor is it the framing of a collective body. It is a *multiplication* of connections and disconnections that reframe the relation between bodies, the world they live in and the way in which they are 'equipped' to adapt to it [my emphasis]."[27]

Rancière's focus on the interaction between art and spectator and on the spectator's engagement also form the theoretical basis for Claire Bishop's *Artificial Hells*, a critique of what she has termed "the social turn," the trend among artists to use social situations to produce politically motivated projects.[28] Concerned about social justice, climate change, and rampant class inequality, artists want their art to make a difference in the real world. These artworks aspire to actually *do* something: open an immigration booth, create a conversation, pose a question in public space, build a school, etc. Often these projects are co-authored with the audience and are participatory by nature.[29]

More recently, in tandem with the reception of Rancière's writings, the popularization of relational aesthetics in contemporary art,[30] and a heightened awareness of forms of affective labor[31] that have become commonplace in the experience economy of the early twenty-first century,[32] theatre and performance scholars have returned to a renewed focus on spectatorship: the role of the spectator, the act of spectating, and different modes of spectatorship, including participatory practices, one-on-one performance, and immersion, among others.[33] Echoing Rancière's "being together apart," in a contemporary art project that constructs "a place for solitude" where a spectator is allowed the necessary space for contemplation,[34] Hans-Thies Lehmann emphasizes how a performance "gains political force largely by virtue of its capacity to generate a 'situation' that precipitates a 'concrete questioning of the self.'"[35] In other words, in what ways might artistic practice allow a genuine space for self-reflection, critical thinking, disavowal, and/or discomfort? Lehmann, like Rancière and Bishop, cautions against a superficial form of participatory spectatorship: "Audience involvement is not to be taken as simple 'participation,' which in an era of game and reality shows has lost its critical potential."[36] Instead, "the political in theatre," Lehmann suggests, "is the momentous undermining of key certainties: about whether we are spectators or participants; whether we perceive or are confronted with perceptions that function 'as if' or for real; whether we dwell in the field of aesthetic make-believe or in real actuality."[37] Lehmann identifies this tension as "a grey zone of overlapping experiences and perceptions," which, he adds, "can happen in extremely different ways."[38] The examples I highlight later fall into this grey zone, specifically because they forge a connection between the aesthetic realm and its on-site reception (the present "art" audience), but also a relation among different groups of spectators with varying degrees of separation (namely those unintended ones) that trouble what is real and what is "as if." Rather than speculating about new audience experiences or new modes of spectating, the cases I discuss offer strategies of *aesthetic distribution* that presuppose, as Rancière terms, "the loss of destination," specifically sited as a relationship between what happens on- and off-site among *other*, unanticipated spectators.

In his book *Passionate Amateurs: Theatre, Communism, and Love*, which engages with the labor of theatre and its practice as a form of communism (a term he uses to refer both to Marxist ideology and community, of being alone with others), Nicholas Ridout describes Nature Theatre of Oklahoma's performance of *No Dice!* to illustrate how this "kind of communicative labor [their show]" "might constitute a mode of political action in the theatre."[39] What is significant here is Ridout's emphasis on *in* the theatre. He writes,

> We might hold on to the possibility that the political action of the theatre will take place *in* the theatre, rather than seeking to expand itself into any other part of the so-called real world. This is to insist, once again, that the theatre does not stand to one side of the "real" world or offer an alternative to it: the theatre is a real place, where real people go to work, and where their work takes the form of "conversation."[40]

Refusing to see the political as happening outside of or as separate from the aesthetic sphere, Ridout emphasizes theatre's realness, in particular as a set of relations where people come together, to labor. Art does not point to reality, it *is* reality.

In an interview I conducted with Lola Arias, she describes the process of art making as dialogic (which she credits to Bishop): as "social intervention for generating utopian models of working and thinking and living together."[41] For Arias, as for Ridout, the "work" of art might constitute its political action, where art, as she says, is "a matter of entering into a conversation with others."[42] The meteor in *El Chaco en Kassel* and the performers' embodied testimonies in *Mi Vida Después* pointed to certain realities *and* created them, by fostering conversation with others. They made art from the real, and also, simultaneously, *intervened* in the real, by establishing a communicative kind of off-site spectatorship that existed not as independent from the work, but, on the contrary, *in conversation* with it.

The Object Meets the Artists

When Faivovich & Goldberg were approached by Documenta 13 director Carolyn Christov-Bakargiev in 2009, they had been doing research in the Chaco region of Argentina for over three years. Located one thousand kilometers north of Buenos Aires, the region is mostly known as the site of El Campo del Cielo, which refers to the massive group of meteorites that hit it almost five thousand years ago. These originated from the area of the solar system between Mars and Jupiter known as the asteroid belt, and are thought to be 4.5 billion years old, in other words, older than Earth itself. Although El Campo del Cielo has long been revered by indigenous communities, it was officially recorded as having been "discovered" by Spanish colonizers in 1576, and not until the late 1700s did scientists believe that the meteors did not in fact come from the earth, but from the sky.[43] There was a succession of excavations in the region in the decades following the 1960s, when there was a renewed scientific interest in meteorite research and conservation.[44] During this period numerous meteorites either disappeared from the region (there is both a legal and contraband meteorite business) or were taken from the site in the name of science (with one-way tickets).

Faivovich & Goldberg first encountered the region as children, when they visited the Planetario Galileo Galilei, a spaceship-like building designed in 1966 by architect Enrique Jan. They have always been fascinated by space exploration and as friends were obsessed with one meteorite in particular—El Taco—one half of which is on permanent view at the outdoor entrance to the planetarium. The search for the missing half became the source for the first part of their ongoing project called *A Guide to Campo del Cielo*, which combines science, conceptual art, mapping, photography, history, and journalism to research Argentina's Campo del Cielo meteorites and their cultural impact. One of their actions, for example, included proposing a 3-D commemorative stamp of various meteorites from the region, which was issued by the Argentine postal service in 2007. Faivovich & Goldberg's curiosity about El Taco led them to the Smithsonian, where its other half was stored, a slice of it having been removed and put on display in the meteorite hall. In 1962, when a farmer bumped into what came to be called El Taco at its original point of impact, the meteor was unearthed and sent to Mainz, Germany. There, it was cut in half, and redistributed to the United States and Argentina. The two pieces had since been conserved in completely different conditions: one lay outside in the rain and everyone could touch it, the other had never been displayed to the public and was held indoors.

In 2010 Faivovich & Goldberg brought the two pieces of the meteorite together for the first time since their separation. Their exhibit at the Portikus gallery in Frankfurt featured an installation titled *Meteorit "El Taco"* that reunited the two halves, but only for the duration of the exhibition.

The pieces would go back to their respective "homes" when it was over. For the reunification of this "cosmic readymade," as Portikus director Daniel Birnbaum called it,[45] the artists left a gap in the middle of the two parts, exactly the size of the slice cut off and on display at the Smithsonian. It was just enough of a gap for spectators to walk, sit, or lie down between the almost-halves of this intergalactic object that had been separated by the will of humankind.

Faivovich & Goldberg have a hands-on, hands-off approach: hands-on when it comes to the journey, interacting with any leads that could take them to the next clue, similar to investigative reporters searching for a narrative or producers making something happen; hands-off in terms of distancing themselves from that narrative enough to ensure that they would not alter its outcome. They are mobilizers, which for El Taco meant moving the rocks from place to place, both institutionally and physically, across national and cultural frontiers. They are ethnographers, participant observers willing to get their hands dirty without necessarily giving an interpretation of the facts they have carefully assembled. They facilitate a

El Chaco en Kassel, 2012. dOCUMENTA (13): The Guidebook. *Courtesy of Faivovich & Goldberg.*

framework that accumulates the voices that speak on behalf of the object. In the El Taco book, Starling points out the recurring themes in the project, such as "ideas of patrimony in relationship to the meteorites"[46] and prods the artists to discuss such issues further. Although Faivovich & Goldberg assume the role of mere witnesses, spectators of the object's fate, it's impossible to forget that they are the ones editing the conversation, meticulously placing it at the conclusion of the book. They are thus cognizant of their role in shaping the story they deem to be staying "back" from and very much acknowledge how their actions become part of the historical narrative. As Goldberg explains,

> We need to let the images appear as unmediated as possible so you can read the differences between what the meteorite was like sitting in the field it was found in . . . or between how it appears in the snapshot of a visitor of the planetarium or in a 1980s newspaper. . . . At a certain point we appear within that system as image-makers ourselves.

Faivovich & Goldberg with a mock-up of El Chaco, Friedrichsplatz, Kassel, November 3, 2011. *Courtesy of Faivovich & Goldberg.*

Goldberg, a photographer trained in New York's International Center of Photography (ICP) and heavily schooled in the photo-documentary tradition of Robert Capa and Henri Cartier-Bresson, is keenly aware of the delicate balance between observer and observed, witness and spectator. At what point does the observer become an implicated subject within the story he/she investigates, and therefore experiences? Faivovich & Goldberg not only admit their role as image-makers but also contextualize their work within the discourse of colonialism, geopolitics, national heritage, cultural patrimony, institutional support networks, and indigenous rights. The artists' motivations, as well as their own intervention with this object that they purported to stand back from, however, would soon come under scrutiny in the next installment of their project.

El Chaco en Kassel was conceived as the second part of their meteorite series. El Chaco, the heaviest of the meteors at roughly 37,000 kilograms, would be transported from its original crash site in Argentina to Germany. The meteor would be installed for the duration of the art festival and returned to its place of origin in the hopes that, as Gabriela Speranza writes, it "would perhaps collaborate in the campaign of Chaco Province to have Campo del Cielo declared a World Heritage Site," and reverse the "direction of the classic colonial route of the looting of indigenous heritage by means of a south-north-south trajectory conceived in South America."[47] A large part of the project would comprise the institutional and intercontinental collaboration required to transport such an object, not to mention the massive logistical nightmare. Most important for the artists was the conversation about the meteor's legacy and the achievement of unanimous approval for its voyage from the numerous communities connected to it, including: the local government (Chaco province), representatives of the Moqoit Council (the indigenous Moqoit Nation), and the community board of Gancedo (that guards the meteorite). Once Documenta 13 confirmed their financial backing, Argentine and German institutions began the plans for the meteorite's journey.

Because Argentine law prohibits the removal of meteors and their fragments from its provinces, the Chamber of Deputies of Chaco had to approve the bill proposed by parliament to authorize the loan, in order to dislocate the meteor. The closed session took place on December 29, 2011, and turned into a heated political and philosophical debate on the meaning of art, the role of imperialism ("We are the owners, not the Germans!"[48]), the importance of cultural patrimony ("The resource is ours! It stays in Chaco!"[49]), and the fear of loss ("they are going to cheat us once again, but in a more sophisticated way"[50]). With a renewed sense of national pride, including on the part of many who were discovering the meteor for the first time, the Chamber passed into law Article 1 by a margin of one vote (fourteen in favor, fourteen against, with the chairman breaking the tie), which legally approved the loan and the transport of the object to Kassel. This hearing convened one of the project's first off-site audiences: those at the hearing did not witness the piece in Kassel, as the on-site audience would have, but nevertheless they engaged with the object *as* art.

With the new law in place, El Chaco was ready to begin its voyage, except the opposition—those who had voted against the loan in the original vote—took their concern and outrage to the media. A simple Google search leads one to the myriad newspaper articles, letters to the editor, and opinion pieces, that were published soon after the Chamber's decision approving the meteor's temporary transfer. Debates ensued about whether to send or not to send the meteor to Germany. Some believed El Chaco should fabricate an exact replica—a fake—to ensure continued interest in the meteor in a foreign land. Others insisted that it would never come back, and that the whole "art" thing was a pretense for stealing it, similar to past North American ruses. Local news soon sparked debate on social media, which brought in activists and academics, among them social anthropologist Alejandro Martín López who specializes in Moqoit culture (but is not of the tribe himself), to stop the transfer. His petition objected to the project's "deeply colonialist attitude," its pretense as art, and appealed to "those who have the money to seek to promote the value of the meteorite *within its place of origin*."[51] They recommended using the "many technological tools" we have at our disposal today to "permit the artistic appreciation of this meteorite without moving it from its cultural landscape." Preventing El Chaco's journey was now a protest movement deploying the same anticolonialist rhetoric and nationalistic pride that prompted the objects' transfer in the first place. Who were the meteor's spokespeople? Whose interests were on the line? Who were its interpreters? What was meant to be a temporary relocation of a "cosmic readymade" as art exhibit, was now a complex web of relations that would make its way to Kassel, but without the actual meteor.

In fact, what would have constituted one of the single heaviest and oldest objects transported for the purposes of art, thus caused a public media frenzy—and prompted Faivovich & Goldberg to cancel the meteor's scheduled trip in an official email dated January 26, 2012, to Documenta's curator, Carolyn Christov-Bakargiev. "We already began to work on an alternative gesture that includes what lay at the heart of our initial proposal," they wrote, "without removing any specimen from the Chaco region."[52] On the surface, it would seem as though El Chaco's myriad spectators had won the fight against the appropriation of indigenous culture by what they regarded as a pair of privileged, white, upper-middle-class artists from the capital, Buenos Aires, whose project amounted to no more than a capricious (or quixotic!) desire in the name of art (and its collectors). In a twist worthy of a sci-fi thriller, in March 2012 Faivovich & Goldberg received a copy of a letter addressed to the Chaco governor. In it, the Moqoit people, self-described as the "leaders, associates, and members of diverse communities who above all are legal representatives of community organizations and associations,"[53] explain how:

> We have examined the question carefully with all due seriousness and in full knowledge of the importance of this heritage for our people, which makes us proud because for the first time we feel our cultural identity so strongly as the Moqoit people. We see the meteorite as a gift from God, one that means there must be divine intention for our people, the people of the Chaco, and for our country Argentina. Among the authorities of our communities, we also respect the stance of those of our brothers who are not in agreement, but they are not legitimate in any way and therefore it does not enable them to make any decisions. Honorable Governor, we wish to inform you that the decision to cancel the project and not show the meteorite in Germany brought us much pain, sadness, and regret.[54]

More than a staging of El Chaco in Kassel, its production unveiled an intricate script whose various actors related to the meteor's drama in different capacities. *The Weight of Uncertainty* became the new title of Faivovich & Goldberg's installation at Kassel, which physically demarcated the absence of the meteorite and was accompanied by transcripts, images, and photos that documented the object's interpreters—off- and on-site participant spectators—including the artists themselves. More than a project about a meteorite or about national heritage or national frontiers or even postcolonialism, the failure of *El Chaco en Kassel* generated a range of spectators for the nonevent, who had participated in a conversation surrounding the object of art, and in the process, participated in the creation of a new object of art, *The Weight of Uncertainty.*

The Artists Meet Their Past

Mi Vida Después, which premiered on March 26, 2009, at Buenos Aires's Teatro Sarmiento, was part of director and curator Vivi Tellas's *Biodrama* cycle of stage biographies.[55] For the cycle, Tellas commissioned productions based on the lives of people currently living in Argentina, what she has called "a return of the real in the field of representation."[56] The only restriction was that the subjects must be living so that the artist could collaborate with them. The aim was to use theatre as a form of investigation and research, both in terms of generating new content, as well as experimenting with blurring the lines between reality and fiction, a process that would influence Lola Arias's work significantly.[57]

As part of the series, Tellas herself also originated a number of signature pieces, which she titled Proyecto Archivos.[58] Often an emotional process, as she revealed in an interview with Julie Ward, she guided nonprofessional actors through a method of exploration, remembering, and research, to form scripts and productions that would tell their stories.[59] The premise is that each individual not only holds an archive but *is* himself or herself the archive, embodying a reserve of experiences, texts, and images, not unlike what Diana Taylor has written about as an embodied act of transfer, a performed archive, in *The Archive and the Repertoire*.[60] This process, present in all of Tellas's work, would be what Arias would eventually use in *Mi Vida Después*, collaborating with performers as the repositories and vessels of the past, shared with others in the present. The charge to find theatricality in the everyday world and use nonactors to tell their own stories was thus already prominent in the Argentine theatre world by the time Lola Arias premiered *Mi Vida Después*.[61]

In her own trajectory, Arias recounts this use of the real in theatre as formative. She began experimenting with the nonrepresentational, using babies and animals, for example, who cannot pretend to be something or someone else. In 2007, she decided to have one of the performer's babies present onstage in *Striptease*. This created an entirely new set of task-based issues for the actors to deal with, like how to prevent the baby from crying so the show could go on. They had to stay in character and deliver their lines while simultaneously caring for this real being: changing his diaper, picking him up, placing him in the crib, and playing with him. As Arias explained to me regarding *Striptease*: "That piece is key to a change in my work because it marks when I start to try to stage something that goes against fiction."[62] *Mi Vida Después* is a continuation of this investigation.

The play might take place in a theatre, but the experience is real for both the performers and spectators: performers tell their own stories, in Argentina, to Argentine audiences. The bodies onstage *are* themselves the sites of reconstruction where memory becomes materialized.

Like lawyers and experts in a courtroom, the performers in *Mi Vida Después* use an array of physical evidence onstage to reconstruct the lives of their parents including personal video footage, TV episodes, photographs, shreds of clothing, toys, souvenirs, letters, journals, postcards, newspaper clippings, birth certificates, and phone recordings. This is a form of journalism theatre, where the theatre is the mise-en-scène of the resulting, and ongoing, investigation. As they narrate the stories and reenact events, the performers display the documents by holding them up to the audience and showing them on overhead projectors, as one might do with a trial exhibit brought before a jury. Pablo Lugones puts on what he says are his grandfather's boots "as if time had never gone by" to dance the Argentine malambo, like his father and grandfather did before him.[63] Liza Casullo, daughter of the late Nicolas Casullo (a famous writer and professor who died during the run of the show) and former newscaster Ana Amado, wears a replica of the Chanel suit her mother wore nightly on TV. Clothes rain on Casullo from the ceiling as she attempts to deliver the headlines her mother had to utter, a cover for the real news of abduction and torture and a way

Lola Arias's *Mi Vida Después* (My Life After). *Photo by Lorena Fernández.*

to mask her own clandestine activities as a militant.[64] Mariano Speratti shows us toy cars on the overhead projector—"Bugatti Type 35C"—which stand in for the cars his father, Horacio Rodolfo Speratti, used to repair and collect. We also learn that his father used the cars to conceal weapons for the Peronist youth. Later in the show, holding a vintage audio cassette player, Speratti tells us that his dad was kidnapped by the armed forces in a major operation on June 6, 1976, at the age of forty-one.[65]

According to the show's marketing materials, *Mi Vida Después* asked three simple questions:

Lola Arias's *Mi Vida Después* (My Life After). *Photo by Lorena Fernández.*

Who were my parents when I was born?

What was Argentina like before I learned to speak?

How many versions are there about what happened before I existed or when I was so young that I can't remember?[66]

These are at the heart of the myriad stories we witness in *Mi Vida Después*. The performers, like preschool children role-playing adult life, reenact versions of family histories, anecdotes, and memories, to see what sticks, what fits, what remains. Referring to children of Holocaust survivors, these are what Marianne Hirsch has called "the generation of postmemory," who carry not the lived experiences themselves, but the "post-memorial" work of trauma.[67]

Thus the performers in *Mi Vida Después* make sense of the present moment through the once removed histories of their parents. As part of the postdictatorship generation, they draw upon events that they did not experience firsthand but either heard about through their relatives or were aware of because of their parents' involvement, interweaving personal narrative with public documentation of major historical events. The ensemble speaks directly to us, complicit in the fact that they are testifying right here, right now. In speaking about *Biodrama*, Tellas explained its specificity in relation to Argentina's history:

> In Argentina it's very difficult—the years of dictatorship, and I insist on this because it's very difficult—*desaparecidos*, people being killed, tortured and you just can't get over it yet. It's like you know the value of your life and your experience was very . . . like you weren't worth anything. So my project on *Biodrama* is also putting a light on that. Your experience has value and it's unique. Your experience is what you have and nobody can take that away, so how can we do some poetic theater work with that.[68]

In *Mi Vida Después*, it is this experience that is put forth front and center. Historical trauma is embodied, remembered, and shared onstage. There is a sort of showy "I am demonstrating something to you now" quality to all the performances throughout the piece that acknowledges the audiences' own act of witnessing. There is a simultaneous embrace of theatricality—the magic "as if," the recourse of pretend—as well as an antitheatrical affinity with the lecture format that cries out, right in our face, "This is true!" Rather than considering itself a "history lesson" about Argentina's past, Arias wanted to use the performers' microhistories, their lived reality—as prompted by Tellas's *Biodrama* experiment—to challenge theatrical representation. "If we want to make political theater," Arias recounts in an interview in *Bomb* magazine, "the form itself also has to be put into question."[69]

Arias was thus keen on selecting performers whose parents represented a broad spectrum of political perspectives. To choose the cast, which she characterized as a "very strange process, almost CIA-like," she would "call actors and non-actors and say things like, 'I know that your father disappeared, but I don't know which political party he belonged to.'"[70] The ensemble ranged from children of guerrilla activists and exiled intellectuals, to children of the military or right-wing sympathizers. As Cecilia Rosa writes in her review for *E-misférica*, "The piece include[d] the testimonies of those who are not usually considered victims,"[71] which is rare in Argentine representations of this period.

One of these embodied testimonies, unbeknownst to Arias and the cast, would find its own off-site audience, and would eventually be accepted as actual testimony in the case against Luis Antonio Falco, generating its own off-site spectatorship. As Arias told me, "another important factor in my work is how the real starts to affect the piece and how the piece begins to affect the real. The writing continues to change as time goes on and as the performers' lives evolve. The piece incorporates these changes, which are always contemporary."[72]

Mi Vida Después featured actress Vanina Falco, whose biological father, Luis Antonio Falco, was on trial at the time the show premiered in 2009, for abducting her brother, Juan Cabandié, during Argentina's military regime. Cabandié's biological parents, Alicia Alfonsín and Damián Abel Cabandié were abducted from their homes on November 1977, when Alicia was five months pregnant. They were then transferred to the clandestine detention and former torture center Escuela Superior de Mecánica de la Armada, otherwise known as ESMA (now a memorial site), where Juan was born in 1978.[73] Falco, a former intelligence officer who worked for the Argentine Police, falsified birth papers and brought the infant to his home, raising him as his own with his wife and their daughter Vanina. It wasn't until 2003, when Juan was twenty-five, that he began to doubt his identity.[74] Cabandié alerted the Abuelas de Plaza de Mayo, who conducted a DNA test that identified him as the child of Alicia and Damián, the seventy-seventh grandchild recuperated by the Abuelas.[75]

Nine minutes into the show, Vanina takes the microphone, downstage right, and speaks directly to us, as we see what appears to be a vintage photograph projected on the large screen behind her. The actors who place the photograph on the overhead projector are visible to the audience. "This is the album of the photos from my childhood," she announces. As she describes each image, the other actors draw on the photographs with a red pen, like a teacher would in a classroom setting while explaining a lesson:

> 1976. My uncle [*they draw a red circle around the uncle's face*], my grandfather [*another circle*], and my father [*circle*]. All policemen. They have police faces, police moustaches [*they draw red moustaches on the moustaches*], police attitudes [*they draw a circle around the hands on their waists*]. My father never wore a police uniform because he was in the secret police and worked undercover. That's me, at the bottom [of the photo], sitting in front of my birthday cake, with a strange line cutting through my head [there is a shadow in the photograph]. [We see a second photo: a woman next to a toddler, bathing a baby.]
>
> 1978. This is me when I was three, watching as my mother bathes my brother. In the photo you can see that I am very happy but very confused. I don't quite understand where my brother came from. I don't remember seeing my mother pregnant. [We see a third image.]
>
> 1980. Me hugging my brother. He's the person I love the most in my family. We were always alike. The same green eyes. The same brown hair. Even the same smile. But five years ago we found out that we aren't in fact brother and sister.[76] [*Vanina looks back at the image as it is cut in half*].

The play progresses, and we hear all the performers' stories, as well as Vanina's memories of the different faces of her father. One hour into the show, Vanina gathers dossiers from the floor, places documents into folders, and says:

Screenshot of Vanina Falco reacting to her brother's trial against their father, Luis Falco.

When my brother found out that my father had stolen him, he took him to court. This trial has been going on for five years and it still hasn't finished. So we still don't know how my dad got my brother, or what kind of work he did for the secret police. These are the documents for the trial. Do you want to see them?

Clearly, we do. The cast joins her, gathering on a couch downstage left, and sits beside her. Vanina hands them the folders. They take turns reading from the official dossiers:

LIZA: Statement by Luis Falco, your dad. *She reads from his testimony in court.* Having advised the doctors of our decision to adopt a baby, on the 4th of April 1978, I was informed that a boy had been born who was available for adoption. I did not hesitate to tell my wife that our long-awaited son had arrived, and in order to make the situation less traumatic, I deliberately neglected to request information regarding his birth parents.

VANINA: It's impossible he didn't know where that baby came from. In fact, I remember he brought him home in his arms.

PABLO: Luis Antonio Falco brought Mariano Andrés Falco to the family home stating to the deponent that he had taken responsibility for the adoption procedures.

LIZA: Didn't your mom ever ask where your brother came from?

VANINA: Yes, she says he told her he was the son of a girl who couldn't keep him.

PABLO: How old was your brother when he started to suspect he wasn't part of your family?

VANINA: Well, he started . . .

CARLA: There's something about that here. *She reads.* For some years the deponent suspected that he had no biological relation to Luis Antonio Falco. He was also surprised that while there were photographs of his newborn sister, of the pregnancy, there were none of the deponent. In 2003 . . . *She looks to Vanina.* How old was your brother?

VANINA: 25

CARLA: He asked his mother if he was her son and she told him that he was. Six months later she admitted that he was not. *Carla looks to Vanina.* Where's your statement?

It is in this moment, as we witness this live reading of testimonies taken from Falco's trial, which was actually occurring during the run of *Mi Vida Después*, that Vanina explains her own absence at trial: "I wanted to make a statement, but the law says that a child cannot make any statement against his or her own parents. I would have to take him to court myself." Because of this witnessed moment of truth told in public, on-site *in* the theatre, Falco's lawyers were able to convincingly argue to approve her appeal and accept her performance as her official word, off-site. Staged truth became witnessed truth. Theatre performed a form of "retroactive justice," as Brenda Werth writes in *Theatre, Performance, and Memory Politics in Argentina*.[77] On- and off-site audiences were connected through Vanina's embodied testimony, as both essentially interacted with the same performance, which had materialized the relationship between on- and off-site spectators:

> When we began the show, [Vanina] began a fight to have the right to testify. And after we did the show, the lawyer asked how it was possible that the court would not provide her a place to speak but that she was giving her testimony in a theater. In this instance, the theater was fulfilling a necessary function the court refused her. And, thanks to this argument, the lawyer was able to actually change the law.[78]

In 2011, Vanina's father was condemned to eighteen years in prison, the maximum penalty for appropriation of a minor and stealing an identity. More than just blurring the boundaries between fact and fiction, *Mi Vida Después* intervened not only with shaping how a public might consider its past but also had real implications in terms of changing the law and generating a site of spectatorship outside the theatre that interacted with Vanina Falco's testimony onstage. This transformed, as Ward aptly argues, "the reality of the individual stories told in the play into the reality of an entire country." The piece realized an off-site reception concurrent with the one inside the theatre, generating—*and* connecting—multiple spectator sites where Vanina Falco's performance resonated.

Spectator Sites

A few years ago I interviewed Helen Cole, formerly live arts curator at the Arnolfini arts center, now director of the In Between Time Festival in Bristol, England, for a special issue of *Theater* on performance curating (the same issue with Arias's interview). Cole told me about a research project she had begun years earlier, in 2008, which she had initiated for the purposes of archiving performances as she was leaving her position at Arnolfini, one of the top contemporary art galleries in the United Kingdom, and transitioning to being an independent curator.[79] In order to trace the developments of decades of performances, and somehow measure its impact, she asked individuals from the Arnolfini audiences to share with her a moment of performance that had been important to them. "I deliberately didn't define what I meant by performance," she told me. "I wanted them to decide what they meant by it" (Cole, 63). The responses ranged from memories of conventional performances that "might happen in an arts setting like a theater or a gallery space" to a moment that related to a performance; for example, "they might talk about something that happened in their family or something they'd come across in the street" (Cole, 91–95). In other words, "they were really talking more about being audience members than they were about the event itself," Cole emphasized.

What initially began with twenty audio recordings eventually grew to over eight hundred by 2011, when Cole decided to theatricalize a selection of these into an ever-evolving sound and light installation that she titled *We See Fireworks*, described as "a curated collection of memories of past performances or performative moments whispered softly into the darkness." For the exhibit, which toured internationally (although I unfortunately did not experience it firsthand), Cole filled the room with vintage lightbulbs that represented each memory and would flicker on and off as people listened to the recordings. As the spectator entered the dark room, "they listened to eight of those recordings, and then they were taken from that very comfortable space into another adjacent space that was set up like a recording studio, and in that space I asked them to donate a memory of their own to the archive. So we've ended up with this viral collection, one memory informing another memory" (Cole, 64).

Essentially, *We See Fireworks*, which self-generated fragments of audience experience as it toured, is very much a work that materializes spectator sites, and simultaneously generates new ones, ad infinitum. As you listen to people describe a performance you did not see and never will, you are imagining that performance through the mind of the other. You are both yourself *and* the other spectator. You are the off-site spectator for the original performance as well the on-site for the *We See Fireworks* event, somehow both present and absent simultaneously. You are interacting with the performance's lived memory and its disappearance, even as you witness its permanent trace. "I was trying to unravel that idea of 'audience'—the importance of audience members in the performance experience—by bringing their voices into this installation." In *We See Fireworks*, the off-site audience *was* present. It was actively involved in the production of this newly formed artwork. The spectator and the *other* spectator—that unintended audience—were one and the same.

4. Temporal Sites
Moving Site, Moving Time

To trouble linear temporality—to suggest that time may be touched, crossed, visited or revisited, that time is transitive and flexible, that time may recur in time, that time is not one—never only one—is to court the ancient (and tired) Western anxiety over ideality and originality.

—Rebecca Schneider, *Performing Remains: Art and War in Times of Theatrical Reenactment*, 2011

There is no beginning, middle or end. The narrative happens over the course of the whole performance so you might come in 4 hours after it started and see the very beginning of the play, or you might come in at the very beginning just in time for the end.

—Jim Findlay, *Huffington Post*, 2014

Dealey Plaza

A few years ago I visited the site of John F. Kennedy's assassination when I happened to be in Dallas for a conference. Dealey Plaza was less than ten minutes away from my hotel, so I decided to check it out. I had only two hours to spare. Tickets to The Sixth Floor Museum were sold out. The museum, named after the sixth floor of the Texas School Book Depository (TSBD), where three spent cartridge shells were discovered with a sniper's perch and rifle within forty-five minutes after President Kennedy was shot, recreated the crime scene in the actual space where it had occurred. I had really wanted to see it, to stand in the very place where history had been made on November 22, 1963. I settled for the $2.50 cell phone audio tour of the museum's surroundings around Dealey Plaza. With the detailed map in hand, I listened to the descriptions I had downloaded on the museum's app at all of the stops. These included "the grassy knoll" on the northwest side of the Plaza, famous for the myriad conspiracy theories that claim it as the place where another assassin may have stood; a pedestal that marks where Abraham Zapruder unexpectedly filmed what became the only color movie of the assassination; the X on the street at the precise location where President Kennedy was fatally shot as the motorcade was headed toward the Triple Underpass, itself another site where many witnesses stood and later gave multiple testimonies of what they saw unfold that day. Due to conservation efforts—the place was designated a National Historic Landmark in 1993—very few things, other than traffic lights perhaps, have changed since that fatal day in 1963. The site was oddly familiar. All of the precise locations of President Kennedy's assassination were there, materialized in front of me, locations I had only seen recreated in movies such as Oliver Stone's 1991 *JFK* as well as countless documentaries that used footage from Zapruder's film. The audio guide helped to take me back in time as I physically retraced the crime scene in the now, imagining the events as they had unfolded, in the exact places where they had occurred.

This "on-location" context, or triggering of memory of a historical moment thanks to a specific location where the event in fact took place, is common. The preservation of physical sites, in particular where painful histories occurred, such as former German Nazi concentration and extermination camps, former slave plantations and slave cabins,[1] genocide memorial sites in Rwanda,[2] former torture centers in Latin America, and countless war memorials where battles were fought, is an ongoing practice to help remember the past for future generations. Many of these sites include photographs or archive material, sometimes remnants of clothes or objects that serve as testimony. Some places have survivors, who recount their experiences as living proof of what happened.[3] While the aim might not necessarily be to relive traumatic experiences, but more importantly, to not forget them so they may not be repeated, the physical interaction with a location's history very often does have an affect on its visitors. A location and its context—in particular its relation to the past—becomes a crucial factor in determining the experience an individual might have while visiting that site.

In her book *Performing Remains*, Rebecca Schneider writes about live reenactment, which she describes as "the practice of re-playing or re-doing a precedent event, artwork, or act."[4] Her focus is on both civil war reenactments ("replayed war" [Schneider, 2]) and time-based art ("replayed art" [Schneider, 2]), the latter of which, as Schneider emphasizes, has "exploded in performance-based art" (Schneider, 10). Schneider distinguishes the practice of reenactment from living history: whereas reenactment mostly refers to the replay of events as accurately as possible, living history refers to "the activity of enacting a past way of life where there may be no 'event' of record"

(Schneider, 187). This distinction is important, since it indicates how reenactment references a specific event. Her interest, be it in art reenactment or battle reenactment, lies in those live reenactments that strive for literal precision, where reenacting a past event *just so* means the re-living of that event. As Schneider writes, "they will have touched time and time will have recurred." This constant interplay between "what really happened" in relation to "keeping the past alive" is what Schneider calls "the syncopated time of reenactment, where *then* and *now* punctuate each other" (Schneider, 2). She argues how in these cases performance itself *is* the archive, disappearing *and* recording simultaneously[5] ("the past is not [entirely] dead, since it can be accessed *live*"). Schneider politicizes the "stakes of reenactment,"[6] by troubling the linear temporality of chronological time: "What if time (re) turns? What does it *drag* along with it?" (Schneider, 2) she asks, suggesting, instead, that time may indeed be "touched, crossed, visited or revisited, that time is transitive and flexible, that time may recur in time" (Schneider, 30).

My own JFK tourist experience at Dealey Plaza was clearly not a reenactment. At least not in the way "reenactment" is traditionally defined as a redoing of a previous event. Although I may have been reliving an event in my mind that was not the actual event but the event reimagined from books, movies, and the media, it was more of a live retelling of sorts, an itinerant retracing of footsteps, with the help of a curator's voice on audio. And yet there was something about being physically present in that location, in the act of moving through that space—listening to the audio guide, retracing steps, seeing the events play out in my mind as I visited the landmarks—that had caused the past to reappear, if only in my imagination. The site in this case was the very location where the event happened, so I was very much on-site, and yet experienced the event *off-time*. Its temporal presence had depended on its specific (geographic and historic) location in conjunction with my embodied choreography through the space. My off-time moment referenced a real event that had occurred not only without me but also before my time.

Like Schneider, I am drawn to the relationship of embodied practice to time: bodies *in* space, as they move in a particular location that cites the past, or stops time, or stalls it, repeats or loops it, or perhaps even projects toward a future. I am interested in how activating space (on-location space, specifically) through the manipulation of bodies in performance (both performer and spectator bodies), dislocates time and renders a nonlinear, "off-time" temporality in the now, *on-site*. Rather than focus on the reenactment of a specific event, however, I'd like to examine aesthetic practices that manipulate time through an *embodied* encounter with space. Where does the performance "take us," both literally (physically) and metaphorically? What alternative approaches to space *on-site* propose alternative conceptions of time?

Temporal Reconsiderations

In his book *Shakespeare, Theatre, and Time*, Matthew D. Wagner addresses the nature of time in theatre. Grounded on Edmund Husserl's ideas on time consciousness—the counterintuitive notion that it is our individual subjective experience of time (phenomenological time) that regulates and grounds objective time (clock time) and not the other way around[7]—Wagner argues that theatre, by its very ontology, "fosters temporal discordance," since it presents us with "both time schemes at once" (Wagner, 15). The theatre, irrespective of the intentions of the playwright, director, or actor, makes us aware of both clock time and inner time, simultaneously. In Wagner's words, theatre shuttles us back and forth between each, "by not reconciling the one with the other or explaining one in terms of the other" (Wagner, 18). Theatre therefore "helps us *experience*" Husserl's notion that "clock time is not real time, in spite of its prominence in our everyday lives" (Wagner, 18). Temporal dissonance is only one aspect of Wagner's bigger project, which is to counter the linear perception of time as we experience it in the theatre. The other important quality to theatre's out of joint-ed-ness is what Wagner identifies as "an amplified 'thickness' or density" (Wagner, 28). Explains Wagner: "Between the two [Husserl and Heidegger], we have a useful and apt way to think about the phenomenon of the theatrical present: it is a way of being present that, largely because of the theatre's temporal frame, strongly incorporates the past and the future" (Wagner, 29–30). This temporal density, as Wagner calls it, which characterizes every present moment as it is experienced in the theatre, is largely unavailable in our everyday lives: "In the life of the theatrical event, birth and death stay with us, are present to us, in much more palpable and direct ways than they are otherwise" (Wagner, 31).

Wagner's "thick present," while rich in its undoing of a chronological temporality in theatre as it is experienced *live*, moment to moment, is nevertheless aligned with an ahistorical framework. In her book *The Past Is the Present; It's the Future Too: The Temporal Turn in Contemporary Art*, Christine Ross argues that contemporary art's "temporal turn" is visible in the aesthetic practices that "connect temporality and historicity."[8] Ross examines practices that, she argues, bring historicity *into* the present, which she claims are unique in their encompassing "both a contemporalization (of temporal passing) and a reactivation (of historicity)."[9] For Ross, artists involved in this "temporal turn" are not only shifting away from conceptualizing time as continuous, or linear, but also, and simultaneously, questioning the modernist notion of history as progress. They are instead moving "*towards* a post-metaphysical 'presentifying' aesthetics of reorientation of modern conventions of historical time."[10] In other words, Ross is getting at those aesthetic practices in the visual arts that help us *feel* time, so as to consider the possibility of a different kind of past-in-the-present.

Ross's work on alternative temporalities is tied to a critical historicity that is continuously reinvented, reinterpreted, and possibly reimagined and therefore reoccurring, time and time again. It is akin to Schneider's account of a nonlinear temporality in reenactment that works against Western capitalist formulations of time as progress. Schneider is also very much interested in a nonchronological temporal possibility where performance, as opposed to a disappearing act (an allusion to Peggy Phelan's *Unmarked*), *is* the record of the thing it alludes to. I'd like to consider how the possibility of an "*off-time*" time at site, as I introduced earlier, is an alternative temporality that is aligned with such nonchronological underpinnings. I will focus on three performances whose alteration of space, either fixed in a specific geographical location (tied to a historical moment), or sensorial in an immersive installation, enabled us to experience time differently. Branislav Jakovljevic, in his introduction to a special issue of *Performance Research* on time, reminds us how "experimental performance [has been] invested in a search for alternative temporalities" since the early twentieth century, "with the invention of irregular times of performance, from durational performance, to marathon theatre, to ritualized action" all of which can be seen "as an expression of performance's inherent foreignness to the abstract time of the clock and the calendar."[11] In the examples that follow, which vary widely in scope, I examine how the specificity of location—on site—affects both Wagner's notion of temporal dissonance, as well as Ross's critical historicity. How might the manipulation of space mobilize time? What forms of *off-time* experience were rendered due to the audiences' embodied experience in those spaces?

Moving Off Time

On August 13 and 14 of 2003, a one-hour long performance called *Geyser Land*, conceived and directed by video artist Mary Ellen Strom and choreographer Ann Carlson, took place in a twenty-five-mile strip of land between Livingston and Bozeman, Montana. A total of about thirteen hundred audience members (about 350 at a time) boarded a ten-car passenger train operated by Montana Rockies Rail Tours, "a classic 50's carrier à la Hitchcock," as the *New York Times* described it, complete "with dome cars, a classy dining car, a club car and vestibules in which Dutch doors open halfway so that the mountains rushing by seem almost touchable."[12] The train's architecture was reminiscent of "those great family vacations!" as was advertised, with windows designed for 360-degree viewing of the outdoor scenic landscape. En route, the passenger spectators witnessed large-scale video projections of roaming and now-absent buffalo onto the mountains surrounding the traveling train and Eadweard Muybridge's animal motion studies. Passengers arriving at the Bozeman depot observed scenes from the 1895 film *Arrival of a Train at the Station* by the Lumière Brothers, and Edwin Porter's *Great Train Robbery* from 1903 projected onto an abandoned refrigerator truck, as well as short scenes appropriated from classic Western films such as *Western Frontier Horizon* (1937).[13] Passengers also saw *tableaux vivant*—archival photographs from the turn of the twentieth century to 1972 that were strategically restaged by Ann Carlson, with live performers on the spots where the images were originally taken—spaced throughout the landscape outside the train.[14]

Presented by the Myrna Loy Center in Helena, Montana, in conjunction with the Montana Arts Council and the Livingston Depot Center, *Geyser Land* was part installation, part historical reenactment, part community project, part train ride, and part living sculpture, as the artists described it.[15] It was a conceptual tour experience that used both the natural scenery and the train ride as the performance space in order to re-examine, in the present, a contested historical narrative of conquest and colonization. The location was chosen precisely because of its loaded, and often ignored history regarding the treatment of Native Americans (the Northern Plain Indians known as Crow Nation) who were pushed out of Yellowstone Park and allowed back in the park after the Civil Rights Act of 1964. The Bozeman Pass, as the artist statement explains, "remained one of the longest contested sites between white settlers and the non-treaty Northern Plain Indians, which ended when the Northern Pacific Railroad forged a tunnel through the pass in 1880."[16] In other words, the removal of the Northern Plains Indians was directly linked to the existence of the passenger train the audience boards as part of the performance and its attraction as a tourist site. Both film and transcontinental railroad industries were new experiences for people at the turn of the twentieth century. Contemporary audiences were in a moving train observing the moving images—similar to the way that original passengers had discovered for the first time the landscape (and film) as moving picture. This layering of experiences sets the audience of *Geyser Land* on another sort of time travel, where both cinema and the moving landscape are experienced as if anew.

A little over a year after *Geyser Land*, from September 8 to 11, 2004, another form of multisite and itinerant performance took place over a two-hundred-mile route in southeastern Kentucky. *RFK in EKY*, conceived and directed by Los Angeles Poverty Department (LAPD) founder John Malpede, was a "real time, site-specific intermedia performance" event that recreated, thirty-six years later, Robert F. Kennedy's original 1968 War on Poverty tour in the region.[17] The performance, produced with LAPD's co-director Henriëtte Brouwers, alongside Appalshop (an arts and media organization in Whitesburg, which is a town of sixteen hundred in the heart of eastern Kentucky), included a procession of motor vehicles, two official hearings of the Senate Subcommittee on Employment, Manpower, and Poverty (held at Vortex and Fleming-Neon, Kentucky), roadside visits with individual families, walking tours of Liberty Street and strip mine sites, a stop at the former one-room schoolhouse in Barwick, and verbatim reenactments of RFK's interviews and speeches on streets, in courthouses, and at the local college with actor participants.

Using the original landscape and its community (with an all-local cast of hundreds), *RFK in EKY* invited participants to reflect on present-day conditions of Appalachia and alternative visions for the future by engaging with this familiar, and in this case, local, historical event. It is an example of what Scott Magelssen calls "invocational simming," where audiences both enact and rehearse for a future reality and advocate for it, embodying the change they want to see.[18] *RFK in EKY* reenacted encounters and speeches from the most significant events of Robert Kennedy's highly publicized poverty tour in Appalachia, which occurred one month before he announced his presidential run and four months before his assassination in 1968. In Malpede's words, *RFK in EKY* was an opportunity "to revisit the essential and still pertinent questions raised in the original visit" during a pivotal election year, a few months before George W. Bush was to be re-elected for a second term as president of the United States.[19]

Unfortunately, due to distance and expense, I did not experience either *Geyserland* or *RFK in EKY* firsthand—which points to the critical element of site specificity in both pieces.[20] Their unique and critical location targeted the local community and its residents as the audience members, who were participant performers, as I will soon discuss. To uproot the productions and perform them elsewhere would have been impossible, and more significantly, pointless. These were performances whose site specificity was wholly ingrained in the land: in its history, its access (or lack thereof), its people and culture, and its community. What is particularly striking about both these performances, besides their enormous scale—both took four years to make, included casts and crew of over a hundred people, required an extensive budget, and produced lengthy documentation and multimedia archives—is how both activated time through wide open, porous, neglected, and rural spaces. *RFK in EKY* used the region's sites to enable people to circulate and recontextualize their own surroundings, creating landmarks of perhaps forgotten architectures. *Geyser Land* created a tourist experience to revisit and question historical formulations of the landscape. In both of these performances, the dramaturgy of reenactment was completely linked to the dramaturgy of site (what story the space revealed), allowing content and place to merge in recreating a significant moment in history *as* future-present. Both *Geyser Land* and *RFK in EKY* are connected to a new historicity: a way of looking at the past (through specific location and embodiment) that challenges that past *as* progress. As Strom and Carlson explain, "The project, among other things, sought to challenge and dismantle the notion of history as a continuous development."[21] Malpede, in his artist statement, also counters the aim of reenactment as a nostalgic act, seeking instead "to inject history with critical thinking" through this one-time, four-day performance. In both cases, the dramaturgy and simultaneity of events changed not only the way its audience/participants perceived space but, more significantly, the way they perceived its history in relation to the present. As Jan Cohen-Cruz observed of *RFK in EKY*, "I felt like I was time traveling, back and forth, between 1968 and now."[22] Both of these productions manipulated time precisely by immersing audiences spatially.

Another, very different performance, one that I'd nevertheless also like to consider in relation to *Geyser Land* and *RFK in EKY* as another spatially activated "off-time" immersion, is *Dream of the Red Chamber*, an installation for a sleeping audience directed by Jim Findlay, conceived and written with Jeff Jackson, which I saw in New York City in 2014. For the performance, which was loosely based on the epic eighteenth-century Chinese novel of the same name (*Shítóu jì*) by Cao Xueqin, also known as *The Story of the Stone*, Findlay and his team built an underground environment that was a cross between a den-like brothel and a luxurious spa, filled with forty red-sheeted cots—all in the basement of the Brill Building in the middle of Times Square. The audience could come and go at any time between 5:00 P.M. and midnight. We could sleep, and were in fact encouraged to do so during the show—hence the late viewing hours and, on other days, additional overnight performances that lasted until 6:00 A.M.

If *Geyser Land* and *RFK in EKY* took inspiration from historical events and staged them on location, circulating audiences not only through motor vehicles, buildings, landscapes, and pathways but also displacing them through time, *Dream of the Red Chamber* suspended time, daring us to surrender to it by asking us to embrace what seems like the most passive state par excellence, sleep. In addition, by encouraging audiences to come and go as they pleased (physically and metaphorically), and creating a place where we were in fact encouraged to tune out, *Red Chamber* enabled us, paradoxically, *to wake up*, to be present in the here and now, between altered states of consciousness. It allowed me to contemplate the possibility of dreams as reality, and reality as a dream: an *off time* where presence and absence are one and the same.

Before delving into each of these performances in detail, however, let's first look at the notion of movement and mobilities in space and time.

Mobilities in Space and Time

In her book *Performance, Transport, and Mobility: Making Passage*, Fiona Wilkie addresses different modes of transport, including walking, boats, trains, automobiles, and airplanes, as well as performances that either take place inside such systems of transport or whose content is shaped by them. Focusing on a range of performances that "work against the logic of uninterrupted flow," Wilkie demonstrates how these encourage spectators "to register their passage as a complex activity,"[23] essentially fostering a form of criticality. As such, Wilkie argues, they *make passage*, and develop a means of shaping how we might experience transit. She writes, "Performance not only responds to but can also produce mobilities, reshaping existing models of engendering new, alternative possibilities for movement."[24] Wilkie connects the notion of transit to the mobility turn in the social sciences, which analyzes social practices in terms of movement instead of spatial rootedness,[25] and is keen to unveil what David Creswell terms the "'historical conditions that produce specific forms of movement.'"[26]

Prior to *Making Passage*, Wilkie wrote about site-specific practices, most notably in the United Kingdom, as well as itinerant performance.[27] As her research developed, Wilkie explored the ways performance addressed issues of mobility and transport, even when "grounded" in a specific location. She articulated an important shift in site-specific practices from *inhabiting* a place to *moving through* spaces,[28] as artists began to transport audiences from one place to another. In a special issue of *Contemporary Theatre Review* on "Site-Specificity and Mobility," Anna Birch emphasizes how "site" is "more mobile than the discourse generally permits," and explores the concept of mobility as an engagement with the action of moving in order to "upset the 'fixedness' of site's specificity."[29] As Henri Lefebvre famously argues in *The Production of Space*, space, which is socially constructed, actively shapes an event; the space itself is never fixed; it continuously evolves as a social entity.[30] Wilkie, who also contributed to this collection with "Site-Specific Performance and the Mobility Turn," argues how contemporary site practices might incorporate "other ways of being on the move."[31]

Wilkie highlights the embodied activity of movement and circulation of audiences that goes beyond walking—beyond the psychogeographic mapping practices or sound walks—encouraging us to think about less visible figures on the move (the refugee, the migrant, the vagrant, the nomad) and the various modes of moving practices: "Even when site-specific practice is conceived as intrinsically tied to physicality and meanings of one site, and therefore in some ways immobile, attending it often requires a different kind of mobility of its audience than the usual modes of theatre-going."[32] She highlights three ways in particular: audience transport to/from site, journey *as* mode of performance, and invitation to think about what it means to be in transit. I find Wilkie's audience-centered approach a useful tool for looking closely at how *Geyser Land*, *RFK in EKY*, and *Dream of the Red Chamber* dislocate and therefore mobilize time and audience/participants, and how both are contingent upon the other. The audience for *Geyser Land*, which invoked the chronotype of the train narrative, is encouraged to move about on a moving train, and is thus doubly mobile. Likewise, the audience in *RFK in EKY*, akin to the campaign narrative, was encouraged not only to move with the RFK motorcade from Vortex to Fleming-Neon to Hazard but also to mingle with one another during the various stops along the way. In *Dream of the Red Chamber*, we were encouraged to come and go as we pleased, to lie down on the beds, rest or sleep, walk around, to close our eyes and dream. Such forms of circulation, as David Wiles writes, "play upon the spectator's sense of lived time."[33] These events are not only itinerant in the locational sense, journeying us through spaces, from one place to another, but also in their time dimension, either traveling multiple time periods in the here and now, or enabling us to feel different rhythms of time simultaneously.

Of course, movement through space is always temporal, in the sense that it takes actual time—a precise measurable unit of duration in which one can get from place A to place B—which is why the "mobility turn" in Wilkie's language is one that necessarily implicates the temporal. Audience mobilities, the circulation of audiences, are thus already temporal structures that get laid over a number of mobilities. These include historical mobilities—RFK moving across Appalachia, tourists moving across Yellowstone—but also more metaphorical mobilities, like Cohen-Cruz's feeling of time travel, as well as my own sensation in *Red Chamber* of moving from being fully awake, to drowsing off, no longer knowing whether I was dreaming or not. I had the constant sensation that time was suspended. There are also literal (and negative) mobilities, such as the displacement of native populations to make way for the railroad, which *Geyser Land* emphasizes, as well as *im*mobilities, blocked social mobilities, and a lack of access to upward mobility, a theme concurrent in both *RFK in EKY* and *Geyser Land*. Temporal sites are thus spaces where time is *moved*: activated, revisited, and questioned, but also moved to a standstill. They are both material (the actual location as it is preserved, such as a childhood home, Dealey Plaza, a battlefield, crime scene, etc.), and immaterial (in the sense that they are created by the interaction of a spectator/participant *in* that space). The temporal sites created in and by performance are both temporary—ephemeral, in the moment—and permanent, since they may change how we view and/or remember a site's relationship to its history. Joseph Roach, in *Cities of the Dead: Circum-Atlantic Performance*, shows how embodied memory, the *doing* of acts with one's body, what he terms "kinesis," can rewrite the course of history *as it is remembered*. These acts of surrogation, how a culture reproduces and re-creates itself, thus alter collective memory.[34]

Whereas the Montana Pass of *Geyser Land* and the southeastern Kentucky region of *RFK in EKY* are "fixed" geographical sites, these performances rendered them (temporarily) mobile by orchestrating interactive, immersive, and itinerant theatrical devices that embodied, and therefore generated, an elasticity of time. *Dream of the Red Chamber* moved its audience to an alternative consciousness of *being* "in time." In these performances, audiences circulate, their movement is choreographed *in time*: they are moved, *not* moved, lulled to sleep, or left to roam, all of which have specific political implications—insofar as these movements–or lack thereof—invoke specific temporal sites that, as Schneider suggests with performance art and war reenactments, *counter* the linear, nostalgic clock narrative and call instead for a criticality, a remaking, a re-creation, a possibility of seeing not necessarily again, but anew.

With this focus on ways of moving and moving bodies in and through space, then, we can now turn to how these performances *moved* us, temporally speaking.

Time Moves in Multiple Directions at Once

As soon as audiences, who paid $40 a ticket, boarded the spacious passenger train in *Geyser Land*, they were readily placed in a position of leisure. Strom and Carlson established the spectators' role as tourists from the onset, encouraging them to move around the train and circulate like the travelers from decades ago, as had been the original intention set by the train's architecture. The audience heard the following message when they entered the train:

> The Northern Pacific had the new American passenger cars that completely differed from European compartmentalized cars. The cars were wide open and designed to allow passengers a great deal of mobility during the trip. They were encouraged to move around, to change seats, to sit with someone new. A traveler was free to go and sit down next to whomever they liked and to change places again and again. So, we encourage you to move around the train during the next hour.[35]

This active role was critical for engaging audiences not so much as voyeurs to the past, but as tourists aware of a constructed narrative, that, as Strom and Carlson explain, "points to the railroad as a tool of colonialism."[36] It is worth noting that Montana Rockies Rail Tours had promoted trips in the Montana region as providing passengers with "never-ending views of the spectacular scenery."[37] In *Geyser Land*, Strom and Carlson cleverly usurp this scenery to reclaim another vision of what it is we are looking at, and reclaim what has gone for so many years either ignored or forgotten.

Even before boarding the train, spectators at the Livingston depot experienced simultaneity of events happening around them, all the while understanding that something was anachronistic. They encountered Northern Cheyenne tribe members dancing in traditional dress, a group of local ranchers playing their regular poker game (performing as themselves), and the *tableaux vivant* of *Three Women and a Porter*, circa 1902 (photographer unknown), where four performers (Wayne Mansaw, Ann Johnson, Megan Schneeberger, and Kristi Topham-Petty) enacted the postures of the photographer's subjects, who appear to be three white, upper-class women, wearing replicas of early twentieth-century dress, attended by an African-American railroad porter. As the audience boards the train then, there is already a framing of historical class and race divisions, a mixture of what was then and what is now, and how that past inexorably informs the experience of the present.

Like *Geyser Land*, the role of the audience in *RFK in EKY* was carefully mapped out, in this case oscillating between the role of spectators of a reenactment event (past) and participating *as* spectators in the reenactment itself (present). In other words, as Cohen-Cruz wrote regarding her experience of the piece, *RFK in EKY* drew "everyone present into its world as a participant, snapping us back into the present, and then reeling us back 36 years again."[38] Throughout the four-day performance, where there was no admission fee and one could join at any moment, actors and spectators mingled with each other. Spectators would become part of the 1968 crowd. To get into the mood, everyone was invited daily for pancake breakfasts at Appalshop media and cultural center in Whitesburg to meet and greet, borrow sixties-style costumes, and get their hair styled. The mobility between sites was not only encouraged but had been strategically chosen so that conversations could evolve amongst actor/participants. The project archive details this aim, explaining how "the audience costuming solidified a kind of *temporal community*, a citizenship in the recreation that transcended individual differences—opening up a broader public space and encouraging deeper interactions [my emphasis]."[39] In addition, the distance between each stop was important for giving people enough time to interact with one another—"a critical processing arena" as their archives called it—enabling them "to share information and perspective" after visiting each site together.[40] Cohen-Cruz's travel notes are particularly helpful for bringing such unscripted moments to life, which are ultimately the kinds of conversations the project was aiming for:

> On Thursday I meet a local guy. . . . We get to talking about politics and he says eastern Kentucky is Republican now because of the religious values they preach. I ask him about the separation of church and state and he pauses. And I think that this moment is only possible because 1968 brought us together in 2004.

Circulation between *RFK*'s sites was a key element in exchanging ideas and providing multiple sightlines, transforming the space of time *for* and *by* the audience.

Motorcade arriving in Whitesburg, Kentucky, as part of *RFK in EKY*, September 2004. *Photo by Shawn Poynter. Courtesy of Henriëtte Brouwers.*

From left to right in the center foreground, RFK aide Peter Edelman (played by Mitty Owens), the real Peter Edelman, and Senator RFK (played by Jack Faust) in *RFK in EKY*, September 2004. *Photo by Shawn Poynter. Courtesy of Henriëtte Brouwers.*

Even as the local community witnessed the reenactment, they also belonged to it. As part of *RFK in EKY*'s development, project staff designed and implemented a series of "Memorabilia Gatherings" prior to the performance dates, where community members were invited to share their stories on video or audiotape and have their photos and letters scanned.[41] Many of these were subsequently published in the *RFK in EKY Times*, a physical newspaper distributed to audience participants throughout the course of the four-day event. Some of the performance's stops formally included the sharing of such recollections from the community. For example, at a preserved one-room schoolhouse in Barwick (which at the time held approximately thirty-two students from grades kindergarten through eighth grade), rather than recreate the events from 1968, Malpede instead decided to use the space for public conversation.[42] Audience participants entered and watched a video projected onto the wall of Kennedy's original visit to that school, where he moved from desk to desk, knelt at their level, and whispered to each child individually. The audience then heard former teachers and students speak about that visit. Peter Edelman, longstanding antipoverty activist and Kennedy's legislative assistant who helped to plan and presided in the original 1968 tour, introduced Bonnie Jean Carol, who was still teaching kindergarten in a Head Start program at Chavies in 2004, and Zona Akemon, the school cook. The three of them, along with John Malpede, stood in the front, reminiscing about that time, as audience members listened:

PETER: How hard was it to teach in a one-room school?

BONNIE: I enjoyed every minute of it. It wasn't hard.

PETER: Well maybe we should've kept it up!

BONNIE: It wasn't hard at all.

ZONA: They had to learn to work for themselves in a one-room school. They learned to study for themselves, didn't they Bonnie?

BONNIE: Sure did.[43]

Bonnie and Zona, then spectators to RFK's visit, now find themselves discussing their memory of the event as present-day spectators listen. As Bonnie and Zona continue to recall the conditions under which they taught, Edelman invites those audience members who were present at the original visit. The transcript reads,

P: Are there any of your students who are here today?

B: Yeah. Where are ya? J.D.

J: Come on up. Come on up here.

(Applause)

Jimmy Darrell Farler (J.D.), watching in the audience, was one of the children whom RFK spoke with at those desks, and recalled to a local newspaper how Kennedy had softly told him, "You can be what you want to be."[44] In these passages, we see the fluidity in which spectators of the original event in 1968 are now called upon as narrators.

Another component to RFK's *off-time* experience occurred through the portrayal of those performers who enacted a past generation. Phyllis Buckner, for example, who played her mother, Betty Terrill, reflected:

> I think that, you know, by doing this, it has showed that eastern Kentucky has moved up some, but it needs to continue to grow. We need more stuff here. Just like they wanted in '68. We still want it. We don't have a factory in Wolfe County today. So, if the children here, when they grow up, get a job, they have to leave to get a job. I don't want my

Motorcade on a strip mine at the Yellow Creek Mining Site, Knott County, Kentucky, as part of *RFK in EKY*, September 2004. Conversation with Dough Melton from B&W Resources Inc. Strip Mine. *Photo by Carmela Castrejon. Courtesy of Henriëtte Brouwers.*

child leavin'. I don't want my grandchildren leavin'. I want them here. So, you know, it's basically, like it was in '68. There's still no industry here. And farmlands are gettin' slower.[45]

What is significant here is how this "postshow" testimony stands as an encounter with its past that signals a need for improvement moving forward. Terrill points to an immobility that has been present in eastern Kentucky, where lack of industry has caused many to leave (an example of negative mobility). The act of performing in the present on-site enabled a live engagement with past issues the community was still struggling with, such as a lack of jobs and the region's economic decline. Actors cast were spectators not only to these past selves but also to the issues they raised.

If *Geyser Land* and *RFK in EKY* moved us "off time" in terms of a nonchronological temporality, where the past reappears in the present, *Dream of the Red Chamber* activated a different kind of temporal awareness, where nonlinearity was primarily due to a suspension of time. In this space, time was cyclical, and images, sounds, words, and sensations seemed to reappear, in an endless loop, in both dreams and reality.

Submerging Time, and Time Again

When I went to *Dream of the Red Chamber*, I got off the subway stop at Times Square. I tried my best to walk through the usual chaos and cacophony of traffic, tourists, massive digital screens, flashing billboards, and New York residents briskly walking past me. I focused on the directions indicated by the Google Maps app on my iPhone and very intently ignored the tour operators trying to sell me city bus tours, the watch peddlers with briefcase showrooms, the surreal life-size SpongeBob SquarePants and Minnie Mouse asking me to pose for a picture, the multiple requests for loose change. It was still light out. When I finally made it to 1619 Broadway, the performance's site, it was suddenly quiet as soon as I entered the building. It reminded me of that feeling you get when you dive into a pool, and slowly go under, submerging yourself in the fullness of silence underwater. A red carpet signaled a long corridor, which was lined on both sides with old-style cathode-ray-tube TVs planted on the floor leading to an open-steel staircase on the far right corner. The monitors displayed that grainy snow static that used to show up when something was wrong with the TV's reception. I remember thinking this was my brain after seven blocks in midtown Manhattan. I was glad for the mental pause. Time began to slow down.

We've all been there: a moment of extreme rush—being late to the theatre, dashing to the airport, scrambling to get the kids to school in time for work, racing to an exercise class. Once we get to that point of arrival, the feeling of relief somehow changes our internal clock. We breathe. We notice that breath. Everything seems calmer. I went down to the basement level, where I stood with other audience members in front of a large, sheer white curtain lit by red lights that shone through from the other side. The sheet blocked from view what we were about to experience. Two box office staff gently asked us to take off our shoes. They held aside the curtains and invited us into the main area, a large rectangular space that was approximately forty-five feet by sixty-five feet, fully carpeted and surrounded entirely by those same white, translucent, crushed-voile curtains, which prevented us from seeing the walls that were about ten feet away from the playing area. The space was very inviting; I felt a strong urge to enter and walk around. Cots, actually rollaway beds, filled the room, and both spectators and performers milled about the space. The fact that we were underground, below Times Square, somehow contributed to my experience of this off-time dimension, as if I had been physically cut off from the madness and mayhem that was happening "up there." I was now fully submerged underwater, moving closer toward the deep end.

In the epigraph to this chapter, I quote Findlay explaining how the piece operated like a durational performance or art installation. "We show it durationally," he says,

> so the show starts at 5 P.M. and goes until midnight some days and from 5 P.M. to 6 A.M. others. . . . There is no beginning, middle or end. The narrative happens over the course of the whole performance so you might come in 4 hours after it[']s started and see the very beginning of the play, or you might come in at the very beginning just in time for the end.[46]

We were thus privy to a world that existed without us, and would continue, *always*. The endlessness, or more precisely, the *appearance of* endlessness in this performance enabled time to feel suspended, as if we were submerging in time. In this scenario, we were "absent" voyeurs (absent in the sense that many of us would, in fact, fall asleep). It was as if what we were experiencing had been happening forever in a constant loop and would continue once we were gone. Time, in *here*, was at a standstill, and yet it was forever present.

Unlike immersive experiences where audiences are encouraged, sometimes even coerced, to either interact or engage in some form of exchange with the performers, *Dream of the Red Chamber* had an unbreakable fourth wall. Performers, whether portraying a character or not, never looked at or acknowledged us. We were in a dreamland whether we were asleep or awake; they existed whether we were there or not. The performance did not depend on our intervention or engagement. On the contrary, the live installation gave the feeling that it was happening *in spite* of our presence, a kind of dreamscape or "as if" world occurring before our eyes. Although we shared the physical terrain with the performers, we nevertheless maintained separate worlds where one was clearly the observer (when awake), and the other, clearly the observed. Okwui Okpokwasili, one of the *Chamber* ensemble members, described the sensation of playing in this world: "Only occasionally did I feel watched, but mostly I felt part of a sea, or a floating world that didn't demand any more than being in an unending present. . . . I found it freeing to perform for a sleeping audience."[47]

Of course what makes this piece stand out from other immersive environmental worlds is the fact that here the performance is meant to induce sleep. "We prefer that you not pay attention," Findlay emphasized, offering that

> one of the big things we found early on when we started doing research for this is once you disrupt that normal relationship between audience and performer, where the audience pays attention and the performer has a responsibility to be entertaining, once you disrupt that there's a whole new set of parameters that come into what it is to experience a work of art.[48]

In the underbelly of the megalopolis, where time moves at a speed that is supposedly in positive correlation to its productivity, it is counterintuitive to claim, as *Red Chamber* does, that *rest* might be as, or even more, productive than action. It is, however, quite compelling to contemplate how enabling sleep, an altered state of consciousness, might be more difficult, and perhaps even more demanding, than getting your audience to watch intently. Asking us to deliberately *not* pay attention will have us doing the opposite, kind of like telling a child "not to touch." Spend some time in New York City subway cars and you will notice how much effort urban dwellers put into effacing what is right in front of them, working hard to detach themselves from what is present. Video games, iPods, smartphones, books, magazines: we have long used handheld distractions to distance ourselves from our surroundings, which themselves are products of capitalist fantasies, all vying for our attention—Debord's worst society-of-the-spectacle nightmare come true.[49] We are daily sleepwalkers. Where do we turn to escape, or wake up? *Red Chamber* refocuses our gaze on *how* we experience, rather than *what* we see, hear, or feel, and allows us to become aware of our own submersion in an alternate, cyclical, *ever-present* temporality that counters the notion of linear time.

Various screens multiply and magnify the actions of performers Christina Campanella and Kaneza Schaal in *Dream of the Red Chamber. Photos by Paula Court.*

Juxtaposition, Loops, and Temporal Consciousness

Two final elements of these productions' ability to mobilize our sense of time has to do with the juxtaposition of images, video, and transcripts from the past with today's physical sites, as well as the looping of video stills and sound composition.

In *Geyser Land*, the projected images of buffalo onto the landscape serve as an example of this off-time layering. Once "tourists" boarded the train they noticed some young passengers. Crow Nation children of differing ages, who live on reservations south of Billings, "occupied" the train prior to everyone else's boarding. Given that the Crow had been pushed out of Paradise Valley (as it is often called), Carlson and Strom invited them early on to the process, and they were one of the first community partners. During the journey, the children, dressed in modern clothes, walked slowly in unison from one end of the train to another, a defiant omnipresence that says "I am present, was always present, and will remain." A Crow music group called Fights Alone performed in the club car, as did Bentley Spang, a performance artist who was born on the Crow Indian reservation. With the backdrop of Dan Dobson's original sound score, Crow elder and spiritual leader Heywood Big Day told stories that related the region to his ancestors' lives. As they view projections of buffalo onto the landscape, the audience listens to their tour guide narrate how his own great grandfather witnessed the "coming in of the Europeans and the pioneers," and how they moved the herd of buffalo out in order to build the railroad.[50] The images of buffalo on the landscape, in Strom's own words, "ghosts the buffalo,"[51] superimposing their presence (as past) onto the scenery. We learn what other tours might omit telling us: "It is estimated that 15 million buffalo roamed this region. By 1882 there were 7 million remaining, by 1890 there were 300 left inside the confines of Yellowstone Park. Indians were moved to reservations that were continuously decreased in size."[52] While the buffaloes provided subsistence for the Indians, the United States Army encouraged their killing precisely to diminish the Indian population and make it "safe" for tourists. By projecting these images onto the landscape, and narrating the reasons behind their disappearance, Strom not only juxtaposes the past and present but enables the audience to become aware of temporal reinventions of truth for the benefit of certain communities over others.

The second stop of Day Two in *RFK in EKY* was at the Vortex Community Church, next door to the one-room Vortex School, where Kennedy held the first of two hearings for the Senate Subcommittee on Employment, Manpower, and Power. The school, which is now demolished, held only five students at the time of RFK's visit. Both testimonies were from local residents and were entered into the official Congressional Record. These transcripts are the scripts Malpede and his team used for the re-creation.[53] As a staged theatrical performance, it was, like any congressional hearing, long, tedious, and monotonous (the Vortex hearing was itself forty-five minutes). What is particularly compelling about them is how the issues raised then, of quality of life for example, were still pertinent to the community now. More than mimic or try to be authentic, the hearings (and their rehearsals) provided a space to reflect on where things stood today, in particular in terms of issues around education, health care, and job growth. The reenactment of the transcripts on-site—their *off-time* performance—had enabled obvious contemporary parallels. Another moment occurred during a speech, in a packed room with standing room only, at Alice Lloyd College in Pippa Passes, where Kennedy had addressed students on education and the Vietnam War. The re-creation *now* had eerily striking parallels with the War in Iraq; and the reasons why citizens were against the Vietnam War *then* resonated with the community in 2004.

The project, though not a big-budget re-enactment, as Malpede himself observed (it cost about $300,000, raised by Malpede and Michael Hunt[54]) was nevertheless a packed four-day affair, which itself became a part of Kentucky's history, embodied over time. This "enabling" of multiple journeys—between architectures, between landmarks, between events, between ideas—was no coincidence, but rather a highly orchestrated inducement of time travel. Malpede maintained varying degrees of flexibility throughout the performance, and structured the reenactment itself as "a set of different modalities of experience at each event site."[55] As he explained in his "Final Artistic Statement," "the, in process, decision to structure the event in this way was a significant improvement over the idea of sustaining a 're-creation' throughout and then bookending the re-creation with 'issues, events and public conversations.'"[56] Malpede thus allowed pauses between stops that enabled audiences to linger. As with Kennedy's tour in 1968, the goal was not one of arrival, but a point of entry into ongoing conversations about improving economic conditions and battling poverty, constantly going back, and forth, and toward the future. This happened as participants voyaged through varying geographical and historical sites, rediscovering together that civic engagement was embedded throughout the dramaturgical structures.

Whereas *Geyser Land* and *RFK in EKY* juxtaposed images, video, and transcripts from the past with today's physical sites to induce an alternative temporality, *Red Chamber* generated an installation of real-time video stills that played with scale, repetition of text, choreographic loops, as well as a trance-like melodic soundscape, to create an off time, on-site. Throughout the night, down the stairs of the Brill Building, just a couple of feet below the ground from Times Square, we heard birds chirping, female voices whispering into amplified microphones, tinkling bells, and distinct flute and carriage-bell sounds—sometimes played live by Christina Campanella.[7]

Jamie McElhinney's sound design accentuated a heavy yet melodic bass drone that filled the room, with speakers placed even under the beds. At each of the six performances throughout the run, a different song composed by Elysian Fields was inserted into the sound environment, at a unique point for each show. Throughout the night, we were gifted with exquisite arias, recordings of Maria Callas, mostly from Puccini and Verdi. Lying on one of the cots, drifting in and out of sleep, I imagined these hymns lifting me up. I felt utterly weightless. The experience was not unlike sound meditations, where participants are surrounded by vibrations that potentially induce trancelike states. In an interview with the *New York Times*, Findlay explained how he and Jackson were inspired by a visit to composer La Monte Young and visual artist Marian Zazeela's *Dream House*, a sound and light environment originally conceived in 1969, re-created and open to the public in downtown New York since 1993. Similar to *Dream House*, *Dream of the Red Chamber* played with repetitive cycles of sound in ways that distanced us sharply from the urban world that was only steps away, leading us deeper into a state of calm the longer we stayed.

The environment had a visual component that similarly led us on a journey, surrounding us with projections at many levels. There were TV monitors set among the beds at audience level, two suspended flat-screen TV monitors, and two larger projections—onto the curtains—at opposite ends of the room. The screens showed a constant flow of changing imagery: close-up shots of live actions, objects, and textures were purposefully disorienting, playing with scale. Singly, the performers would walk a few steps toward one of the tiny, hidden, live-camera feeds and display something—grapes, pearls, red beads, hair, dark-painted nails, a shawl—as if they were surgeons using an endoscope to examine the interior of an organ, to reveal what the naked eye otherwise could not see. These repetitive revelations became quite sensual. We could see the performers' fingers slowly caressing each object. By opening our eyes our focus would dramatically shift in an instant, from sounds heard in our sleep (I can still hear the words *monk*, *rainwater*, *twelve*, and the phrase *ten years to prepare* as if it was yesterday) to a grape that looked like it was the size of a car. Everything was out of whack. Had I already lived this moment? Had I already been here before? Would I still be here *then*?

Temporal Sites

In the conclusion to *Performing Remains* Rebecca Schneider reiterates how turning to the past is not necessarily a "nostalgic" act, but also a cross-temporal one (designating a "camp" or queer sensibility that suggests a political efficacy in "turning, revolving" the "linear track").[58] Reenacting the past, she explains, does not connote an impossibility of return (as nostalgic) but is an "affective journey" that "bears a political purpose for a critical approach to futurity unhinged from capitalist development narratives of time."[59] In this sense, both *Geyser Land* and *RFK in EKY* conjure historical narratives of events in the *now* to re-create a rupture in the contemporary evaluations of the past *and* future. Both are performances predicated on ruptures of time, reconstructing the past so as to generate and shake up alternatives for generations to come. It is not coincidental that both artists use a mirror as a metaphor for describing their aims. Malpede talks about the project as a simultaneous "deconstruction and reconstruction" of Robert Kennedy's visit explaining how *RFK in EKY* "not only recreates an historic moment, it holds a mirror to it."[60] In an interview with the *Billings Gazette* of Montana, Mary Ellen Strom explains how, with Ann Carlson, they were "trying to 'mirror back' the contemporary moment."[61] Their use of space on location was predicated on moving us not only through time, back and forth to and from the past and present, but also to conjuring a feeling experiencing an *off time*. While *Dream of the Red Chamber* does not tie a specific historical moment to its geographic location, it enables a form of countering time, an opposition to a chronologic rhetoric of productivity at its own "location." *RFK in EKY* and *Geyser Land* and *Red Chamber* used structures of mobility to deal with issues of time, essentially making us aware of both its passage and its rupture. These three interstitial performances generated temporal sites that moved us, on-site and *off* time.

5. Urban Sites
Landmark Performance

> Gentrification is a process that hides the apparatus of domination from the dominant themselves. Spiritually, gentrification is the removal of the dynamic mix that defines urbanity—the familiar interaction of different kinds of people creating ideas together.
>
> —Sarah Shulman, *Gentrification of the Mind: Witness to a Lost Imagination*, 2015

> As theatre-makers we are constantly engaged in dialogue and in the development of collective identity. When you are outside of a theatre space, that just becomes more intense and political, and more interesting. The infrastructure becomes a partner *and* a player in whatever performance you make, especially in the city—you can't avoid that.
>
> —Gülgün Kayim, *Performance and the City*, 2015

Ghouls in the Gowanus

On October 15, 2014, I attended *The Dreary Coast*—a site-responsive, immersive theatre work that took place on Brooklyn's Gowanus Canal. The production was written and directed by Jeff Stark—an underground theatre impresario known for his large-scale, low budget, off-the radar, collaborative, do-it-yourself (DIY) performances in unfrequented locations throughout New York City. *The Dreary Coast*, developed by Stark over the course of four years, used elements of Greek and Roman mythology, Dante's *Inferno*, black metal music, as well as the canal's history to take its audience on a journey through one of the most polluted waterways in the United States. Roughly thirty of us arrived at a previously undisclosed location—a neighborhood bar. After a few drinks, we signed a fairly scary waiver form (in case we fell in the water). About a dozen people draped in cream-colored hooded cloaks and wearing wild, heavy eye makeup arrived ringing hand bells. Without speaking, they escorted us to a raw space next door, on the second floor of the adjacent building. We held hands and formed a circle as part of a silent, and very creepy, ritual-like "hooding" ceremony, where they gave everyone the same robe to put on. After a slow procession down the fairly empty streets, with our newly donned cloaks, we arrived on the Second Street boat landing. Ghouls and demons named Spikebeard and Lusthoney taunted us as we waited for the boat to arrive. "Woe you miserable losers! Put your heaven by!" they shouted, and insulted my partner: "How about this guy? He looks like a talent scout at a graveyard. Haaaaaa!" Once we were sitting in the canoe, they relished their shared death jokes:

SPIKEBEARD: Hey, eh, why do they put fences around cemeteries?

LUSTHONEY: Whaa?

SPIKEBEARD: Because they're dead . . .

LUSTHONEY: Hit 'em! Hit 'em![1]

We were now ready to embark on our journey as deceased souls through the kingdom of Hades (convincingly played by the hefty Zero Boy, a longtime East Village performer). Fifteen of us climbed carefully into the canoe. Due to capacity limits, the other fifteen spectators would walk on land, along the canal's side, observing the action from afar—and yes, canoe-rider tickets were more expensive. Our guide through hell was Charon, the ferryman of the River Styx (E. James Ford) who falls madly in love with Persephone

Jeff Stark's *Dreary Coast*, 2014. *Photo by Tod Seelie.*

(Ava Eisenson) and tries, unsuccessfully, to rescue her from Hades. Charon would lead us, the souls of the newly dead, on an exquisite tour of this eerie underworld on the banks of the infamous Gowanus Canal.

The performance was quite grandiose for its portrayal of this beautiful yet horrific spectacle of an industrial waste site, in spite of its DIY production model. The landscape was the star. The cast and crew for the production, which included Sarah McMillan (costume designer), George Graham (composer), and Swoon (boat designer)—numbered over fifty, a sizeable group for coordinating an outdoor performance. Whenever possible, they met on-site to rehearse. Timing was another logistical concern. As Stark explained, they had to coordinate the start time and curtain calls to match rising and falling tides. Otherwise, they would not fit under the canal's bridge.[2] (There is one scene in which we mortals pass under a bridge while a chorus of about a dozen singers walks above us.)

The production was low budget and self-financed, most of the money coming from a crowd-sourced Kickstarter campaign; its realization depended on the enthusiastic support of many volunteers. Boat tickets for the three-week run of the performance sold out before the show premiered. As he does with all his work, Stark does not ask for permits, carrying his do-it-yourself culture through to all aspects of production. His self-titled "trespass theatre" deliberately bypasses cultural gatekeepers, institutional

Jeff Stark's *Dreary Coast*, 2014. *Photo by Tod Seelie.*

grant-making organizations, corporate sponsors, and whatever local governing board issues legal permission to use the public space his performances occupy.[3] "It is liberating not to wait for an institution to make decisions," he told me, "but I spend a lot of time thinking about raising money," which is not surprising.[4] Because he does not ask producers or local authorities for sponsorship, instead forming relationships with people in the neighborhood and groups who use the same space, Stark himself considers his form of theatre "radically unsustainable." For this piece, and others he has done, the descriptor is in keeping with the environment in which he has chosen to stage the work: a polluted canal in a neighborhood with drastically increasing rents.

For those unfamiliar with the Gowanus neighborhood in South Brooklyn, it is bordered by the fancier and more expensive Park Slope neighborhood to the north, and Carroll Gardens to the south. The area became an industrial and shipping zone after the New York legislature authorized the construction of the canal in 1849, which transformed the Gowanus Creek into a 1.8 mile-long commercial waterway. What was once a busy transport hub became a sewage outflow (excrement included) and a major waste site for the coal gas plants that settled there.[5] Urban legends tell of the local Italian mafia dumping dead bodies in the canal, apparently because it was so polluted no one would go near the place. Stark—who has lived in the Gowanus since the late 1990s, when artist and community activists began moving into the neighborhood and turning many of the warehouses into art and manufacturing spaces[6]—described the Canal to me as "raw sewage, combined with industrial waste, and despair."

Stark was inspired to create *The Dreary Coast* when he went on a canoe tour of the Gowanus in 2004, one of the myriad tours offered by Ludger Balan, then the director of the Urban Divers Estuary Conservancy (otherwise known as "The Divers"). His organization, similar in spirit to The Gowanus Dredgers Canoe Club, which still exists, did activist-art-type events (focusing attention on the canal in an effort to get the city to clean it up[7]) in which participants would scuba dive to the bottom of the canal and do live video transmission. The idea behind this action was to take advantage of a clause in the regulations of the Environmental Protection Agency (EPA), created in 1980 to manage the cleanup of hazardous waste sites across the United States, which said that it must regulate a body of water to its use. In other words, if people fish there, then the EPA has to make sure the fish are safe to eat. The Divers, hoping to make them regulate the canal, decided to scuba dive in it—horrible for the health of the divers, but potentially a legitimate reason to demand that the EPA clean it up. Stark recalls his boat experience with Ludger: "It was a profound experience for me. I was watching Ludger and thinking, 'This is a horrifying place.' . . . This guy is like a tour guide through hell, and I suddenly realized, he's like Charon."[8] It was during that tour that Stark heard about the man who dumped benzene, a known carcinogen, into the canal for twenty years. As audience members in *The Dreary Coast*, we also learned about that man and how his former gas station—the benzene drop site—is now the very site where a Whole Foods stands.

In March 2010, the EPA finally declared the canal a Superfund cleanup site, paving the way for a $500 million cleanup project. Thus, by the time *The Dreary Coast* premiered in 2014, the Gowanus was a contested urban site, very much in the news as a neighborhood in transition, with news headlines like "Not Even Toxic Waste Can Stop Gentrification: NYC's Superfund Neighborhoods Are Booming" and "The Once and Future of Gowanus."[9] Indeed, the New York City Department of Planning changed the zoning laws on Fourth Avenue from commercial to residential in 2010, the same year the EPA declared the canal a Superfund site, and by the time *The Dreary Coast* premiered in 2014, some of the changes were evident. According to the Furman Center's 2013 State of New York City's Housing and Neighborhoods, the Gowanus Community Board saw more than 4,400 new residential units come on line between 2000 and 2013,[10] averaging 50 percent higher than the rest of Brooklyn for price per square foot.[11] To make way for a number of these expensive housing projects, artists were evicted when a building's new owner did not offer lease renewals to make way for new luxury condos, as *Hyperallergic* reported in October 2015.[12] While Gowanus's "growing" creative culture is a profitable asset, it is at the expense of the very artists who initially settled there and established it as a "creative culture," as well as the displaced small businesses and those they employ.[13]

The Dreary Coast's Gowanus location was thus the site not only of a soon-to-be-cleaned-up but still heavily polluted waterway but also the site of real estate speculation, artist evictions, and rezoning laws. The neighborhood was teetering on the brink of massive transformation, from an industrial art complex to an upscale residential neighborhood with an "urban feel," what Airbnb, coincidentally, described as "steadily stockpiling cool art spaces."[14]

For audiences less familiar with Gowanus's history, *The Dreary Coast* certainly put it on the map. The performance is just one example among many that, I want to suggest, marked the land at a moment when that land was critically in transition: at the brink of either being redeveloped or vanishing in the face of so-called urban improvement. I'd like to consider how such productions both *landmark* the sites they occupy and are themselves landmark performances and agents of change.

We can envision a map of New York City labeled to mark specific performances that took place across the city's neighborhoods: a "theatrical" voyage through New York's urban transformation. Given the historical contexts of such productions, these performances map urban change. Their site specificity is implicated in the very "trans" of the urban environment—the moving across, beyond, and through—that they purportedly want to save. They are entrenched in the changes in their respective neighborhoods, bringing to the foreground issues around art and gentrification, performance and the city, in ways the artists themselves might not have conceived. In retrospect, they are *landmark* because they left their own traces in sites that either no longer exist or that have changed so much that they are barely recognizable. Before describing these three performances, which occurred between 1990 and 2005 in New York City, I'd first like to address some of the larger issues surrounding performance and the city.

Performance and Gentrification

It is not uncommon for artists to seek out undeveloped or underutilized urban spaces—neighborhoods and architectures in transition. Perhaps the main reason is that they are cheap, but it is also because they have transformative potential: urban artists have a different vision for what a space is and what it could be. Theatre, of course, has a long history of using the city for performance, a history charted by Stanton B. Garner Jr.—"from the Soviet restaging of the winter palace in Petrograd to Max Reinhardt's outdoor productions of *The Merchant of Venice*"—in his chapter "Urban Landscapes, Theatrical Encounters: Staging the City" in Elinor Fuchs and Una Chaudhuri's anthology *Land/Scape/Theatre*.[15] Tracing the genealogy of what he calls "contemporary urban environmental theatre," Garner delineates how "the city has regularly formed part of an avant-garde redefinition of performance space."[16] Indeed, some performances, in particular, site-responsive theatre projects that integrate either a piece of architecture or a specific neighborhood, are often inextricably related to the economic and political interests of the spaces they occupy, even as they claim otherwise, as Michael McKinnie, in particular, indicates in his book on the economics of site-specific performance.[17] If earlier, more politically oriented groups like the Living Theatre, the Performance Group, Bread and Puppet Theater, as well as other "activist urban performance," such as William Pope.L's crawls and Fluxus Street Events, were claiming the urban milieu as performance landscape in the early sixties and seventies, the landscape of politics around performance in New York City today is markedly different.

As public space in New York City became more difficult to access after 9/11, in terms of obtaining liability insurance and permission for groups to gather, real estate prices have risen relentlessly, the range of live-art sites and the diverse types of events staged throughout the five boroughs has left us with some virtually unclassifiable performances. They run the gamut from the off-the-grid, unmarketed, illicit, "trespass theatre" events like *The Dreary Coast*, to well-financed, higher-profile ventures like the live-art initiative at Times Square Alliance that seeks to expose contemporary artists to a wider platform (counting 360,000 potential spectators a day). Production companies like Dancing in the Streets, in existence since 1984 and now based in the South Bronx, have foregrounded the use of public urban spaces for performance and community engagement, compromising between securing the necessary permits in order to "occupy" city space.

While some theatre, as Jen Harvie asserts, aims "explicitly [to] intervene in and change conventional urban process," many of the partnerships that facilitate and fund art and performance in the city (whether in public, private, or privately managed public spaces) operate without challenging the urban process itself.[18] For example, developers David and Jed Walentas, the father-and-son team known for their rapid "revitalization" of the DUMBO waterfront neighborhood in Brooklyn, understood that investing in cultural capital—like giving free or discounted space to performing arts groups and venues such as GAle GAtes and St. Ann's Warehouse in the late nineties—would quickly raise the economic capital of what is now one of the most expensive zip codes in New York City.[19] Anita Durst, the daughter of Douglas Durst (copresident of the Durst Organization, which has owned and developed real estate in Manhattan since the early 1900s), founded the nonprofit organization chashama in 1995 to secure space for artists in New York City that would otherwise be vacant. The program proved so successful, securing more than a hundred thousand square feet worth approximately $3.1 million for artists all over the city, that other organizations followed suit. The Lower Manhattan Cultural Council (LMCC) began Swing Space in 2004, modeled after chashama's A.R.E.A. (Accessing Real Estate for the Arts) program. While chashama and Swing Space have indeed helped to secure temporary space for thousands of artists in New

York, where they could develop new work and animate unused spaces, they nevertheless operate under an overarching system of uneven power relations whereby control of space is dictated by market concerns. While chashama and LMCC do not profit from these partnerships of artists and locations, the Walentas benefit from this system, as do other developers. In a 2005 interview with *Theater* on the arts and real estate, Durst explained:

> Landlords are latching on to the economic model: bring arts into a community, create a multi-arts center, and you'll start gentrification. Arts organizations bring in energy, and then landlords can raise rents. We stay ahead of that model because we're always moving. Chashama gets into the areas that aren't doing so well, revitalizing currently empty real estate and, when the area becomes sustainable, we move out.[20]

What seems like a win-win situation is in reality more of a catch-22 scenario whereby an artist needs access to a site in order to produce work, yet by doing so might already be compromising the process and ultimately contributing to the very gentrification that will eventually drive them out. While chashama may "stay ahead of that model," the model itself persists.

Much has been written about the relationship between art and urbanism and contemporary art and the politics of space. Arguing how the culture industry played a significant role in gentrifying the Lower East Side, the late urban geographer Neil Smith wrote how the "rawness of the neighborhood had in fact been part of its appeal."[21] "Art dealers and patrons, gallery owners and artists, designers and critics, writers and performers," he wrote in his now widely disseminated book *The Urban Frontier*, converted "urban dilapidation into ultra chic."[22] While Smith avows that some artists worked explicitly to counter gentrification, and many became victims of the very process they helped to precipitate, he nevertheless concluded that "however wittingly or otherwise, the culture and real estate industries worked together to transform the Lower East Side."[23] In other words, regardless of how artists position themselves, the interests of capital—which prioritize the buying, improving, and selling of redeveloped property for profit—dominate the systems under which art and the culture industry operate.

In 1987, even before Smith, Rosalyn Deutsche, and Cara Gendel Ryan published "The Fine Art of Gentrification," which articulated the intricate connection between the art world and the real estate market, asserting that "despite their bohemian posturing, the artists and dealers who created the East Village art scene, and the critics and museum curators who legitimize its existence, are complicit with gentrification on the Lower East Side. To deny this complicity is to perpetuate one of the most enduring, self-serving myths in bourgeois thought."[24] Deutsche continued to question the interests of art in the city in her book *Evictions*, in particular how the rise of Public Art during the 1980s and early 1990s often operated under the guise of "democracy" but actually served to legitimize existing urban conditions as inevitable. Establishing a contrast with art as decoration—"aesthetic movements that design the spaces of redevelopment"—she laid the groundwork for "interventionist aesthetic practices" where art would be a "*site* as well as a *stake*" in urban struggle, engaging with and revealing the conditions that defined that space.[25]

The use of performance *in* the city and, in tandem, the use of the city *as* performance, has run amok in every corner of New York: the margins, the center, Manhattan, Bushwick, Broadway, Coney Island, Times Square, underground subway tunnels, overhead bridges, abandoned warehouses, borough parks, the Woolworth building. *To experience the city anew. To appropriate the city. To reframe the city. To make it poetic.* Whether unknowingly or unabashedly referencing a slogan that originated as radical political intervention in the mid-fifties/early sixties—from Debord's vision for *la dérive* and the Situationist International call for reframing one's passage through the city—the pursuit of experiences beyond the mainstream is filled with contradiction. On the one hand, we could say we have the more official production venues in New York *staging* dissidence, yet partnering with developers/landlords to "house" the performances—handling the permits, partnerships, and insurance liabilities. Articulating the need for a cultural materialist analysis of theatre in the urban sphere in *Theatre and the City*, Jen Harvie observes how such materialist criticism can "unveil how Western urban theatre is complicit with neoliberal capitalism, contributing to fostering uneven urban economic and social development, and how its creativity is limited by its complicity."[26] On the other hand, we have the actual dissidents who are creating do-it-yourself, participatory, often spectacular events and/or trespass experiences that occupy spaces outside the art and entertainment establishment, highly attuned to *playing* in the city, in reaction to the institutionalization of play. As Nicolas Whybrow points out in his introduction to *Performance and the Contemporary City*, it was Henri Lefebvre's 1968 book *The Right to the City* that called for a "participatory citizenship" that envisioned "a role for art that creatively produces the city in the interests of its citizens."[27] And yet these events are simultaneously often appropriated into the lure and creative appeal of New York, often for large profit returns.

Today artists continue to bring people to "blighted" spots, sometimes illegally, without permits, often because they are unwilling to risk being denied the permits and losing the opportunity to do the work. On the surface, artists' attraction to places that aren't entirely occupied seems dangerously parallel to developers' pretense that they have just "discovered" a neighborhood. But as Matt Bolton writes in the *Guardian*, "The temptation to conclude that art is a useless mode of critique in a post-Fordist 'creative economy' is strong, but must be resisted,"[28] especially as artists are becoming increasingly aware of the ways aesthetic and event production, including the financing of shows and space promotion, are themselves part of a larger network of capital interests.[29] As Gülgün Kayim, co-founder of Minneapolis-based performance collective Skewed Visions[30] and former director of Arts, Culture, and the Creative Economy for the city of Minneapolis says in the epigraph to this chapter in relation to performance outside conventional theater spaces: "The infrastructure becomes a partner *and* a player in whatever performance you make, especially in the city—you can't avoid that."[31] Kayim is among a growing number of artists and art administrators who are highly attuned to the ways art production can operate for a more equitable kind of urban revitalization that promotes permanence and stability for the communities living there. I will come back to Kayim's work, as well as other contemporary artists who are making art in ways that counter displacement, engaging communities that would otherwise be excluded from the urban planning process, at the conclusion to this chapter.

My point here, however, is not to glorify performances that occupy a public place on the brink of so-called urban development, or even to argue that they produce so-called counternarratives that stand to resist the forces of gentrification. My point here is instead to trouble how we view performance in relation to the urban landscape. By contextualizing what form of "urban" these vanishing mise-en-scènes unveil, whatever their intentions may be—to make money or initiate change—we can talk about the kind of city they implicitly propose or support. What narrative of "urban" is being performed? What city is either desired or produced through such performances? What communities, regardless of geographical specificity, are present, or silenced? As David Harvey argues in his "Right to the City" manifesto, urbanization is and has always been a class phenomenon. "The question of what kind of city we want," he declares, "cannot be divorced from that of what kind of social ties, relationship to nature, lifestyles, technologies, and aesthetic values we desire."[32]

In her book *Gentrification of the Mind*, Sarah Schulman evaluates the intellectual consequences of the displacement caused by gentrification, emphasizing the impact on queer politics after the AIDS crisis. "Spiritually," writes Schulman, "gentrification is the removal of the dynamic mix that defines urbanity—the familiar interaction of different kinds of people creating ideas together."[33] Schulman argues that it is not only neighborhoods that are gentrified but also what we know of our history, and what we consider our politics. We can extend this argument to theatre history and its historiography, in terms of what we choose to remember about certain productions, in particular shows that occurred at moments of heightened transition in what are considered high-gentrifying locations (considered prime for gentrification).[34] As an avid New Yorker who has lived here since the late 1990s, I often walk through neighborhoods and wonder what role theatre history might add to the legacies of those landscapes. While many performances were not necessarily meant as "aesthetic interventionist practices," to use Deutsche's terminology, at the time of their production, their site specificity cannot be separated from the changes occurring at the sites, and the people *living* at those sites. The performances I identify as landmark were entrenched with New York City's spatial history in ways that marked its passage at a moment when that land was literally in transition: either at the brink of becoming redeveloped or vanishing in the face of so-called urban improvement. These urban dramaturgies remain as ephemeral acts with permanent traces.

The Teepee in the Shantytown

On August 17, 1993, bulldozers plowed through "the Hill," the unofficial name of one of the oldest shantytowns in New York City, located at the corner of Canal and Chrystie Streets right at the foot of the Manhattan Bridge. "Its fifty or so occupants were uprooted in an early-morning action that officials said was for their own safety," Ian Fisher of the *New York Times* reported the following day, "crushing into bits of plywood and muddy rags one of the most visible symbols of homelessness in Manhattan."[35] The Hill had been one of the last remaining homeless encampments left around New York City in a decade where homelessness had skyrocketed. David Dinkins, who as Manhattan borough president had run in 1990 on a platform for the homeless, vowing to champion their rights and the city's obligation to house them, quickly changed gears once he took office as mayor.[36] His tenure is characterized by a cohesive and aggressive campaign to rid the streets of the homeless. In just three years, the city "bulldozed homeless encampments, barred 'unauthorized persons' from public spaces and tentatively embraced the Transit Authority's eviction of disorderly homeless people from the subways, even in winter."[37] The series of shantytowns erected on vacant lots throughout the city, often made from tents, cardboard, wood, and scavenged material that would provide shelter, were often called "Dinkinsvilles," a comparison to the "Hoovervilles" of the Depression era.

The Hill's 1993 demolition was one of many in New York City.[38] Two years prior, in June 1991, shortly after a Memorial Day concert organized under the "Housing Is a Human Right" slogan, city crews infamously destroyed another homeless encampment in Tompkins Square Park (evicting between two hundred and three hundred park dwellers and demonstrators) in the East Village. The fight over the park, which peaked with the violent police riot of August 1988 when Mayor Koch's administration unsuccessfully attempted to rid it of, as he called them, the "insipid conglomeration of human misfits," is described in detail in Neil Smith's book *The New Urban Frontier*. In Smith's chapter "Class Struggle on Avenue B: The Lower East Side as Wild Wild West," he chronicles how Tompkins Square Park became "the site of the most militant anti-gentrification struggle in the United States" and a "symbol of a new urbanism being etched on the urban 'frontier.'"[39] As real estate developers moved in to colonize even the margins of Manhattan, resulting in ever-increasing rents, the gradual replacement in entire neighborhoods of one class with another, and no alternative housing options for those displaced, first the Koch and then the Dinkins's administration unapologetically continued to represent those apartment-dwelling neighbors who complained about filth, crime, and drug dealing. Dinkins went so far as to claim that Tompkins Square Park had been "stolen from the community by the homeless."[40] The $2.3 million renovation of the park began almost immediately after the 1991 demolition of the encampment. Urban renewal was predicated on "cleaning up" the city without attacking the roots of homelessness or providing affordable housing options for those displaced by increasing rents.

It was amidst this turmoil that Thieves Theatre, which had staged Jean Genet's *Deathwatch* (with prisoners at the Illinois State Penitentiary) and *Marat/Sade* (with former mental patients in Toronto) prior to coming to New York, presented Heiner Müller's *Despoiled Shore Medeamaterial Landscape with Argonauts* in early September of 1991 at the Hill. Dramaturgically, the production had two levels, as Thieves' founders Nick Fracaro and Gabriele Schafer explained to me.[41] The first was the theatrical staging of the play itself for a limited audience of fifteen, and the second was a teepee, which housed the play and its creators from November 1990 through May 1993. This "three-year-long enactment and para-theatrical performance of the Müller piece," as Fracaro described it, had a much larger impact, with "more than 78,000 vehicles and 350,000 people crossing the Manhattan Bridge during an average day . . . gazing at the evolving living history of the teepee in the shantytown."[42]

Thieves Theatre's vision for site-specific and "zeitgeist-specific" theatre making, as they called it, called for the incorporation of the real-life context of the subjects with whom they were working. This had been the case with *Deathwatch* (they performed with the prisoners) and *Marat/Sade* (they lived in the Toronto halfway house with the subjects). Fracaro and Schafer wanted to expand the potential impact of theatre in an urban

Thieves Theatre's teepee at the Hill, 1991. *Photo by Margaret Morton, copyright OmbraLuce LLC.*

environment as they explored where to stage Müller's text, which called for "the naturalism of the scene." They decided that making an Indian teepee in homeless territory would create a strong juxtaposition of an image of survival—the teepee marking that 1990 was the hundredth anniversary of the Wounded Knee Massacre—against the backdrop of the shanties of Dinkins's abandoned, homeless New Yorkers. As they explained to me, New Yorkers' attitudes toward the homeless seemed to be shifting from sympathetic to disparaging, while at the same time there was still a romanticism, albeit superficial, regarding the Native American and "living on the land," evidenced by the novel and subsequent Hollywood success of *Dancing with Wolves* in 1990.[43]

The tall teepee stood out among the shantytown's wood and paper shacks, bringing renewed visibility to the Hill—the kind of visibility the

Thieves Theatre's teepee at the Hill, 1991. *Photo by Margaret Morton, copyright OmbraLuce LLC.*

Dinkins administration was determined to suppress. Made of seventy-eight US domestic mailbags that had been ripped open and sown together by Schafer, the structure was held up by seventeen pine trees the artists collected upstate. At eighteen feet tall and twenty feet in diameter, it was hard to miss. The Thieves' production rejected the theatrical establishment choosing instead, as C. Carr reported in an interview, "to 'embody and articulate' the voice of the disenfranchised" in *their* land.[44] "The performance ended with us removing the cover of the teepee, thereby reminding the audience that they are sitting in a shantytown under the night sky, and thus also reminding them that 'homes' of any kind are neither permanent nor safe and that we all have a false sense of security."[45] Erecting a teepee in that place and staging *Argonauts* inside it grounded Müller's play in living history. The material the artists wrote around Müller's play talked about the history of Manhattan and the site of the shantytown in particular. The tepee and its performance also marked the land with an alternate poetics, a "warring landscape," as Fracaro called it, even after the Hill was long gone. Connecting Gertrude Stein's famous quotation from *The Autobiography of Alice B. Toklas*—"a landscape is such a natural arrangement for a battlefield or a play that one must write plays"[46]—and Müller's desire, in Fracaro's words, to "stage battles," Thieves Theatre's *Argonauts* embodied the tension inherent in the continuing urban struggle for land, from the homeless of the Hill to those fighting eviction by landlords and developers—a struggle that persists to this day in New York City and elsewhere.

Father amid the Meat

In June 1990, the late theatre visionary Reza Abdoh mounted *Father Was a Peculiar Man*—a seminal urban site-specific piece written by Mira-Lani Oglesby and produced by Anne Hamburger, founder of En Garde Arts. *Father* spanned four city blocks in the vicinity of West Twelfth Street and Ninth Avenue, a neighborhood known as Meatpacking District, now trendy and home to the High Line park,[47] luxury designer stores, and the new Whitney Museum. When *Father* premiered, the site was a sketchy destination, dark and desolate, notorious for its semi-abandoned warehouses and its stench, extremely different from the gleaming, manicured destination it would eventually become. Actress Juliana Francis-Kelly, who was barely out of college and had never been to or heard of the place before she was cast in *Father*, recalled how "meat was still being packed there, though the industry seemed small, family-operated, and on the decline."[48]

Inspired by Dostoyevsky's classic *The Brothers Karamazov*, *Father* was staged in sixteen different locations, in this area below Fourteenth Street. More than sixty performers rehearsed daily on location in the streets, "with interns watching out for traffic," as Francis-Kelly told me, as well as "indoors, in what had been the meat lockers—creepy, cement rooms with giant

Reza Abdoh's *Father Was a Peculiar Man*. Courtesy of Anne Hamburger and En Garde Arts.

freight elevators that we opened by pulling an old rope." The audience, who numbered around two hundred per night, circulated through the streets—witnessing a full marching band, Jackie Kennedy riding in a red Cadillac convertible, a cemetery, and a 120-foot banquet table that spanned the length of West Twelfth Street, over which was suspended an enormous meat cleaver. In *Death of Character*, Fuchs described the chaotic staging: "From which we gleaned horrific fragments of physical abuse, sodomy, drunkenness, rape—paused for a song or two—and concluded with martyrdom and death."[49]

Besides the smell, the Meatpacking District was also known for its marginalized population, which consisted of many transgender sex workers who had survived the AIDS crisis of the mid-1980s. In the 1970s there were few legal residences in the neighborhood, which, according to the *New York Times*, made possible the "raucous night life" that would flourish there later on, catering primarily to the queer community,[50] clubs like L.U.R.E. (Leather, Uniform, Rubber, Etc.), J's Hang Out (shut down by the city's Department of Health for "unsafe sex" in 2002), Hellfire Club (a BDSM sex club), and the Clit Club (the lesbian hangout and performance venue), none of which exist today. Just five years prior to *Father*'s premiere and near its location at 835 Washington Street, the Koch administration's Department of Health closed the gay sex club the Mineshaft, contending that it permitted "high-risk sexual activity" linked to the spread of AIDS.[51]

The Mineshaft was notorious for the sexual promiscuity of its downstairs spaces, with dungeon-like rooms. Mayor Koch said of the Mineshaft when it was brought down: "It must be horrific, horrendous in its actuality to witness."[52] Instead of finding a cure for AIDS and promoting HIV education, New York City and the federal government responded to the epidemic by closing gay clubs, a move that only served to foster bigotry toward homosexuals. Images from Abdoh's production stand out in relation to this history:

> The spectacle culminated in a hellish installation staged on the second floor of a warehouse building. In this cement and brick setting, spectators were free to browse on their own in three dark rooms, which were fitted out with various profane and sacred tableaux in obscene proximity. For instance, a scene of a fashion mannequin lying under a circular saw blade with blood on her neck was near a scene of hooded monks praying. In the second room, the actor playing a green-skinned Ivan lay naked, chained to his nightmare bed, tormented by clothespins pinching his

Washington and Little West Twelfth Streets, 1985. *Photo by Brian Rose.*

Washington and Little West Twelfth Streets, 2013. *Photo by Brian Rose.*

flesh. At the other side of the room, naked men stood in a bathtub with shower attachment, washing themselves and each other. They kissed in gay embrace, then pissed into the water they were standing in, or the other way around.[53]

Abdoh's own life paralleled the lives of many in the district: he had tested positive for HIV a year earlier in 1989 and had been outcast by his father because he was gay. On May 11, 1995, he died of AIDS at the age of thirty-two.[54] "Various segments of society with different energies converge here," Abdoh explained in an interview, "and yet they maintain a strange balance. Teen-age hustlers, transvestites, drug pushers, yuppies, young night-clubbers and the police warily co-exist in an area that brews the dark elements in our nature."[55] With its images of death, blood, suffering, pain, and redemption, as well as its allusions to pop-culture icons, its ensemble dances, and marching-band music, *Father* mirrored the disparate worlds both past and present coinciding in the Meatpacking District. It was a meditation of sorts on the lure of capital against a backdrop of AIDS and the disenfranchised, typical of neighborhoods "recently discovered" or on the brink of becoming gentrified. Embracing both the history of the district and the reality of its marginalized community, *Father* left not just a theatrical legacy, but an equally important lasting impact on the urban fabric of New York City. The performance brought audiences to the neighborhood who might otherwise not have ventured here and exposed them to the images of destruction and death that were at the time drawn from the very real horrors endured by the gay community.

A Pool for the People

Agora, another large-scale—albeit very different—urban, site-specific performance, was also closely linked to the shifting demographic and landscape. Featuring over forty dancers in an energetic combination of dance, acrobatics, and theatrical imagery, it took place at the then-abandoned fifty-thousand-square-foot McCarren Park Pool in Williamsburg, Brooklyn. The show, performed from September 13 to October 1, 2005, and followed by a second version (*Agora II*) one year later, opened the site to the public for the first time in twenty years. Conceived, directed, and produced by choreographer Noémie Lafrance and her nonprofit organization Sens Productions, it was a civic performance on a grand scale, inviting the audience to experience a moment in this monumental and highly contested, public space in the heart of the rapidly gentrifying Williamsburg and Greenpoint neighborhoods. *Agora* tested the complex relationship of such a production: on the one hand, reimagining city space via performance as a transformative catalyst, and, on the other, leveraging the politics of art production and public space specific to New York City. *Agora* exemplifies the challenges of producing such a work after 9/11, when safety and liability issues were more strictly regulated, and private interests and real estate speculation increasingly controlled public space, in particular in relation to art production.

Agora's performances had over ten thousand people crowding the dilapidated area over the company's three-week run. The empty pool came to life for the one-hour duration of the show. Thirty dancers, costumed by designer Karen Young in the range of pedestrian garb seen on a Brooklyn street—longtime residents and hipster newcomers—moved inside the enormous space. Besides the core ensemble, whose members filled the space with numerous tableaux, there were separate "featured" numbers, interspersed throughout in a structure similar to a lineup of circus acts, with additional guest appearances by performers Leigh Garrett, Miss Saturn, Elizabeth Streb's dance company, and the Young Dance Collective. All kinds of performers converged at the pool, filling the space with vignettes: a couple of kids at one end spraying graffiti on the walls and smashing bottles; a woman sunbathing on a lawn chair set on a patch of grass; a man wheeling his armchair, functioning television set, and living-room lamp around the pool; lots of roller skating and biking; dancers partnering with skateboarders; people kicking soccer balls and beach balls; others filling buckets of water into an inflatable kiddie pool. Other images seemed to resemble gentrified hipster Williamsburg: a couple fighting; snazzy hula hoopers; a celebrity wannabe in fancy sunglasses; Saturday-night partiers. For the final tableau, the performers dressed in bright-colored clothes and formed a lively street fair, inviting audience members to come inside the pool and join them. In an interview with Lafrance, she explained how the piece was meant to foster public exchange in public space, culminating with the invitation for the audience to come together in the *agora*, to project themselves into the future of the pool.[56]

The pool, which could accommodate sixty-eight hundred bathers, was the last of eleven enormous public pools built in 1936 by Robert Moses, the highly criticized New York City "master builder" whose controversial urban renewal practices under the Works Progress Administration (WPA) are heavily documented in Robert Caro's biography.[57] The pool-building project was conceived as the largest of its kind in the United States during

Agora performance, 2005. *Photo by Richard Termine. Courtesy of Noémie Lafrance.*

Agora performance, 2005. *Photo by Suzanne Gervais. Courtesy of Noémie Lafrance.*

the New Deal, and was promoted as a means of democratizing access to recreation. After forty-eight years, the pool was closed down in 1984 due to lack of funds and remained shuttered at the urging of neighbors amid a bitter and racially charged community debate over its use. For years, "the old guard" community members from Williamsburg and Greenpoint (mainly people of Polish, Italian, and Irish backgrounds) wanted the pool demolished. The agenda was to keep young people out who came to the pool from other neighborhoods. According to an interview with Junior Nieves, a fifty-one-year-old Time Warner repairman who grew up in Greenpoint, it was not uncommon for riots to break out: "The Puerto Ricans were on one side, the Polish were on the other, and all hell was breaking loose."[58] Amid such racial and ethnic tensions, the Friends of McCarren Park emerged as the community group that wanted the pool destroyed; an alternative group, the McCarren Park Conservancy, wanted to save it, though they had not been successful in raising the funds for its renovation.

Enter Noémie Lafrance, a resident of Williamsburg since the early 1990s, whose fascination with this empty and fenced-off area brought attention from both the public and city authorities to the plight of the pool. Not coincidentally, it also paved the way for a new wave of corporate partnerships, which was met with strong opposition from local residents who

McCarren Park Pool, before the renovation. *Photo by Chad Nicholson. Creative Commons Attributions Share License.*

resented the fact that a corporate, private outsider was brought in. Seeing the renewed interest in the space, and the possibility for future tenants, the Parks Department got the multibillion-dollar media conglomerate Clear Channel (and its Live Nation Inc. subsidiary[59]) involved and asked Sers Productions to partner in its renovation.[60] Over the course of the next few years after *Agora*, up until the summer of 2009 when it was closed for renovation, the McCarren Park Pool became one of the most popular concert venues in New York City.

As Lafrance rehearsed *Agora* in the spring of 2005, the Brooklyn areas surrounding the park were rezoned for housing to accommodate new high-rise developments, pricing out many old-time residents as well as the older generation of artists.[61] By 2007—a year after *Agora II*, during the height of the real estate boom and right before the housing market crash—the perimeter of McCarren Park had become "a hotbed of residential development," according to David Maundrell, broker and president of aptsandlofts.com, "with 400 units becoming available at McCarren Park alone."[62] Maundrell's real estate agency, along with Prudential's Douglas Elliman, sold the luxury condos developed by North Development Co. at Bayard Street, which was adjacent to the park. After the rezoning took effect, everything on the perimeter of the park was developed. A *Washington Post* article from 2007 reported on a Fannie Mae dossier that "found mortgage lending in Williamsburg [had] increased in recent years at twice the national average," with most of the dollars going to upper-class families.[63] Many of the artists who had initially "settled" in Williamsburg were among the second batch of people forced out as a result of the increasing rents and new developments. The first had been the "old guard" of Euro-American and Puerto Rican populations, mostly of lower income, that had lived in Williamsburg and Greenpoint for generations. Rents in these areas rose exorbitantly.[64]

In general, *Agora* felt more like a rock concert than a formal dance event. I remember the audience, the crowds, the lights, the music, the images, the ambience, more than the actual dancers, their movements, or the choreography. I remember the rain that night and waiting under our umbrellas amidst the crowds of people waiting to get in. But what I recall the most is the actual pool, its size, its beauty, its vastness. It was a sheer thrill to witness such a spectacle, almost like a mass baptism—minus the water. In hindsight, this was both the performance's success as well its shortcoming. How could one performance do justice to such a large space? To such a large and diverse community? The pool eventually reopened as a state-of-the-art recreation center in the summer of 2012, after a $50 million renovation through Bloomberg's PlaNYC initiative. Visions of what the abandoned space should become had always differed among the various communities of Williamsburg, in particular as its population shifted. The debate over the space and the performance became part of the neighborhood's recent history, in particular the rapid gentrification that had all but evicted so many of its residents since the late 1980s.

Artists and Residents as Agents of Change

Over the past decade, I have seen a growth of both performance *in* cities and the performance *of* cities, characterized primarily by the opposing voices claiming a stake in the "reframing" of the city. Whether these ephemeral live acts are rehearsed scenarios, improvised happenings, impromptu gatherings, organized political events, or festive encounters, the various displays and approaches of performance in the city serve as distinct examples of urban dramaturgies. The proliferation of die-ins, rallies and protest marches, and the politically motivated blocking of traffic across cities nationwide, are striking examples of urban dramaturgies that take over public space. Likewise, we can read the ways that cities themselves are marketed as stages for entertainment, consumption, and art, often for the benefit of the few. We can also, as I have done here, look at how a range of theatrical productions that occurred at a specific moment of urban transformation, integrate the *trans* of the urban environment into their legacies. Whereas the "transformative" is often something seen as a positive force in performance, it is equally important to consider how transformation might obliterate history, and might even, and quite literally, displace people. Rereading these performances through a geographic-specific and historic-specific lens amid their urban landscape recontextualizes their role in the city.

Within institutions, official discussions around performance and the city nowadays often center on something called "creative placemaking"—a term that has come to the fore in the last decade to describe practices that place art and culture at the center of urban change, characterized as "when public, private, not-for-profit, and community sectors partner to strategically shape the physical and social character of a neighborhood, town, tribe, city, or region around arts and cultural activities."[65] Two of its main principles, as delineated by ArtPlace America (itself a highly funded ten-year collaboration "among a number of foundations, federal agencies, and financial institutions" to position art as a vital component of community planning[66]), assert that creative placemaking "creates opportunities for people of all income levels and backgrounds to thrive in place," and that it "supports economic diversity in the community, providing multiple points of entry and interaction for people of all incomes."[67] In theory, creative placemaking stands in opposition to the institutionalization of "public art" so critiqued by Deutsche in the 1990s, and seems to be a more engaged form of participation in the urban struggle for determining and creating an equitable city. It remains a contentious term, as Gülgün Kayim, in her keynote address at the Mid-America Theatre Conference acknowledged: "I've heard the words 'creative placefaking,' . . . 'placekeeping.'"[68] Nevertheless, its participants continue to reposition art and culture at the forefront of a more equitable form of city planning.[69] Kayim herself took her skills as a theater maker to her position as the director of Arts, Culture, and the Creative Economy for the city of Minneapolis. During her tenure, she worked with artists to develop ways to enhance engagement with communities that would otherwise be excluded from the urban-planning process, developing initiatives such as Creative CityMaking.[70] The program hired artists to apply their artistic skills to develop alternative ways to communicate residents' needs and desires with city officials. In her address, Kayim described the impact of this initiative:

> I have learned—especially in the space of racial equity—that translating data into a dance, a performance, or a song is a better way to engage communities that have been underrepresented in planning and evaluation processes and who have a great deal of suspicion around the rigid, analytical models that traditional evaluation has taken—especially in the realm of quantitative evaluation. We're asking for qualitative evaluation to begin to shift that difference. Our artists have done things like data jams, collectively analyzing material that they've gathered. They've used video to collect stories and then transcribe that video and collectively looked at it from lots of different perspectives. They have done performances and asked communities to come and locate themselves within a map of the city in the spaces they feel sad and happy—as simple as that. We've spatialized all that information, handed it to the Department of Planning, and now we're using that information for the city's comprehensive plan, which is a legal document that the city is required to produce for housing, land use, transportation—many of the tangible things that the city is required to plan for.[71]

As Kayim's example illustrates, an awareness of the process of gentrification as uneven development has served as a springboard for partnerships and collaborative practices between artist and communities, so that performance does not simply happen in the city, but operates with the city in a way that helps to change the very systems that create such uneven development. Artists such as Theaster Gates, Rick Lowe, and Mark Bradford, have pioneered alternative models of interventionist arts practices in urban areas. Their projects—Dorchester Projects in Chicago's South Side, Project Row Houses in Houston's Third Ward, and Art + Practice Foundation in Leimert Park in Los Angeles—simultaneously revitalize the city and work against the forces of displacement, creating permanent change with and for the communities that live there.[72] "What if art was of the neighborhood, and not outside it?" asks Bradford as the question that propels his work. These artists have created models of art spaces that foster permanence for its residents. These community-based, art-activist initiatives both comment on and alter the city's transformation. They are setting the stage for new ways of making and creating art that propel change in the city for and by its participants.

Artists' participation in the process of city building over the years has taught them that they must be critically aware of problematic partnerships and funding sources that might run counter to their agendas, promoting class and racial divides.[73] Their work at a contested urban site can bring both the welcome of city agencies and the unwelcome attention of developers. Increasingly aware of such issues, contemporary performing artists, like their counterparts in the visual arts, are deciding what production, funding, participatory, and process-oriented models their performances should take. Aaron Landsman's *Perfect City* exemplifies this shift in practices. Landsman, who trained as a theatre artist and toured extensively with performance company Elevator Repair Service, has been staging work that engages community activism and addresses social issues, in particular as these concern ownership of the city, sustainability, urban planning, and gentrification. From 2012 to 2013, he developed *City Council Meeting* (which he created with Mallory Catlett and Jim Findlay), a participatory art project locally tailored to confront community issues at each location.[74] For *Perfect City*, Landsman decided to take his art activism to a new level, establishing a more long-term form of community engagement in the likes of Theaster Gates, Rick Lowe, and Mark Bradford, to help foster a more equitable and participatory form of urban revitalization. Working collaboratively with students from the Lower East Side, who are credited as co-authors of the project and retain equal control, as well as activists, artists, and urban planners, *Perfect City* is conceived as a twenty-year project—"a think tank, an arts collective" that creates "long-term creative strategies to respond to displacement and gentrification."[75] The work-in-progress iteration I saw at The Graduate Center's Elebash Hall as part of Prelude NYC 2016 had me sitting around a table set up on the stage next to a mixture of *Perfect City* collective members and spectator-participants. Other audience members could observe from their seats. What unfolded was a streaming set of ideas, concerns, questions, manifestos, lectures, and explanations regarding how cities change and what we could do to contribute to the urban-planning process.

Like many of the projects I highlight in this book, *Perfect City* shifts the focus from an emphasis on a physical location in the city to the systemic ways and processes by which urban sites are created, distributed, and controlled. *Perfect City* demonstrates a more inclusive, invested, and progressive approach to art making in the public sphere. It does not claim a particular location; it is *of* a community, not *in* a community. It creates the transformation it envisions. It is an example of a landmark performance in that it fosters permanent change—literally *marking* the land—through a long-term participatory process. In this sense, landmark performance can

Roundtable performance for Aaron Landsman's *Perfect City*, 2016. *Photo by Paula Court.*

function to equitably redistribute urban resources amongst social classes, by creating artworks that play a part in permanent urban transformation. Such contemporary landmark performances offer a way for local residents to not only reflect on urban issues but also to engage in the process as agents of the change they want to see.

Epilogue

Not so long ago I took my students to the African Burial Ground National Monument, located not far from where I teach in downtown Manhattan on Broadway between Duane and Reade Streets. The African Burial Ground was accidentally discovered in 1991, during construction of a thirty-four-story General Services Administration (GSA) federal office building,[1] when archaeologists initially found a number of graves twenty-five feet below the ground. This eventually led to the discovery of slightly over four hundred skeletal remains of men, women, and children, as well as burial artifacts that had been interred in what a 1755 map of Manhattan designated the "Negro Burial Ground." As the *New York Times* reported, "The evidence created a conceptual quake, transforming how New York history is understood and how black New Yorkers connect to their past."[2] The discovery of so many bodies brought to light this forgotten history of unwilling immigrants forced into slavery, who, at the time, made up 20 percent of New York's population. It sparked political debates surrounding the designation of the site as a sacred and national landmark. Controversy ignited in the community in the months following the discovery, in particular against the government's brash decision "to exhume and preserve the remains while proceeding with its nearly $300 million construction project."[3] African American groups fought to preserve the dignity of those buried and to honor their legacies, and their protests and actions eventually led to a halt in construction and a revision of the building's plan. Thanks to the community's resistance, in 1993 the burial ground was placed on the National Register of Historic Places. GSA contracted Howard University to conduct the research and analysis of the bone fragments found at the site,[4] all of which were reinterred in a ceremony adjacent to the new building in 2003 (which was ultimately constructed on a slightly shrunken plot of land to make way for a memorial). Three years later the site was finally recognized as a national monument to be administered by the National Park Service.[5] Architect Rodney Leon designed an "Ancestral Libation Chamber" memorial in 2007 at the location where the 419 bodies were reinterred, which also serves as a "Sacred Place," where an estimated twenty thousand remains of

Africans are currently thought to be buried.[6] A $4.4 million visitor center, meant to explain the site's significance, the one I visited with my students, opened in 2010.[7]

The African Burial Ground is the oldest cemetery of African American descendants ever to be found in North American soil. It is a site where thousands of Africans buried their dead during the 1600s and 1700s. As the *New York Times* reported when the bodies were found, "After what mean years they had on earth—enslaved, impoverished and ostracized—black New Yorkers in the 18th century were consigned to a desolate graveyard beyond the city walls."[8] The burial ground was quite literally out of town, outside the city's borders. It struck me as I visited that I was standing on what had originally been an *off site*. Not only had blacks been barred from burying their dead inside the city (a map of Manhattan in 1776 shows the "Negros Burial Ground" outside the city's limits), but the memory of the location itself had been buried along with the thousands of bodies interred there, who, not coincidentally, had their heads facing yet another *off site*: Africa. It was the voices of the multiple African American groups that fought to *mark* the site, pay tribute to its people, celebrate their legacy, that had made what was once an "off site" *present*.

I bring up my visit to the African Burial Ground because it so obviously highlights the persistence of *off sites*. These don't disappear with time. On the contrary, they nag at us and have prior claims on space. It strikes me that in this moment, as we witness a massive refugee crisis, a far-flung rise of populism and oppressive white nationalism, an obsession with border patrol, an increase in incarceration and detention centers, and a flurry of dangerous isolationist policies and agendas regarding world trade and decreased funding for foreign aid, that we are moving toward a backward world that prioritizes and glorifies borders, limits, zones, *walls*, and essentially, forced *im*mobility in all its forms (social, class, cultural, gender, you name it). These are scary times in which, instead of the site *bound*, or site *specific*, we might want to look *beyond* sites in order to make what is *off*, what is *out of bounds*, present, moving away from exclusionary sited practices.

Contemporary artists will increasingly focus their attention on the relation *between* sites; searching for ways to relocate or even dislocate a determined, or preconceived "site," whether this be a site of knowledge, or discipline, or historiography, or even, a physical location. Itinerant architectures will be replaced with "transposed" experiences, or the transfer of experience to a different place and context. In Copenhagen, for example, the Alhadj Djumaa, a fishing boat that left Egypt in 2013 for the Italian island of

Lampedusa carrying 282 Ethiopian and Eritrean refugees, is now the host of Lampedusa Cruises. The tour experiences, conceived by arts collective Fix and Foxy (Teun Catelein, Tue Biering, and Jeppe Kristensen), are led by locals and refugees from Ethiopia, Eritrea, Sudan, and Syria. Because of its proximity to Tunisia, Lampedusa was critical in the European migrant crisis, becoming a landing spot for boatloads of tens of thousands of refugees who came from Africa and the Middle East, thousands of whom died trying.[9] However, "contrary to what you might expect," the artists state, "we sail for pleasure."[10] They offer VIP Tours ("tours with locals and former refugees to brunch together"), Canal Tours ("our guides will tell you the hidden history of Amsterdam through the eyes of its immigrants and outsiders, including their personal migration story"), and Shuttle Service ("the most compelling service of our company, transferring people").

Another example is *A Mile in My Shoes*, an experience produced by the Empathy Museum, one among a growing number of museums created around a concept rather than a building.[11] This experience-based exhibit, created as part of London's LIFT Festival in the summer of 2016, invited participants to literally step into someone else's shoes and, as the *New York Times* explained, "embark on a mile-long physical, emotional and imaginative journey to see the world through their eyes":

> While walking, visitors listen on iPods to professionally produced 10-to-12-minute-long recordings narrated by the shoes' owners, who range from a prostitute to a surgeon to a drug dealer turned artist to an immigrant who is in the country illegally. . . .
>
> After walking and listening, visitors are invited to an adjacent space to reflect upon and discuss what they experienced and learned about these individuals. A few days later, the "shoe box" is whisked off to a new location.[12]

In speaking about the rationale behind this form of moving installation in her own work, Jessica Turtle, co-creator of the Museum of Homelessness, related how this is about "creating events where you're taken on a journey."[13] Rather than "space-less," these museums are actually *creating* spaces for otherwise marginalized communities or remote and/or foreign situations and simultaneously developing new forms of exhibit building that defy the more conventional gallery space, building experiences that help us relate to one another in real time and bringing people together.

The search for ways to make *off sites* presenced, embodied, and experienced, through live forms, has become of crucial importance. *Off sites* tend to run counter to official sites, but nevertheless are connected to them. The presence of *off sites* therefore allows for transpositions between sites. They are more fluid. More inclusive. I began this book thinking about how site specificity allows for the creation of new spaces for performance and new forms of theater. In my introduction, I suggested that contemporary approaches to site specificity address both new forms of theatre *and* generate new spaces simultaneously. I had originally assumed that any epilogue to this book would address new technologies, such as avatars, advances in virtual reality, and how a variety of digital spaces might allow for the creation of alternative *off sites*. But our current moment suggests that developing experiences that create a real coming together, an experience that offers a *relation* between sites—as opposed to divided by exclusionary systems of power *on* a specific site—will become more and more important. By way of an ending I offer the notion of *off sites* as a way to think about progressive political strategies through performance in times when democracy itself is under threat. How will artists continue to make *off sites* present? What can performance offer in terms of making *off sites* visible? Shifting our perspective to the presence of *off sites*, and moving *beyond* the site specific, it seems to me, brings to light what is buried underneath.

Notes

Bibliography

Index

Notes

1. Off Sites: A New Journey through Other Spaces

1. Quoted from Mike Pearson's "Special Worlds, Secret Maps: A Poetics of Performance" in Fiona Wilkie's "Mapping the Terrain: A Survey of Site-Specific Performance in Britain," *New Theatre Quarterly* 18, no. 2 (2002): 142. See also Mike Pearson, *Site-Specific Performance* (New York: Palgrave Macmillan, 2010); Mike Pearson and Michael Shanks, *Theatre/archaeology: Reflections on a Hybrid Genre* (New York: Routledge, 2001).

2. Joanne Tompkins, "The 'Place' and Practice of Site-Specific Theatre and Performance" in *Performing Site-Specific Theatre: Politics, Place, Practice*, ed. J. Tompkins and A. Birch (New York: Palgrave Macmillan: 2012), 1.

3. Nick Kaye, *Site-Specific Art: Performance, Place, Documentation* (New York: Routledge, 2000).

4. Tompkins, "'Place' and Practice," 1.

5. Richard Schechner, "Extensions in Time and Space: An Interview with Allan Kaprow," *TDR* 12, no. 3 (1968): 153–59.

6. Gary Younge, "Don't Let Trump Fool You: Rightwing Populism Is the New Normal Video," *Guardian*, January 16, 2016, accessed January 29, 2016, http://www.theguardian.com/commentisfree/video/2016/jan/06/dont-let-trump-fool-you-rightwing-populism-is-the-new-normal-video?CMP=fb_us.

7. For more on neoliberalism and globalization, see David Harvey, *A Brief History of Neoliberalism* (Oxford: Oxford University Press, 2007); Saskia Sassen, *Losing Control? Sovereignty in the Age of Globalization* (New York: Columbia University Press, 2015); Joseph Stiglitz, *The Price of Inequality* (New York: W. W. Norton, 2013).

8. Quoted from Bertie Ferdman, Ryan M. Davis, and Anne Erbe, eds., "Works Sited: A Forum," *Theater* 43, no. 2 (2013): 27.

9. In November 2015, the twenty-first annual Climate Change conference, more commonly known as COP21, generated what is called the Paris Agreement, in which 195 nations set a path to ensure that the temperature did not increase more than two degrees Celsius. UNFCCC, http://newsroom.unfccc.int/unfccc-newsroom/finale-cop21/. In June 2017, Trump announced that the United States would withdraw from the Paris Agreement.

10. Ferdman et al., "Works Sited," 31.

11. For more information on ecological awareness and the ecological crisis of today's world, see Timothy Morton's *A Dark Ecology: For a Logic of Future Coexistence* (New York: Columbia University Press, 2016).

12. Michael Fried, *Art and Objecthood, Minimal Art: A Critical Anthology* (New York: E. P. Dutton, 1968), 125.

13. Kaye, *Site-Specific Art*, 2–3.

14. Michael Kirby, "The New Theatre," *TDR* 10, no. 2 (1965): 23–43.

15. See Sabine Breitwieser's *Carolee Schneemann: Kinetic Painting* (Prestel, 2016).

16. Oldenburg, for example, whose works included *Autobodys* (1963, in a car park), *Injun* (1962, in a Dallas farmhouse), and *Washes* (1965, in a swimming pool), observed how "the place in which the piece occurs, this large object, is part of the effect, and usually the first and most important factor determining the events (materials at hand being the second and players the third)." Dewey also experimented with live performance. His *City Scale* (1963) took place in city streets where spectators were led through a series of occurrences and places, such as a model undressing at an apartment window, a car ballet in a parking lot, and a singer in a shop window.

17. See Rebecca Schneider, *The Explicit Body in Performance* (New York: Routledge, 1997) and Moira Roth, *The Amazing Decade: Women and Performance Art in America: 1970–1980* (Los Angeles: Astro Artz, 1984).

18. It is important to mention that cross-disciplinary experiments in dance, visual art, and music, were as much of a crucial influence on all of these artists. Yvonne Rainer's early choreographic pieces, along with the founding of the Judson Dance Theater, paralleled the influence of minimalist art practice, along with the earlier chance experiments of John Cage and Merce Cunningham at Black Mountain College. See Sally Banes, *Terpsichore in Sneakers: Postmodern Dance* (Middletown, CT: Wesleyan University Press, 1987); Vincent Katz, *Black Mountain College: Experiment in Art* (Cambridge, MA: MIT Press, 2013).

19. Richard Serra, "*Tilted Arc* Destroyed," *Art in America* 77, no. 5 (May 1989), quoted in Kwon, *One Place after Another*, 12. Incidentally, an article in *Hyperallergic* discusses how artists, other than Richard Serra, have fared under the Visual Artists Rights Act, a federal law that "prohibits any defacement, mutilation, alteration, or destruction of fine art," in claiming that their work was destroyed when removed from the location for which it was tailored. In 2006, reacting to Boston-area sculptor David Phillips's lawsuit, the US Court of Appeals ruled that "the plain language" of the law "does not protect site-specific art." "The harm presented," the court wrote, "is decontextualization." See Daniel Grant, "Why 'Site-Specific Isn't So Specific,'" *Hyperallergic*, November 26, 2014, accessed June 10, 2016, http://hyperallergic.com/158338/why-site-specific-isnt-so-specific/.

20. Suzanne Lacy, *Mapping the Terrain: New Genre Public Art* (Seattle, WA: Bay Press, 1995).

21. Robert Irwin, "Being and Circumstance: Notes towards Confidential Art," in *Being and Circumstance* (Larkspur Landing, CA: Lapis Press, 1985), 9–29; republished in Claire Doherty, ed., *Situation* (Cambridge, MA: MIT Press; and London: Whitechapel Gallery: Documents in Contemporary Art), 43–44.

22. Miwon Kwon, *One Place after Another: Site Specific Art and Locational Identity* (Cambridge, MA: MIT Press, 2002), 14. In particular, she describes the work of artists like Mel Bochner (*Measurement* series, 1968–69), Hans Haacke (*Information*, 1970), Mierle Laderman Ukeles (*Maintenance* series, 1973–74), and Michael Asher (*73rd American Exhibition* at the Art Institute of Chicago, 1979), all of whom began to unveil and expose the cultural confinement within which artists functioned, as well as how the spaces of art (galleries and museums) came to exist.

23. Shannon Jackson, "When 'Everything Counts': Experimental Performance and Performance Historiography," in *Representing the Past: Essays in Performance and Historiography*, ed. Canning and Postlewait (Iowa City: Iowa University Press, 2010), 246.

24. Kwon, *One Place after Another*, 26.

25. Tadeusz Kantor, *A Journey through Other Spaces: Essays and Manifestos, 1944–1990*, ed. and trans. Michal Kobialka (Berkeley: University of California Press, 1993), 76.

26. See Marvin Carlson, "The City as Theatre," in *Places of Performance: The Semiotics of Theatre Architecture* (Ithaca, NY: Cornell University Press 1993), 27–28.

27. Marvin Carlson, "site-specific theatre" entry in *The Continuum Companion to Twentieth Century Theatre*, ed. Colin Chambers (New York: Continuum International Publishing, 2002), 253.

28. Incidentally, in Jan Cohen-Cruz's edited anthology *Radical Street Performance: An International Anthology* (New York: Routledge, 1998), Ngũgĩ wa Thiong'o explains how the spirit of street performance as public forum is one of African theatre's unique characteristics, writing that "legitimate theatre, according to the colonists, was performed indoors, in the colonist's constructed theatres, in the universities and only occasionally, under the supervision of Europeans, in the streets and communities of the indigenous population." Theatre in this case signaled a different kind of high art agenda, in this case both a practice and architecture of colonization. Ngũgĩ wa Thiong'o, "The Language of African Theatre," reprinted in Cohen-Cruz, *Radical Street Performance*, 238–44.

29. Kantor, *Journey through Other Spaces*, 33.

30. David Wiles, *A Short History of Western Performance Space* (Cambridge: Cambridge University Press 2003).

31. In particular his productions of *Acropolis* (1964) and *The Constant Prince* (1965).

32. See especially Richard Schechner, *Environmental Performance* (New York: Hawthorn Books, 1973), and "6 Axioms for Environmental Theatre," *TDR* 12, no. 3 (1968): 41–64.

33. As with avant-garde staging techniques, environmental staging became common in mainstream commercial theatre. During the 1980s, "environmental theatre" was used to characterize such productions as *Tony and Tina's Wedding* (1985), where audiences were invited to participate as guests in a Mafioso wedding party, and *Tamara* (1987), an elaborate murder-mystery journey "event" held at the Seventh Regiment Armory on Park Avenue, more akin to Disneyland than to its

politically motivated environmental avant-garde predecessors. Terms such as "theme park," "carnival," "all inclusive," and "fun house" often appear in descriptions of these shows. Experimental off-off-Broadway also used the "environmental" lexicon to categorize their practices. When Fiona Templeton, for example, premiered *YOU—The City* in 1988, a performance that had an audience of one, who was designated as "the client" and taken through a number of places throughout midtown Manhattan in a series of encounters with various characters, it was also labeled "environmental theatre." See Fiona Templeton and Steve Nelson, "YOU-The City vs. Nelson-The Critic," *TDR* 34, no. 2 (Summer 1990).

34. For critiques of these intercultural initiatives, see David Williams, ed., *Peter Brook and the Mahabharata: Critical Perspectives* (Milton Park, UK: Taylor and Francis, 1991); Maria Shevtsova, "Interculturalism, Aestheticism, Orientalism: Starting from Peter Brook's Mahabharata," *Theatre Research International* 22, no. 2 (1997): 98–104; Rustom Bharucha, *The Politics of Cultural Practice: Thinking through Theatre in an Age of Globalization* (Middletown, CT: Wesleyan University Press, 2000).

35. Of particular interest is Mel Gussow's review in the *New York Times* titled "3 Site-Specific Plays in Central Park," dated June 20, 1989. Gussow reviews three plays produced by En Garde Arts and performed on location: Belvedere Castle, Mid-Park at Seventy-Ninth Street; Bow Bridge on the Lake; and the Dairy, Mid-Park at Sixty-Fourth Street. The three productions included *Babel on Babylon*, written and directed by Matthew Maguire; *Bad Penny*, written by Mac Wellman and directed by Jim Simpson; and *Minny and the James Boys*, written by Anna Theresa Cascio and directed by Kevin Kelley.

It is noteworthy that Anne Hamburger chose not to use the term "environmental" to describe her company, even though the term, in the way Schechner had described it, could have been used. (In fact it was still used by reviewers. See, for example, Stephen Holden, "A Carnival of Satire and Savagery, with a Karamazov as Ringmaster," *New York Times*, July 11, 1990. Holden describes Reza Abdoh's *Father Was a Peculiar Man*, which I detail in chapter 5, as "an exhilarating evening of environmental street theater.")

36. Pearson, *Site-Specific Performance*, 5.

37. Ensemble members were "people considered marginal to mainstream society because of physical disabilities. . . . [Some] were recruited through agencies serving the disabled." Stephen Holden, "In Decayed, Empty Nursing Home, a Pageant of the Lame and Hurt," *New York Times*, September 10, 1991.

38. Monk choreographed dances for actual hospital patients and members of her company, and had the audience circulate inside a building—formerly a smallpox hospital designed by James Renwick—that was normally not open to the public. *American Archeology* was produced by Elise Bernhardt, founder and then producing director of Dancing in the Streets.

39. Jennifer Dunning, "Meredith Monk Looks into Roosevelt Island's Past," *New York Times*, September 22, 1994.

40. Pearson, *Site-Specific Performance*, 40.

41. Fiona Wilkie, "The Production of 'Site': Site-Specific Theatre," in *Contemporary*

British and Irish Drama, ed. N. Holdsworth and M. Luckhurt (Oxford: Blackwell, 2008), 100–101. See also Fiona Wilkie, *Performance, Transport, and Mobility: Making Passage* (London: Palgrave Macmillan, 2015).

42. Quoted from Ferdman et al., "Works Sited," 29. Other notable examples include Aaron Landsman's *City Council Meeting* and PearlDamour's (Karie Pearl and Lisa D'Amour) *Milton*.

43. "How to End Poverty in 90 Minutes," accessed June 2016, http://www.sojourntheatre.org/how-to-end-poverty-in-90-minutes/.

44. Ferdman et al., "Works Sited," 29. See also Michael Rohd, "Artist's Notebook: Civic Participation," *Theater* 43, no. 3 (2013): 25.

45. Francine Mary A'ness, "Resisting Amnesia: Yuyachkani, Performance, and the Postwar Reconstruction of Peru," *Theatre Journal* 56, no. 3 (2004): 396.

46. Ibid., 404.

47. Quoted in A'ness, from the program notes for Yuyachkani's October–December 2003 theatre festival, *La persistencia de la memoria* 1–11.

48. Cathy Turner and Stephen Hodge, "Site: Between Ground and Groundlessness," in *Histories and Practices of Live Art*, ed. Deirdre Heddon and Jennie Klein (New York: Palgrave Macmillan, 2012), 91. On p. 110, they also write how "artists continue to oscillate between dislocation and reclamation of place."

49. Doherty, *Situation*, 12. Writing on the evolution of site specificity in the visual arts, particularly in sculpture, Doherty comments: "More often than not the search for the authentic site of a work was frustrated, characterized by dislocation and displacement. Site was dispersed across location and time. Works were *situational* rather than site-specific."

50. Hans-Thies Lehmann, *Postdramatic Theatre* (New York: Routledge, 2006, English translation; German edition, 1999), 108. Lehmann's *Postdramatic Theatre* is grounded in theatre studies legacies, even though he addresses the influence of visual art on theatre. There is no mention, for example, of Victor Burgin's *Situational Aesthetics* from 1969, which defined the trend in contemporary art at the time in terms of "aesthetic *systems*," as opposed to "individual objects," invoking Brecht's thinking to reconsider the mechanism under which art was produced. (Quotes here taken from Doherty, *Situation*, 41, extracted from Burgin.)

51. Kwon, *One Place after Another*, 29.

52. Ibid., 166.

53. See Shannon Jackson, *Social Works: Performing Art, Supporting Publics* (New York: Routledge, 2011) and her chapter "When 'Everything Counts'" in *Representing the Past*, 240–60.

54. Branislav Jakovljevic, "The Space Specific Theatre: Skewed Visions' *The City Itself*," *TDR* 49, no. 3 (2005): 98.

55. Kantor, *A Journey through Other Spaces*, 88.

56. Marc Augé, *Non-Places: An Introduction to Supermodernity*, trans. John Howe (New York: Verso Books, 2005).

57. Lola Arias, "The Work of Art Is a Parasite," interviewed and translated by Bertie Ferdman, *Theater* 44, no. 2 (2014): 33.

58. "Projects: *Room Service (Help Me Make It through the Night)*," Gob Squad, accessed January 29, 2016, www.gobsquad.com/projects/room-service-help-me-make-it-through-the-night.

59. Ibid.

60. "Dominic Huber, *Hotel Savoy*," PS 122, accessed January 5, 2016, www.ps122.0rg/hotel_savoy.

61. Ibid.

62. Turner and Hodge, "Site: Between Ground and Groundlessness," 91.

63. Kwon, *One Place after Another*, 2. Turner and Hodge write, "If we choose to retain a tentative commitment to the idea of a 'site,' it can be qualified by adopting Kwon's proposal that the term 'site-specific' is useful, not so much in order to identify a genre of art, as a problem-idea" (93).

64. Terry Smith, *What Is Contemporary Art* (Chicago: University of Chicago Press: 2009), 6.

65. Ibid., 4.

66. Books, articles, and special editions include Kwon's *One Place after Another*; Pearson's *Site-Specific Performance*; Wilkie's "Mapping the Terrain," 140–60; Andrew Houston, ed., *Environmental and Site-Specific Theatre: Critical Perspectives on Canadian Theatre in English*, vol. 8 (Toronto, ON: Playwrights Canada Press, 2007); "Site-Specificity and Mobility," special issue, ed. Anna Birch, *Contemporary Theatre Review* 22, no. 2 (2012): with contributions by Fiona Wilkie, Cathy Turner, and Deirdre Heddon, among others. Other related titles include D. J. Hopkins, Shelley Orr, and Kim Solga, eds., *Performance and the City* (New York: Palgrave Macmillan, 2011); Nicholas Whybrow, ed., *Performance and the Contemporary City* (New York: Palgrave Macmillan, 2010); Elinor Fuchs and Una Chaudhuri, *Land/Scape/Theatre* (Ann Arbor: University of Michigan Press, 2002); Josephine Machon, *Immersive Theatres: Intimacy and Immediacy in Contemporary Performance* (New York: Palgrave Macmillan, 2013); Juliet Rufford, *Theatre and Architecture* (New York: Palgrave Macmillan, 2014); Claire Bishop, *Artificial Hells: Participatory Art and the Politics of Spectatorship* (New York: Verso Books, 2012).

67. Notably Mike Pearson, Fiona Wilkie, Cathy Turner, Stephen Hodge, as well as Florian Malzacher, whose focus has been more on the European festival circuit.

68. See, in particular, Doherty, *Situation*; Kwon, *One Place after Another*; and Rosalyn Deutsche, *Evictions: Art and Spatial Politics* (Cambridge, MA: MIT Press, 1996).

69. See Jackson, "When 'Everything Counts'" in *Representing the Past*. Jackson's book *Social Acts* also engages with multiple disciplinary legacies in analyzing performance. Nick Kaye's book takes a performance studies interdisciplinary approach.

2. Disciplinary Sites: Situating Theatre

1. In a personal email correspondence dated February 15, 2017, Levine explained how there was a lot of discussion about signage with Creative Time prior to the performances:

> I wanted no signage anywhere—just the moderately confusing map. Creative Time was insistent that at least the uptown locations be find-able, to launch people on their scavenger hunt. . . . I really liked the idea of creating or merging three different audiences: those who knew exactly what was going on, those who figured out that something *must* be going on, and those who passed right by and saw nothing going on.

2. Shannon Jackson, *Social Works: Performing Art, Supporting Publics* (New York: Routledge, 2011), 19.

3. Shannon Jackson, "The Way We Perform Now," *Dance Research Journal* 46, no. 3 (2014): 56.

4. Jackson, *Social Works*, 18.

5. Performa is the brainchild of art historian and curator Roselee Goldberg, billed as "the nation's first and only visual art performance biennial." "Mission and History," *Performa*, accessed 28 February 2016, http://performa-arts.org/about/mission-and-history.

6. Kari Conte, *Mierle Laderman Ukeles: Seven Work Ballets* (New York: Sternberg Press, 2016). Mierle Laderman Ukeles, "Manifesto for Maintenance Art 1969! Proposal for Exhibition 'Care,'" 1–4 (copyright Mierle Laderman Ukeles, 1969; reprinted in Lucy Pippard, *Six Years: The Dematerialization of the Art Object* [New York: New York University Press, 1979]).

7. See John Bell, ed., *Puppet, Masks, and Performing Objects* (Cambridge, MA: TDR Books, 1988, reprinted Cambridge, MA: MIT Press, 1999).

8. Shannon Jackson, *Social Works*, 18.

9. Today the category is called interdisciplinary work and, according to NYFA's website,

> accepts submissions from artists combining or crossing disciplines, either within a single piece or throughout a body of work. This work may draw on traditions from the visual arts, especially those with a performative, political, and/or social aspect. Examples include, but are not limited to: participatory installations or environments, live art, and public art. *Theatre, dance, or visual art that employs traditional methods of exploration are not appropriate for this category* [my emphasis].

"Artist's Fellowships—Disciplines," *NYFA*, accessed July 7, 2015, https://www.nyfa.org/Content/Show/Artists'%20Fellowships%20%E2%80%94%20Disciplines.

10. Claire Bishop, "Unhappy Days in the Art World? De-skilling Theatre, Re-skilling Performance," *Brooklyn Rail*, https://brooklynrail.org/2011/12/art/unhappy-days-in-the-art-worldde-skilling-theater-re-skilling-performance.

11. Robert Quillen and Gavin Kroeber, "Postshow Theatre." *Theater* 44, no. 3 (2014): 19–29.

12. Trish Bednix, "Sarah Michelle Gellar and Selma Blair Recreate 'Cruel Intentions' Kiss," *After Ellen*, last modified May 29, 2015, http://www.afterellen.com/movies/433739-sarah-michelle-gellar-selma-blair-recreate-cruel-intentions-kiss.

13. Robert Ayers, "The Knife Is Real, the Blood Is Real, and the Emotions Are Real," *A Sky Filled with Shooting Stars*, last modified March 10, 2010, http://www.askyfilledwithshootingstars.com/wordpress/?p=1197.

14. David Levine, Marsha Ginsberg, Jason Grote, and Amy Holzapfel, "The Habit of Realism," *Theater* 42, no. 1 (2012): 100.

15. Richard Schechner, *Between Theater and Anthropology* (Philadelphia: University of Pennsylvania Press, 1985), 35–36. (Original citation, 1977).

16. See Michael Kirby, "On Acting and Not-Acting," *TDR* (1972): 3–15.

17. *Art/US*, no. 13, June 2006.

18. Douglas Crimp, *On the Museum's Ruins* (Cambridge, MA: MIT Press, 1993), 17. This emphasis on the "conditions of reception," is what Crimp argued was "site specific" in minimalist art practices:

> The situated spectator, whose self-conscious perception of the minimal object in relation to the site of its installation produced the work's meaning. . . . The idealism of modernist art, in which the art object *in and of itself* was seen to have a fixed and transhistorical meaning, determined the object's placelessness. . . . Site specificity opposed that idealism—and unveiled the material system it obscured—by its refusal of circulatory mobility, its belongingness to a *specific* site.

19. Lee Strasberg, *The Lee Strasberg Notes*, ed. Lola Cohen (New York: Routledge, 2010); Constantin Stanislavski, *My Life in Art*, trans. J. J. Robbins (London: Methuen, 1980).

20. Strasberg, *Strasberg Notes*, 24.

21. Schechner, *Performance Studies* (New York: Routledge, 2013), 125–26. (Original source: Lee Strasberg and Richard Schechner, "Working with Live Material," *Tulane Drama Review* 9, no. 1 [1964]: 117–35.)

22. David Levine, "An Actual Subversion," *Mousse* 41 (2014): 76–77.

23. Ibid.

24. Ibid.

25. Paul David Young, *NewARTtheatre: Evolutions of the Performance Aesthetic* (New York: PAJ Publications, 2014), 24.

26. David Levine, "Artist Project / Actors at Work," *Cabinet* 25 (2007). Also available at http://www.cabinetmagazine.org/issues/25/levine.php.

27. Ibid.

28. David Levine, "Artist's Journal," *Theater* 38 (2008): 30–51.

29. Marvin Carlson, "David Levine's *Bauerntheater*: The Return of the Matrix," *TDR* 52, no. 3 (2008): 35–36.

30. "Habit by David Levine," *Mass Moca*, accessed May 6, 2016, http://massmoca.org/event/habit-by-david-levine/.

31. Levine et al., "Habit of Realism," 100.

32. Wherever the performers were at the end of the six-hour workday, that is where they stopped. In the New York City version, they did a full eight-hour workday. The convention Levine went for was that the length was not measured by the number of loops, but by the number of workday hours.

33. Levine et al., "Habit of Realism," 95.

34. As Levine explained to me in an email correspondence dated February 15, 2017, "*Habit* counted on the actors to grow restless, and therefore inventive. They had license to do anything they wanted, so long as they stayed within the contours of realism. Part of the spectacle/fun for me was watching the variations that virtuosity and restlessness would or could drive them to."

35. Levine et al., "Habit of Realism," 95.

36. Kirby, *The Art of Time: Essays on the Avant-Garde*, New York: E. P. Dutton, 1969, 71.

37. Levine et al., "Habit of Realism," 100.

38. Bishop, "Unhappy Days."

39. Ibid.

40. See, for example, Shannon Jackson's chapter titled "Staged Management: Theatricality and Institutional Critique" in *Social Works*, where she focuses on the work of Allan Sekula, Andrea Fraser, and William Pope.L

41. Andrew Horwitz, "Visual Art Performance vs. Contemporary Performance," *Culturebot*, November 25, 2011. Carol Martin's *Theatre of the Real* (New York: Palgrave Macmillan, 2012) engages with the fabrication of the real in theatre. I will discuss Martin's work at length in chapter 3.

42. Sara Jane Bailes, *Performance Theatre and the Poetics of Failure* (London: Routledge, 2011), 10. Also, from p. 167, "ERS, like the Wooster Group, Mabou Mines, and Richard Foreman before them, produce theatre as an event that thrives on the understanding that the failure of representation (the reiteration that the art work is an 'artificial construct,' it is an 'artefact') must be significant to the development of the theatre event."

43. See Claire Bishop's *Artificial Hells: Participatory Art and the Politics of Spectatorship* (New York: Verso Books, 2012); Nicolas Bourriaud's *Relational Aesthetics* (Dijon, France: Les Presses Du Réel, 1998); Nato Thompson's *Living as Form: Socially Engaged Art from 1991–2011* (Cambridge, MA: MIT Press, 2010); Grant H. Kester's *The One and the Many: Contemporary Collaborative Art in a Global Context* (Durham: Duke University Press, 2011).

44. See Robert Quillen and Gavin Kroeber, "Postshow Theatre," *Theater* 44, no. 3 (2014).

45. Hans-Thies Lehmann, *Postdramatic Theatre* (New York: Routledge, 2006, English translation; German edition, 1999).

46. Such as Jan Fabre, Robert Wilson, Richard Foreman, Romeo Castellucci, Pina Bausch, Gobsquad, Forced Entertainment, Tadeusz Kantor, Fura del Baus, the Wooster Group, and Sasha Waltz, among others.

47. See, in particular, Cathy Turner and Synne Behrndt, *Dramaturgy and Performance* (New York: Palgrave Macmillan, 2007); Magda Romanska, *The Routledge Companion to Dramaturgy* (New York: Routledge, 2014); Marianne Van Kerkhoven, "European Dramaturgy in the 21st Century: A Constant Movement," *Performance Research* 14, no. 3 (2009): 7–11; Peter Eckersall, "Towards an Expanded Dramaturgical Practice: A Report on 'The Dramaturgy and Cultural Intervention Project,'"

Theatre Research International 31, no. 3 (2006): 283–97; Katalin Trencsényi and Bernadette Cochrane, *New Dramaturgy: International Perspectives on Theory and Practice* (London: Bloomsbury Publishing, 2014).

48. In her review of *Postdramatic Theatre*, which appeared in *TDR*, Elinor Fuchs emphasizes Polish/German theatre scholar Andrzej Wirth's underacknowledged influence in the development of Lehmann's term and thinking. Lehmann responded to Fuchs's review. See Elinor Fuchs, "Postdramatic Theatre by Hans-Thies Lehmann. Translated by Karen Jürs-Munby. London: Routledge," *TDR* 52, no. 2 (2008): 178–83, and Hans-Thies Leihmann, Karen Jürs-Munby, and Elinor Fuchs, "Lost in Translation?," *TDR* 52, no. 4 (2008): 13–20.

49. Bailes, *Poetics of Failure*, 18.

50. Elinor Fuchs, *The Death of Character: Perspectives on Theatre after Modernism* (Bloomington: Indiana University Press, 1996). The book contains a reprinting of the essay "The Death of Character," originally published in *Theatre Communications* in 1983. Bonnie Marranca, *The Theatre of Images* (Baltimore, MD: Johns Hopkins University Press, 1996).

51. See, in particular, Bailes's section titled "Failing Terms: Performance and/or Theatre?" in her introduction to *Poetics of Failure*, 18–22.

52. Fuchs, *Death of Character*, 170.

53. Bonnie Marranca, "Book Review: *Happenings and Other Acts*," *PAJ* 56, vol. 19, no. 2 (1997): 115. The "live art" Marranca refers to here is not the live art that Lois Keidan has made prevalent in the United Kingdom.

54. Bonnie Marranca, "Bodies of Action, Bodies of Thought: Performance and Its Critics," *PAJ* 61, vol. 21, no. 1 (1999): 11–23.

55. Ibid., 12.

56. See Bonnie Marranca and Gautam Dasgupta, "Performing Arts Journal Changes Name to PAJ," *PAJ* 58, vol. 20, no. 1 (January 1998): v–vi.

> After publishing this periodical since 1976 as *Performing Arts Journal*, we have decided to change our name simply to "*PAJ*," adding the subtitle "A Journal of Performance and Art" to the cover and masthead. Though we have always been referred to as *PAJ*, in a more formal sense this move further solidifies the efforts, outlined four years ago in the Editorial of PAJ 42, to expand our commentary to art world activities as they articulate key issues in performance and spectatorship. The recent creation of the "Art & Performance Notes" section of the journal also reflects this new direction.

57. Leslie Hill, "Mapping the Territory: Introduction," in *Performance and Place*, ed. Leslie Hill and Helen Paris (New York: Palgrave Macmillan, 2006), 7.

58. Bertie Ferdman, "From Content to Context: The Emergence of the Performance Curator," *Theater* 44, no. 2 (2014): 9.

59. See, in particular, Sally Banes's *Terpsichore in Sneakers: Post-Modern Dance* (Middletown, CT: Wesleyan University Press, 1987).

60. Panel took place on April 24, 2014. Panelists included Roselee Goldberg

(moderator and convener), Claire Bishop, Adrian Heathfield, John Rockwell, Hrag Vartanian, and David Velasco.

61. See, in particular, Adrian Heathfield, *Live Art and Performance* (New York: Routledge, 2004); Amelia Jones and Adrian Heathfield, *Perform, Repeat, Record: Live Art in History* (Bristol, UK: Intellect Ltd., 2012); and Bishop, "Unhappy Days."

62. Horwitz, "Visual Art Performance."

63. Ibid.

64. Lois Keidan, "This Must Be the Place: Thoughts on Place, Placelessness and Live Art since the 1980s," in *Performance and Place*, ed. Leslie Hill and Helen Paris (New York: Palgrave Macmillan, 2006), 9.

65. Beth Hoffmann explains in her essay "Radicalism and the Theatre in Genealogies of Live Art," in *Performance Research* 14, no. 1 (2005): 100–101.

> The descriptor "live art" was used as early as 1979 by the *Performance Magazine* to describe a broad area of work that included fringe theatre, performance art, rock gigs and political performance. "Live art" gained wider currency, alongside "time-based art," through the development of the National Review of Live Art (NRLA), an annual festival which began life in the late 1970s as the Midland Group in Nottingham's "Performance Art Platform."

66. Keidan, "This Must Be the Place," 9.

67. Beth Hoffmann, "Radicalism and the Theatre in Genealogies of Live Art," in *Performance Research* 14, no. 1 (2005): 97.

68. Ibid., 100.

69. Ibid., 100–101.

70. Ibid.

71. Bishop, *Artificial Hells*.

72. Young, *NewARTtheatre*, 6.

73. The other artists are John Kelly, Liz Magic Laser, David Levine, Alix Pearlstein, Janet Cardiff, Gerard Byrne, Georg Bures Miller, Xaviera Simmons, Ohad Meromo, John Jesurun, Pablo Helguera, William Leavitt, Joe Scanlan, Michael Smith, and Elisabeth Subrin.

74. Young, *NewARTtheatre*, 179.

75. Ibid.

76. Armand Gatti, "Armand Gatti on Time, Place, and the Theatrical Event," *Modern Drama* 25 (1982): 71.

77. Ibid.

78. Ibid.

79. Kirby, "Environmental Theatre," *Total Theatre* (New York: E. P. Dutton, 1969).

80. Gatti, *Modern Drama*, 71.

81. Augusto Boal, *Theatre of the Oppressed* (New York: Theatre Communications Group, TCG edition, 1993).

82. Douglas Crimp, *On the Museum's Ruins* (Cambridge, MA: MIT Press, 1993), 17.

83. Kwon, *One Place after Another*, 40.

84. Ibid., 13.

85. John Kelly, Liz Magic Laser, David Levine, and Alix Pearlstein in conversation with Young, *NewARTtheatre*, 14.

86. Florian Malzacher, "Empty Stages, Crowded Flats," Sidsel Graffer and Ådne Sekkelsten, Scenekunsten og de unge [Performing Arts and The Young] (Oslo: Vidarforlaget AS, 2014), 116–27.

87. Ibid.

88. Bishop, "Unhappy Days."

89. See Julia Halperin, "Performers Tell Museums to Get Their Act Together on Fees," *Art Newspaper*, September 22, 2015.

90. Ibid.

91. Richard Schechner, *Between Theatre and Anthropology* (Philadelphia: University of Pennsylvania Press, 1985), 112.

> A performance "takes place" in the "not me . . . not not me" between performers; between performers and texts; between performers, texts, and environment; between performers, texts, environment, and audience. The larger the field of "between," the larger the performance. The antistructure that is performance swells until it threatens to burst. The trick is to extend it to the bursting point but no further.

3. Spectator Sites: Artistic Intervention and the Unintended Audience

1. Kenneth Goldsmith, n.d., Facebook, accessed October 25, 2015.

2. Carol Martin, *Theatre of the Real* (New York: Palgrave Macmillan, 2013), 120.

3. Kima Jones, Twitter post, March 15, 2015, 11:20 A.M., https://twitter.com/kima_jones.

4. Saeed Jones, Twitter post, March 15, 2015, 11:07 A.M., https://twitter.com/theferocity.

5. Rin Johnson, "On Hearing a White Man Co-opt the Body of Michael Brown," *Hyperallergic*, March 20, 2015.

6. Alec Wilkinson, "Something Borrowed," *New Yorker*, October 5, 2015.

7. C. A. Conrad (also known as CAConrad), "Kenneth Goldsmith Says He Is an Outlaw," *The Poetry Foundation*'s Harriet blog, June 2015.

8. Ibid.

9. Johnson, "On Hearing a White Man," 2015.

10. Ta-Nehisi Coates, *Between the World and Me* (New York: Spiegel and Grau, 2015).

11. Martin, *Theatre of the Real*, 119–48.

12. Jesse McKinley, "Theater Addresses Tension over Play," *New York Times*, March 16, 2006.

13. Martin, *Theatre of the Real*, 4.

14. Ibid., 120.

15. In *Learning How to Fall*, T. Nikki Cesare Schotzko considers how the aesthetic realm itself not only functions as a stylized re-envisioning of daily life (in her case with the events of 9/11) but also "inversely, as a viable means by which one might experience and process real-world political and social events." See T. Nikki Cesare Schotzko, *Learning How to Fall: Art and Culture after 9/11* (New York: Routledge, 2015), 8.

16. Christopher B. Balme, *Theatrical Public Sphere* (Cambridge: Cambridge University Press, 2014).

17. Ibid., 15.

18. Jürgen Habermas, *Structural Transformation of the Public Sphere: An Inquiry into the Category of Bourgeois Society*, trans. Thomas Burger and Frederick Lawrence (Cambridge, MA: MIT Press, 1989). Original German version published in 1962.

19. Balme, *Theatrical Public Sphere*, 7.

20. This distanced form of viewing or representational spectatorship through visual reproduction such as photojournalism is what Susan Sontag ponders in *Regarding the Pain of Others* (New York: Picador, 2004).

21. Walter Benjamin, *Illuminations: Essays and Reflections* (New York: Schocken Books, 1968), 217–52.

22. The meteor's intended destination in the Friedrichsplatz Park was alongside Walter de Maria's *Vertical Earth Kilometer* (1977) and trees from Joseph Beuys's *7000 Oaks* (1987). *Vertical Earth Kilometer* is a one-kilometer-long solid brass rod that is five centimeters in diameter, inserted completely into the ground so that only the top is flush with the surface of the earth. It is therefore impossible to see from the perspective of the viewer, who has to imagine the incredibly long rod buried underneath. It is one of the late De Maria's signature land art sculptures. *7000 Oaks*, which Bueys considered "a social sculpture," took five years to complete. The plan was to plant seven thousand trees throughout the city of Kassel, each paired with a columnar basalt stone approximately four feet high.

Both of these projects, like the planned *El Chaco en Kassel*, framed nature as art, and conceptualized art making as a set of actions. They are also art projects whose enormous scale necessitated a laborious and costly installation, and in particular with *Vertical Earth Kilometer*, had almost nothing to show for all the effort except in the spectator's imagination and the work's documentation. For *El Chaco en Kassel*, the intended location of the transported meteorite was primary; the reference to the De Maria and Beuys works and their shared conceptual strategies was a significant factor in the decision to make Kassel the meteor's ultimate destination for Documenta 13.

23. Jacques Rancière, *Emancipated Spectator*, trans. Gregory Elliott (New York: Verso Books, 2011), 13.

24. Ibid.

25. Rancière, *Emancipated Spectator*, 59. The chapter, called "Aesthetic Separation, Aesthetic Community," uses a phrase from Mallarmé's poem titled "White Water Lily," first published in a magazine called *Art and Fashion*. The phrase reads, in French "Separés, on est ensemble." Rancière uses Mallarmé's poem to

analyze another work of art by French artists called *Campement Urbain* (Urban Encampment). He writes, "The tension between being 'apart' and being 'together' is bound up with another tension between two statuses of artistic practice: as a means for producing an effect and as the reality of that effect."

26. In both *Aisthesis: Scenes from the Aesthetic Regime of Art* (New York: Verso Books, 2013) and *Emancipated Spectator*, Rancière critiques Adorno's notion that avant-garde abstraction offers political resistance just because it opposed the status quo. He also critiques the assumption that Brechtian "distanciation" (unveiling the means of production while simultaneously showing the product) is necessarily political resistance.

27. Rancière, *Emancipated Spectator*, 72–73.

28. Bishop stresses new ways of critiquing this type of art that respond not just to its process, but also to its product, stressing that a rewarding social or participatory experience alone cannot account for its aesthetic value. Bishop is among an array of art historians, curators, and critics—notably Grant Kester—who are responding to a changing art world where participation, as spectatorship, has become central to making art—and social change. Whereas for Kester the ultimate goal of participatory art is the promotion of equality and social collaboration per se—its social and/or political efficacy—Bishop finds this problematic, stressing that a rewarding participatory experience alone cannot account for aesthetic value, as the destabilization and questioning of social norms are also essential. Whatever their disagreement over its value *as* art, what is noteworthy is that, ultimately, both Bishop and Kester are concerned with a form of participatory spectatorship whose intent is overtly social and political. See Claire Bishop, *Artificial Hells: Participatory Art and the Politics of Spectatorship* (New York: Verso Books), 2012.

29. Recent notable examples include Tania Bruguera's *Immigrant Movement International* (2010–15), a long-term art project comprising an advocacy group for immigrants; Suzanne Lacy's *Between the Door and the Street* (2013), where hundreds of women gathered on the stoops of a residential block in Brooklyn to initiate unscripted conversations on gender issues; Steve Lambert's *Capitalism Works for Me!* (2011), which had a large freestanding scoreboard and press-button voting podium where passersby could vote on whether or not capitalism worked for them in their lives; and Pablo Helguera's *School of Panamerican Unrest*, another long-term public art project whose main component was a portable schoolhouse structure that was installed at various points along its twenty-five-thousand-mile journey from Anchorage to Tierra de Fuego, to foster discussion and performances on the current political situation. See also Pablo Helguera, *Education for Socially Engaged Art: A Materials and Techniques Handbook* (New York: Jorge Pinto Books Inc., 2011); Nato Thompson, *Living as Form: Socially Engaged Art from 1991–2011* (Cambridge, MA: MIT Press, 2012).

30. Nicholas Bourriaud, *Relational Aesthetics* (Dijon, France: Les Presses Du Réel, 1998).

31. Michael Hardt and Antonio Negri, *Empire* (Cambridge, MA: Harvard University Press, 2001); *Multitude: War and Democracy in the Age of Empire* (New York: Penguin Books, 2004).

32. B. Joseph Pine and James H. Gilmore, *Experience Economy: Work Is Theatre and Every Business a Stage* (Cambridge, MA: Harvard Business Press, 1999). Pine and Gilmore detail how to engage customers (consumers) in experience-led marketing campaigns.

33. See, in particular, Ric Knowles, "Editorial Comment: Spectatorship," *Theatre Journal* 66, no. 3 (2014): xi–xiv; Tom Sellar, "Special Issue: Participatory Performance," *Theater* 43, no. 3 (2013); Gareth White, *Audience Participation in the Theatre: Aesthetics of the Invitation* (London: Palgrave Macmillan, 2013); Allison Oddey and Christine White, *Modes of Spectating* (Bristol, UK: Intellect Books, 2009); Josephine Machon, *Immersive Theatres: Intimacy and Immediacy in Contemporary Performance* (London: Palgrave Macmillan, 2013); Helen Freshwater, *Theatre and Audience* (London: Palgrave Macmillan, 2009); Sonia M. Livingstone, ed., *Audiences and Publics: When Cultural Engagement Matters for the Public Sphere* (Portland, OR: Intellect Books, 2005); Bruce McConachie, *Engaging Audiences: A Cognitive Approach to Spectating in the Theatre* (London: Palgrave Macmillan, 2008).

34. Rancière, *Emancipated Spectator*, 53.

35. Jerome Carroll, Karen Jürs-Munby, and Steve Giles, "Introduction," in *Postdramatic Theatre and the Political: International Perspectives on Contemporary Performance* (London: Bloomsbury Methuen Drama, 2013), 24.

36. Ibid.

37. Hans-Thies Lehmann, "A Future for Tragedy?," in *Postdramatic Theatre and the Political: International Perspectives on Contemporary Performance*, ed. Karen Jürs-Munby, Jerome Carroll, and Steve Giles (London: Bloomsbury Press, 2013), 99–100. Lehmann writes,

> The creation of this grey zone of overlapping experiences and perceptions can happen in extremely different ways. One result of such a practice of shuttling between states is the necessity for the participants to make a decision about the nature of what they live through or witness. They find themselves in a double bind, calling for an aesthetic appreciation and at the same time for a reaction of responsibility, which could be to some degree "real." There remain "grey zones" of indistinction between art and the political, which can be explored, opened, enlarged by theatre practice.

38. Ibid.

39. Nicholas Ridout, *Passionate Amateurs: Theatre, Communism, and Love* (Ann Arbor: University of Michigan Press, 2013), 124.

40. Ibid.

41. Lola Arias, "The Work of Art Is a Parasite," interviewed and translated by Bertie Ferdman, *Theater* 44, no. 2 (2014): 45.

42. Ibid.

43. Carolyn Christov-Bakargiev and Daniel Birnbaum, foreword to *El Taco: The Campo del Cielo Meteorites*, vol. 1, ed. Guillermo Faivovich and Nicolás Goldberg (Stuttgart: Documenta 13 and Hatje Cantz, 2010).

44. "El Chaco," *Documenta (13)*, accessed April 5, 2016, http://d13.documenta.de/#/research/research/view/el-chaco.

45. Foreword to *El Taco*, 2010.

46. Simon Starling, "In Conversation with Guillermo Faivovich and Nicolás Goldberg, May 2010," in *El Taco: The Campo del Cielo Meteorites.*

47. Ibid., 51.

48. Excerpts of the official transcripts from the tribunal sessions were on display at the exhibit, as well as reprinted (and translated) in *Chaco*, vol. 2, ed. Guillermo Faivovich and Nicolás Goldberg (Stuttgart: Documenta 13 and Hatje Cantz, 2013, p. 136–74.

49. Ibid.

50. Ibid.

51. "Open Letter about El Chaco Meteorite," published January 2012. The petition can also be found at https://www.change.org/p/evitemos-que-el-meteorito-el-chaco-sea-trasladado-a-alemania.

52. *Chaco*, vol. 2, 198.

53. "Letter from Jorge Milton Capitanich, Addressed to Governor of Chaco Province," reprinted in *Chaco*, vol. 2, 196.

54. Ibid.

55. Coproduced by Steirischer Herbst Festival; Theater Spektakel Zurich; Internationales Sommer Festival Hamburg; Noordozon Performing Args Festival; and Grand Theatre Groningen.

56. Quoted in Philippa J. Page, *Politics and Performance in Post-Dictatorship Argentine Film and Theatre* (Suffolk, UK: Tamesis, 2011), 133.

57. The cycle, whose complete name was *Biodrama: Biografías Escenificadas* (Staged Biographies), began in 2002 with Analía Couceyro's *Barrocos retratos de una papa* based on the life of the painter Mildred Burton, and prior to Arias's 2009 production included such works by Argentina's foremost theatre artists, including Beatriz Cattani and Mariano Pensotti's *Los 8 de Julio* (2002), based on the life of three Argentineans born on the same day; Daniel Veronese's *La forma que se despliega* (2003), in which a couple deals with the pain of the loss of their child; and Edgardo Cozarinsky's *Squash* (2005), with the well-known actor Rafael Ferro representing his own life.

58. For more information on Proyecto Archivos, visit Vivi Tellas's website, http://www.archivotellas.com.ar/. Pamela Brownell, "Proyecto Archivos: El teatro documental según Vivi Tellas," *E-misférica 9.1–9.2, Sujetos de/al Archivo*, ed. Diana Taylor and Marianne Hirsch, 2012. Alan Pauls, "Kidnapping Reality: An Interview with Vivi Tellas," in *Dramaturgy of the Real on the World Stage*, ed. Carol Martin (New York: Palgrave Macmillan, 2010).

59. Brooke Lefler, "Biodrama as Live Action Documentary, Director Vivi Tellas at University of Oklahoma," *KGOU*, April 15, 2015, http://kgou.org/post/biodrama-live-action-documentary-director-vivi-tellas-university-oklahoma#stream/0. Interview with Julie Ward.

60. Diana Taylor, *The Archive and the Repertoire: Performing Cultural Memory in the Americas* (Durham: Duke University Press, 2003). Taylor has written

extensively on the role of theatre and performance in providing an alternative people's history. Her work has continuously stressed the role of performance as an embodied practice that unveils the difference between the official narratives and records (the archive) versus the lived (personal) histories.

61. Prior to developing this piece, Arias had collaborated with Stefan Kaegi on *Airport Kids* (2008), which featured international children from eight to fourteen years old who lived in small communities in Lausanne, away from their parents and their countries. Kaegi, cofounder of German-based Rimini Protokoll had been the only non-Argentine to take part in Tellas's *Biodrama* series. He created *Sentate* (2003), a dramatized relationship between owners and their pets.

Kaegi and his theatre company are themselves known for what Ulrike Garde and Meg Mumford term "reality theatre," who describe Rimini Protokoll's work as "overtly engaging with the 'facts' of social reality," presenting "'real' contemporary people and their lives on stage, either in person or in a carefully scripted text based on real-life interviews and documents." Ulrike Garde and Meg Mumford, "Postdramatic Reality Theatre and Productive Insecurity: Destabilising Encounters with the Unfamiliar in Theatre from Sydney and Berlin," in *Postdramatic Theatre and the Political: International Perspectives on Contemporary Performance*, ed. J. Carroll, S. Giles, and K. Jürs-Munby (London: Methuen Drama, 2013), 1.

62. Arias, "The Work of Art Is a Parasite," 31.

63. *Mi Vida Después*, 2009, video recording of full-length production, Vimeo (password protected). All subsequent descriptions refer to this recording.

64. Casullo's parents, we learn, exiled to Venezuela and Mexico, where Liza was eventually born; she came back to Argentina in 1983, at the end of the Dirty War. Casullo covers her face with her mother's image as we see the original footage of the *Telenoche* program her mother reported for projected on the large screen behind her.

65. According to desparecidos.org—his abduction was horrific—armed forces surrounded the street and prohibited neighbors from going out and witnessing what they were doing. Speratti's body was never found.

In the show, he calls his three-year-old son to the stage, whom we learn is about the same age as he was when his dad disappeared: "Moreno!" he calls. With his son by his side now, Speratti plays his dad's recordings. In Spanish, we hear the Peronist triumph song *Al triumfo!* But his favorite part, he explains to us, is a recording of his dad saying his name: "Mariano!" The voice lingers, ominously present. With his young son standing before us, it is hard not to see this moment as a resurrection, a triumph of sorts, a reckoning, the voice of the disappeared brought to life. "Say 'Papa!'" the voice begins. "Hello Mariano! Are you there?" No answer. "Mariaaaaaano! Mariaaaaaaaaano!" the voice persists, playfully, as if searching for his son in a hide and seek game. Mariano and his son listen. We witness their presence. The voice persists. *Al triumfo.*

66. "My Life After: 2009," Lola Arias's website, accessed April 11, 2016, http://lolaarias.com/proyectos/mi-vida-despues/.

67. "Postmemory characterizes the experience of those who grow up dominated by narratives that preceded their birth, whose own belated stories are evacuated

by the stories of the previous generation shaped by traumatic events that can be neither understood nor recreated." Marianne Hirsch, *Generation of Postmemory: Writing and Visual Culture after the Holocaust* (New York: Columbia University Press, 2012), 4.

68. Interview with Julie Ward, in Brooke Lefler, "Biodrama as Live Action Documentary, Director Vivi Tellas at University of Oklahoma," *KGOU*, April 15, 2015, http://kgou.org/post/biodrama-live-action-documentary-director-vivi-tellas-university-oklahoma#stream/0.

69. "It must create an experience that is political in and of itself. If we're going to talk about the guerrilla movements, we're not going to put on mustaches and guerrilla costumes and pretend it's the '70s again." "Interview with Elianna Kan," *Bomb Magazine* 128, summer 2014, http://bombmagazine.org/article/10057/lola-arias.

70. Ibid.

71. Cecilia Sosa, "Mi Vida Después: Non-Kin Affects in Post Dictatorial Argentina," *e-misférica* 7.2 "After Truth," ed. Jill Lane and Marcial Godoy-Anativia, http://hemisphericinstitute.org/hemi/en/e-misferica-72/sosa.

72. Arias, "The Work of Art Is a Parasite," 32.

73. "En el 2004 me llaman y me dicen: 'Vos sos Juan Cabandié,'" Megacausa ESMA, Espacio Memoria Argentina, accessed April 13, 2016, http://www.espaciomemoria.ar/megacausa_juicio.php?ju_ID=144&cabezal=megacausa&barra=megacausa&titulo=megacausa.

74. In particular, he had been following in the news the case of the twins Matías and Gonzalo Reggiardo Tolosa, who had themselves been abducted just days after their birth by Falco's close family friend and former police officer, Samuel Miara.

75. "Durante el juicio, Cabandié manifestó que Falco usaba símbolos Nazis," *El Intransigente*, September 18, 2009, http://www.elintransigente.com/argentina/2009/9/18/argentina-27458.html.

76. The actual DNA test was confirmed in 2004.

77. Brenda Werth, *Theatre, Performance, and Memory Politics in Argentina* (New York: Palgrave Macmillan, 2010), 42.

78. Arias, "The Work of Art Is a Parasite," 32.

79. Helen Cole interviewed by Bertie Ferdman, "Careful of Fireworks," *Theater* 44, no. 2 (2014): 63.

4. Temporal Sites: Moving Site, Moving Time

1. Tony Horwitz, "One Man's Epic Quest to Visit Every Former Slave Dwelling in the United States," *Smithsonian Magazine*, October 2013, Web. https://www.smithsonianmag.com/history/one-mans-epic-quest-to-visit-every-former-slave-dwelling-in-the-united-states-12080/.

2. Wild Whispers Africa, "Rwanda Genocide Memorial Sites," 2016, http://www.wildwhispersafrica.com/rwanda/genocide-memorial-sites/.

3. See Diana Taylor, "Villa Grimaldi," http://villagrimaldi.typefold.com/, June 2015, accessed May 29, 2016.

4. Rebecca Schneider, *Performing Remains: Art and War in Times of Theatrical Reenactment* (New York: Routledge, 2011), 2.

5. Schneider, *Performing Remains.* See, in particular, chapter 3, "In the Mean Time: Performance Remains," 87–111.

6. Schneider, *Performing Remains,* 17.

7. Matthew Wagner, "Time and the Theater," in *Shakespeare, Theater, and Time* (London: Routledge, 2012), 13–14.

8. Christine Ross, *The Past Is the Present; It's the Future Too: The Temporal Turn in Contemporary Art* (New York: Bloomsbury Academic, 2012), 6.

9. Ibid., 12.

10. Ibid., 15.

11. Branislav Jakovljevic, "Now Then—Performance and Temporality: Not Once, Not Twice . . . ," *Performance Research* 19, no. 3 (2014): 7.

12. Wendy Perron, "Art/Architecture: A Performance Piece Runs through It," *New York Times*, August 10, 2003.

13. In order to facilitate the massive projections, Strom mounted tailor-made turntables for two 400-pound digital projectors that pan and tilt on one of the train's cars, which had had nine-foot openings on both sides.

14. Such live recreations included park visitors from 1974, workers preparing to dynamite the pass (as passengers entered the tunnel), immigrant workers (known as the Gandy dancers for the way they had to coordinate the rhythms of their movements) laying the railroad ties dated to 1946, and Chief Pax the Hat (as played by Randolph Big Day) entertaining a white tourist circa 1920.

15. "About," *Geyserland*, http://www.geyserland.org/doc_site/geyserland.html.

16. Geyserland website. See also Lauret Savoy, "Wilderness and Civil Rights 50 Years Later: Recognizing the Ties of Race and Place," *Huffington Post*, September 3, 2014; Peter Nabokov and Lawrence L. Loendorf, *Restoring a Presence: American Indians and Yellowstone National Park* (Norman: University of Oklahoma Press, 2004); Robert H. Keller and Michael F. Turek, *American Indians and National Parks* (Tucson: University of Arizona Press, 1999); Mark David Spence, *Dispossessing the Wilderness: Indian Removal and the Making of the National Parks* (New York: Oxford University Press, 2000); Norman K. Denzin, *Searching for Yellowstone: Race, Gender, Family, and Memory in the Postmodern West* (Walnut Creek, CA: Left Coast Press, 2008).

17. "Project Description," http://rfkineky.org/project/about.htm.

18. Scott Magelssen, *Simming: Participatory Performance and the Making of Meaning* (Ann Arbor: University of Michigan Press, 2014), 13.

19. http://rfkineky.org/project/about.htm.

20. I take my descriptions of the two pieces from the extensive digital archive documentation the artists have made available: http://www.rfkineky.org/ and http://geyserland.org/. Where cited, I also use *New York Times* features and reviews of the productions. In addition, the artists gave me DVDs of the productions, which gave me a better sense and feel for the pieces, despite the fact that no DVD can capture the experience of simultaneity that defines these performances.

21. www.geyserland.org.

22. Jan Cohen-Cruz, "Time Travel," *RFK in EKY*, http://rfkineky.org/library/documentation/time-travel.htm.

23. Fiona Wilkie, *Performance, Transport, and Mobility: Making Passage* (London: Palgrave Macmillan, 2015), 17.

24. Ibid.

25. Ibid., 3. Wilkie credits John Urry as the primary influence in this regard. See John Urry, *Mobilities* (Cambridge: Polity Press), 2007. Wilkie also cites the work of geographer Doreen Massey as a strong influence. See Doreen Massey, *For Space* (London: Thousand Oaks; New Delhi: Sage, 2005).

26. Quoted in Fiona Wilkie, "Site-Specific Performance and the Mobility Turn," *Contemporary Theatre Review* 22, no. 2 (2012): 207.

27. Fiona Wilkie, "Mapping the Terrain: A Survey of Site-Specific Performance in Britain," *New Theatre Quarterly* 18, no. 2 (2002): 140–60; Fiona Wilkie, "Wri(gh)ting Walking," *PAJ* 29, no. 2 (2007): 108–12.

28. Fiona Wilkie, "Site-Specific Performance and the Mobility Turn," *Contemporary Theatre Review* 22, no. 2 (2012): 205.

29. Anna Birch, Editorial, Special Issue: Site-Specificity and Mobility, *Contemporary Theatre Review* 22, no. 2 (2012): 199–200.

30. Lefebvre's project detailed how the organization of space—more than economic determinism—functions as ideology. He argued that the very survival of capitalism is due to the creation of a carefully construed spacialization, hidden from critical view: "(Social) space is a (social) product." Henri Lefebvre, *The Social Production of Space*, trans. Donald Nicholson-Smith (New York: Blackwell, 1992), 26. French version originally published in 1974 by Anthropos in Paris.

31. Wilkie, "Site-Specific Performance," 31.

32. Ibid., 208.

33. David Wiles, *Theatre and Time* (London: Palgrave Macmillan, 2014), 70.

34. Joseph Roach, *Cities of the Dead: Circum-Atlantic Performance* (New York: Columbia University Press, 1996), 2. For a discussion of Kinesis, see Joseph Roach, "A Feeling for Risk: Notes on Kinesthetic Empathy and the World Performance Project," *Theater* 42, no. 1 (2012): 7–9.

35. From video of *Geyser Land* (Mary Ellen Strom and Ann Carlson).

36. "Geyser Land," maryellenstrom.com, accessed June 2016.

37. www.purewest.com/montana, accessed August 2012. The website has suspended its operation.

38. Cohen-Cruz, "Time Traveling with RFK," 2004.

39. http://rfkineky.org/library/what-happened.htm.

40. Ibid.

41. http://rfkineky.org/docs/RFKinEKY_Times.pdf.

42. Ibid.

43. Transcript from the event: http://rfkineky.org/docs/barwick-sept9.pdf.

44. Greg Kocher, "Revisiting Poverty," *Lexington Herald*, September 10, 2004.

45. "What Happened, How It Went, and Where It's Going," *The RFK in EKY Library*, accessed June 30, 2016, http://rfkineky.org/library/what-happened.htm.

46. Priscilla Frank, "Don't Bother Paying Attention: This Play *Wants* You to Fall Asleep," *Huffington Post*, May 13, 2014, accessed August 7, 2014, www.huffington post.com/2014/05/13/dream-of -the-red-chamber_n_5312210.html.

47. Okwui Okpokwasili, 2014, email correspondence with author, August 27, 2014.

48. Frank, "Don't Bother Paying Attention," 2014.

49. Guy Debord, *The Society of the Spectacle*, trans. Donald Nicholson-Smith (New York: Zone Books, 1967), 1994.

50. Geyser Land DVD.

51. Perron, "Art/Architecture: A Performance Piece Runs through It," 2003.

52. Geyser Land DVD.

53. All the transcripts can be found on the documentation website. Vortex hearing, for example, is here: http://rfkineky.org/docs/Vortex_transcript.pdf.

54. James Dao, "It's 1968 in Kentucky: Two Days of Political Theater in the Original Settings," *New York Times*, September 1, 2004.

55. www.rfkineky.org.

56. Perron, "Art/Architecture: A Performance Piece Runs through It," 2003.

57. Campanella was one of the six performers who prominently circulated the space during our slumber. She sang (as did Liz Sargent and Okwui Okpokwasili on other nights) beautiful, mostly improvised melisma from an in-ear live feed of another actor reading the Chinese names of the characters in the original *Dream of the Red Chamber* novel.

58. Schneider, *Performing Remains*, 182.

59. Ibid., 182–83.

60. As quoted in Linda Frye Burnham, "When Kennedy Came to Kentucky," *American Theatre* 21, no. 6 (2004): 32–35.

61. Christene Meyers, "Historic Art Event: Photos, Railroading Combined for Tour," *Billings Gazette*, July 5, 2003, accessed March 2016, http://billingsgazette .com/news/local/historic-art-event-photos-railroading-combined-for-tour/article _687b2b0a-05fa-5651-b2a2-7afbb7726dd9.html.

5. Urban Sites: Landmark Performance

1. Jeff Stark, *The Dreary Coast*, unpublished manuscript.

2. Jeff Stark, "The Dreary Coast," *PAJ* 37, no. 2 (May 2015): 50–51.

3. Bertie Ferdman, "Trespass Theater: Jeff Stark on *The Dreary Coast*," HowlRound, November 14, 2014. http://howlround.com/trespass-theater-jeff-stark-on -the-dreary-coast.

4. Ibid.

5. Joseph Alexiou, *Gowanus: Brooklyn's Curious Canal* (New York: New York University Press, 2015).

6. It was around this time that Nathan Elbogen of XO Projects redeveloped a former canning factory built in 1886 into the Old American Can Factory, a sprawling

130,000-square-foot, six-building manufacturing and arts complex, which I remember going to in the early 2000s. The Old American Can Factory is located on Third Avenue and Third Street, in front of the Gowanus Canal and the 56,000-square-foot Whole Foods Market, which opened its doors in December 2013, after a decade in the making. Elbogen joined forces with local residents and The Gowanus Institute, a research group dedicated to creating innovative ways to develop the neighborhood, to express their concern that Whole Foods would change the manufacturing character of the Gowanus and consequently increase rents in the area, which had not yet been rezoned from manufacturing to residential. They proposed an industrial park that would house local businesses and culinary industries, but once Whole Foods received approval from the NYC Board of Standards and Appeals, construction moved swiftly. Erik Ghenoiu, research manager at the Harvard Mellon Urban Initiative at Harvard's Graduate School of Design, credits Elbogen's sensibility as "key in maintaining the pioneering character of the new Brooklyn economy against the forces of gentrification." Erik Ghenoiu, "Post-Industrial Spaces of Production: The New Brooklyn Economy and the Deutsche Werkbund," in Mathew Aitchison, ed., *The Architecture of Industry: Changing Paradigms in Industrial Building and Planning* (New York: Routledge, 2014), 28.

7. Red Dive, for example, a collective founded in 1996 by a group of women artists working in theatre and dance to re-envision how and where performance was presented, created *Peripheral City: Rediscovering the Gowanus Canal* (2002). The audience participated in an adventure tour—a boat ride down the Brooklyn canal led by Captain Bill Sheehan, an expert on the species renewal the canal was undergoing—that was coupled with a live, multimedia performance. With *Peripheral City*, which was reperformed on-site in 2003, the company, whose activities ended in 2006, sought to bring to the fore environmental and social issues regarding the Gowanus Canal.

8. Ferdman, "Trespass Theater," 2014.

9. Gina Bellafante, "The Once and Future of Gowanus," *New York Times*, February 21, 2014; Emma Turetsky and Jarrett Murphy, "Not Even Toxic Waste Can Stop Gentrification: NYC's Superfund Neighborhoods Are Booming," *Gothamist*, August 22, 2014.

10. Furman Center, 2013 Report.

11. In her article "Gentrifying a Superfund Site: Why Gowanus, Brooklyn, Is Becoming a Real Estate Hot Spot" (published in 2015), Rebecca Salima Krisel writes:

> What was historically a booming manufacturing area with active warehouses spilling their waste into the Gowanus Canal is now an industrial site where middle to upper class families, seeking to purchase organic foods, are willing to relocate and settle down. As of December 2014, a two-bedroom condo boasting waterfront views and located just one block away from the Gowanus Canal on Carroll Street was priced at $1,549,000. The average price per square foot for homes in Gowanus is 50 percent higher than the rest of Brooklyn.

Rebecca Salima Krisel, "Gentrifying a Superfund Site: Why Gowanus, Brooklyn Is Becoming a Real Estate Hot Spot," *Consilience: The Journal of Sustainable Development*, 14, no. 2 (2015): 214–24.

12. Jillian Steinhauer, "New Gowanus Landlord Kicks Dozens of Artists out of Their Studios," *Hyperallergic*, October 15, 2015; Kelly Weill, "Artists Struggle to Survive the Artists Boom," *Politico*, December 14, 2015.

13. Winifred Curran, "'From the Frying Pan to the Oven': Gentrification and the Experience of Industrial Displacement in Williamsburg, Brooklyn," *Urban Studies*, 44, no. 8, 1427–40 (July 2007): 1428.

14. Airbnb, "Gowanus, Brooklyn," accessed June 2016, https://airbnb.com/locations/new-york/gowanus.

15. Stanton B. Garner Jr., "Urban Landscapes, Theatrical Encounters: Staging the City," in Elinor Fuchs and Una Chaudhuri, eds., *Land/Scape/Theatre* (Ann Arbor: University of Michigan Press, 2002), 95.

16. Ibid.

17. See McKinnie's chapter "Rethinking Site-Specificity: Monopoly, Urban Space, and the Cultural Economics of Site-Specific Performance" in Joanna Tompkins and Anna Birch, eds., *Performing Site-Specific Theatre: Politics, Place, Practice* (New York: Palgrave Macmillan, 2012), as well as his book *City Stages: Theatre and Urban Space in a Global City* (Toronto: University of Toronto Press, 2007), which addresses the cultural economics of urban performance.

18. See Jen Harvie, "Space: Exclusion and Engagement," in *Fair Play: Art, Performance, and Neoliberalism* (New York: Palgrave Macmillan, 2013), 125.

19. The story behind St. Anne's Warehouse is particularly interesting. As the *New York Times* reported, "In 2011, despite having won the right to build in the Tobacco Warehouse at 45 Water Street, St. Ann's was stymied by a federal-court case in which a few preservation and community organizations contested a decision by the National Park Service to remove the Tobacco Warehouse from classification as federally designated parkland and allow it to be developed." In other words, Susan Feldman, St. Anne's committed founder and artistic director, had to sign an interim lease elsewhere during the time the case went to court and received approval. See Robin Pogrebin, "Susan Feldman and St. Ann's Warehouse Unveil a Permanent Home," *New York Times*, October 4, 2015.

20. Editors, "Real Estate and Theatre Space," *Theater* 35, no. 3 (2005): 147.

21. Neil Smith, *New Urban Frontier: Gentrification and the Revanchist City* (New York: Routledge, 1996), 18.

22. Ibid.

23. Ibid.

24. Rosalyn Deutsche and Cara Gendel Ryan, "The Fine Art of Gentrification," *Portable Lower East Side* 4, no. 1 (Spring 1987).

25. Rosalyn Deutsche, *Evictions: Art and Spatial Politics* (Boston: Graham Foundation / MIT Press Series in Contemporary Architectural Discourse, 1998), 69.

26. Jen Harvie, *Theatre and the City* (London: Palgrave Macmillan, 2009), 25.

27. Nicolas Whybrow, ed., *Performance and the Contemporary City: An Interdisciplinary Reader* (New York: Palgrave Macmillan, 2010), 6.

28. Matt Bolton, "Is Art to Blame for Gentrification?," *Guardian*, August 30, 2013.

29. See, in particular, Sharon Zukin, *Naked City: The Death and Life of Authentic Urban Places*, New York: Oxford University Press, 2010.

30. Kayim co-founded Skewed Visions with Charles Campbell and Sean Kelley-Pegg.

31. Gülgün Kayim, interview by Bertie Ferdman, "Performance and the City," *PAJ* 37, no. 2 (2015): 42–49.

32. David Harvey, "The Right to the City," *New Left Review* 53 (September–October 2008) 23.

33. Sarah Schulman, *Gentrification of the Mind: Witness to a Lost Imagination* (Berkeley and Los Angeles, CA: University of California Press, 2013), 27.

34. According to the 2015 report by the NYU Furman Center, rents all over New York City are rising at rates that have far surpassed income growth of renters. An important characteristic of gentrification is that it is a direct result of municipal policy decisions that favor luxury housing developments (with tax write offs). Over the last decades, city government has intensified its partnerships with private capital, with Mayor Bill de Blasio's promises to increase affordable housing units by 2024 proving increasingly difficult.

During his campaign, Bill de Blasio promised something he termed "mandatory inclusionary zoning," as part of his plan to "save New York City": 200,000 new affordable housing units created or preserved by 2024. As part of the plan, developers would have to separate 25 to 30 percent of new development in specific rezoned neighborhoods for people with low to moderate incomes. The plan is much lower than the promised units at fifteen thousand units, and they are at market rates in poor neighborhoods.

35. Ian Fisher, "For Homeless, a Last Haven Is Demolished," *New York Times*, August 18, 1993.

36. See editorial, "At Last, a Dinkins Homeless Plan," *New York Times*, September 23, 1992.

37. Sam Roberts, "What Led to Crackdown on Homeless," *New York Times*, October 28, 1991.

38. Other shanties destroyed around the city included one at Seventy-Second Street and the West Side highway, a railway tunnel in Riverside Park, the United Nations, Port Authority Bus Terminal, and another near Columbus Circle, all of which had been deemed unsafe by city officials, who claimed they were fire hazards and/or plagued with drugs.

39. Smith, *Urban Frontier*, 6.

40. Ibid.

41. Unpublished interview with the artists, March 2014.

42. Nick Manhattan (aka Nick Fracaro), "Warring Landscapes," RAT Conference, http://ratconference.com/thieves/blog/warringlandscapes.html, accessed June 2016.

43. It is worth noting that the Thieves Theatre's appropriation of a Plains Indian teepee for artistic and political ends stands in sharp contrast to Kenneth Goldsmith's appropriation of Michael Brown's African American body as described in chapter 2. Thieves Theatre did not seek to profit (either in cultural or financial capital) from the work, and integrated themselves in the "other's" land.

44. C. Carr, "The Bohemian Diaspora," *Village Voice*, February 4, 1992. This land, as Schafer and Fracaro explained to me, was very much disparaged by the outside community. Even the Emergency Medical Services (EMS) would not enter the Hill: sick people would have to be carried out because EMS was afraid to go in for fear of getting a needle and getting AIDS.

45. Email from Gabriele Schafer, June 12, 2014. Previously published in Bertie Ferdman, "Off the Grid: New York City—Landmark Performance," *PAJ* 37, no. 2 (May 2015): 23.

46. Gertrude Stein, *Autobiography of Alice B. Toklas* (New York: Harcourt, 1933).

47. For more information on influence the High Line has had in urban planning internationally, see Dave McGinn, "The High Line Effect: Why Cities around the World (including Toronto) Are Building Parks in the Sky," *Globe and Mail*, October 1, 2014. For a critical look at how the High Line operated to exacerbate income inequality in the Chelsea neighborhood, see Diana Budds, "The Other High Line Effect: How N.Y.C.'s Glitziest Park Spread Income Inequality," *Co. Design*, October 24, 2016. The article featured an interview with Marc Levin, filmmaker and director of the documentary *Class Divide*, which focuses on the families living in the Chelsea-Elliot public housing development.

48. Email from Juliana Francis-Kelly, June 21, 2014. Previously published in Bertie Ferdman, "Off the Grid: New York City—Landmark Performance," *PAJ* 37, no. 2 (May 2015): 25.

49. Elinor Fuchs, *Death of Character: Perspectives of Theater after Modernism* (Bloomington: Indiana University Press), 135.

50. Shaila K. Dewan, "Landmark Status Is Sought for Meatpacking District," *New York Times*, June 4, 2001.

51. Joyce Purnick, "City Closes Bar Frequented by Homosexuals, Citing Sexual Activity Linked to AIDS," *New York Times*, November 8, 1985.

52. Ibid.

53. Fuchs, *Death of Character*, 136.

54. For more on Abdoh's legacy and life, see Daniel Mufson, ed., *Reza Abdoh*, PAJ Books: Art + Performance (Baltimore: Johns Hopkins University Press, 1999).

55. Gerard Raymond, "Theater Takes to the Streets," *New York Times*, June 24, 1990.

56. Unpublished interview with Noémie Lafrance, June 2013.

57. Robert Caro, *Power Broker: Robert Moses and the Fall of New York* (New York: Vintage Books, 1974). Since its publication, and especially after Moses's death in 1981, Caro's book has been central to discussions of Moses and his influence. The WPA, which funded the design and construction of the pool, was an emergency public employment program set up during the Depression era at a time when the

US government invested in public works to bring the country out of economic recession. Between the 1930s and the mid-1960s, Moses, who concurrently held jobs as New York City's planning commissioner, chairman of the mayor's Slum Clearance Committee and commissioner of parks, is estimated to have built public works projects that cost $26 billion and displaced over half a million people

58. Tim Stelloh, "Seeking to Recapture the Glory of the Past. Or Maybe Not" *New York Times*, April 9, 2006.

59. Live Nation was a two-year-old spinoff of Clear Channel that generated $4.4 billion in revenue in 2007–8 by running concert tours. In December 2005, San Antonio-based Clear Channel Communications spun off its concert division and called the new company Live Nation, which has since become the largest producer of live concerts in the world.

60. In order to obtain a permit for *Agora*, Lafrance needed to finance the renovations that would make the park safe for the public. Lafrance had a meeting with Julius Spiegel, the Brooklyn borough commissioner, and his chief of staff, Martin Maher, on December 2004, where she was informed that $500,000 was needed to renovate the space. If she wanted to have a performance there, she had to meet public safety standards, which included fixing the numerous trip hazards, getting rid of all graffiti, cleaning up all the scaffolding and decay. She proposed managing the renovation herself at a cost of $100,000, an estimate she had received from contractor Blaine Wolf.

Eventually, the Parks Foundation managed the renovation (under their nonprofit affiliate City Parks Foundation). They had Clear Channel put in $200,000 and Sens Production $50,000. The deal with Clear Channel (and its Live Nation subsidiary) also included $11,700 in a site fee to be paid in 2006. This payment gave the company access to use the pool for a series of seven concerts that began July 26, 2006. The renovations took six weeks and ended up costing a little under $250,000.

61. According to Michael Powell's "A Condo Tower Grows in Brooklyn," *Washington Post*, February 21, 2007:

> When city officials proposed to rezone Williamsburg's last industrial areas, the Polish, Italian, and Latin communities united to demand affordable housing. For the first time they joined forces with the hipsters and artists living in the same neighborhood. Officials agreed in 2006 to make 20 percent of the new apartments affordable for the working class. Unfortunately, because many of the working-class tenants had bad credit, they could not even qualify for affordable housing. The new development is said to have displaced 2,500 residents, even though the number is known to be significantly higher.

62. Linda Collins, "Newest and Tallest at McCarren Park," *Brooklyn Eagle* April 13, 2007.

63. Powell, "Condo Tower Grows in Brooklyn," 2007.

64. According to NYU Furman Center for Real Estate and Urban Policy's Housing and Neighborhood Report, the median monthly rent in 2006 was $900, compared to $3,055 (asking) rent in 2015. NYU Furman Center, "State of New

York City's Housing and Neighborhoods in 2015"; NYU Furman Center, "State of New York City's Housing and Neighborhoods in 2006."

65. Ann Markusen and Anne Gadwa Nicodemus, *Creative Placemaking*, White Paper for the Mayors' Institute on City Design, a leadership initiative on the National Endowment for the Arts in partnership with the United States Conference of Mayors and American Architectural Foundation, NEA 2010.

66. http://www.artplaceamerica.org/about/introduction, accessed September 2016.

67. Ibid.

68. "Creative CityMaking with Gülgün Kayim: 2016 MATC Keynote Address, Minneapolis, MN," in *Theatre/Practice: The Online Journal of the Practice/Production Symposium of the Mid America Theatre Conference* 6, 2017, http://theatrepractice.us/pdfs/Kayim%202016%20MATC%20Keynote.pdf.

69. See Roberto Bedoya, "Placemaking and the Politics of Belonging and Dis-belonging," *GIA Reader (Grantmakers in the Arts)* 24, no. 1 (2013), http://www.giarts.org/article/placemaking-and-politics-belonging-and-dis-belonging.

70. Minneapolis's Arts, Culture, and the Creative Economy program hires three artists/designers or teams to participate in Creative CityMaking Minneapolis (CCM). The program seeks to advance the city's goal of eliminating economic and racial disparities. It is an independent contract opportunity that pays $30,000 over twelve months. See mnartists.org/content/creative-citymaking-minneapolis-0.

71. "Creative CityMaking with Gülgün Kayim," 11.

72. For more on these artists' work and how they are reconceptualizing the urban *through* their art practice, see Nikil Saval's "Three Artists Who Think outside the Box," *New York Times Magazine*, December 3, 2015.

73. Artists Samantha Hill and Ed Woodham decided to leave an NEA-funded artist residency program in Macon, Georgia, called Mill Hill Visiting Social Practice Artist Residency when they realized their work was financially compromised, to the detriment of the very community they had been interviewing. Hill states,

> As we interviewed people from the neighborhood and talked to members of Macon's African American community, it became very clear that Ed and I had been bamboozled and were part of a gentrification "art washing" scenario. As we began to ask for genuine responses off script of the MAAs [Macon Art Alliance] selected voices, we learned that many people in Macon's art community felt marginalized by the narrow vision of the Macon Arts Alliance. Our findings were much different than the rhetoric presented in the Mill Hill Artist Residency call for artists and the Mill Hill web page.

Art in Odd Places, email message titled "Social Practice Artists Ran out of Town," July 27, 2016.

74. See Aaron Landsman and Mallory Catlett's "City Council Meeting," in Special Issue of *Theater* 43, no. 3 (2014) titled "Participatory Performance." *City Council Meeting* included a run at Project Row Houses in 2012, the community-based arts

and culture nonprofit organization founded by Rick Lowe in 1993 in Houston's Third Ward.

75. Kickstarter page: "Perfect City Fall Launch 2017," https://www.kickstarter.com/projects/711603567/perfect-city-fall-launch-2017.

Epilogue

1. To build federal buildings, the government is required to do an environmental impact statement. A map of the area showed the existence of a "negro burial ground" in that location—not only at the site of the 291 Broadway building but one that extended for many blocks.

2. Edward Rothstein, "A Burial Ground and Its Dead Are Given Life," *New York Times*, February 25, 2010.

3. Ibid.

4. "Introduction to African Burial Ground Final Reports," https://www.gsa.gov/portal/content/249941, accessed March 15, 2017.

5. Rothstein, "Burial Ground."

6. "African Burial Ground Memorial," http://www.rodneyleon.com/african-burial-ground-memorial, accessed March 15, 2017.

7. Rothstein, "Burial Ground."

8. David W. Dunlap, "Unfree, Unknown," *New York Times*, December 26, 199[illegible].

9. Hakim Bello, "I Was a Lampedusa Refugee. Here's My Story of Fleeing Libya—and Surviving," *Guardian*, April 20, 2015, https://www.theguardian.com/commentisfree/2015/apr/20/lampedusa-refugee-fleeing-libya-boats-italy.

10. "Introduction," Lampedusa Cruises, http://rederijlampedusa.nl/en, accessed February 2017.

11. See John Hanc, "Museums with Ideas, Goals, and Sometimes Art. But Walls? No," *New York Times*, March 14, 2017.

12. Ibid.

13. Ibid.

Bibliography

Alexiou, Joseph. *Gowanus: Brooklyn's Curious Canal*. New York: New York University Press, 2015.

A'ness, Francine. "Resisting Amnesia: Yuyachkani, Performance, and the Postwar Reconstruction of Peru." *Theatre Journal* 56, no. 3 (2004): 395–414.

Angotti, Thomas. *New York for Sale: Community Planning Confronts Global Real Estate*. Cambridge, MA: MIT Press, 2008.

Arias, Lola, interviewed and translated by Bertie Ferdman. "The Work of Art Is a Parasite." *Theater* 44, no. 2 (2014): 30–45.

Arlander, Annette. "Characteristics of Visual and Performing Arts." In *The Routledge Companion to Research in the Arts*, edited by Michael Biggs and Henrik Karlsson, 315–32. London: Routledge, 2011.

Augé, Marc. *Non-places: An Introduction to Supermodernity*. 2nd ed. New York: Verso Books, 2009.

Auslander, Philip. *Performance in a Mediatized Culture*. New York: Routledge, 1999.

Ayers, Robert. "The Knife Is Real, the Blood Is Real, and the Emotions Are Real." *A Sky Filled with Shooting Stars*. Accessed February 2016. http://www.askyfilledwithshootingstars.com/wordpress/?p=1197.

Bachelard, Gaston. *The Poetics of Space*. Translated by Maria Jolas. 1957. Boston: Beacon Press, 1994.

Bailes, Sara Jane. *Performance Theatre and the Poetics of Failure*. London: Routledge, 2011.

Balme, Christopher B. *The Theatrical Public Sphere*. Cambridge: Cambridge University Press, 2014.

Banes, Sally. *Terpsichore in Sneakers: Postmodern Dance*. Middletown, CT: Wesleyan University Press, 1987.

Bay-Cheng, Sarah, Chiel Kattenbelt, Andy Lavender, Robin Nelson, eds. *Mapping Intermediality in Performance*. Chicago: University of Chicago Press, 2010.

Bay-Cheng, Sarah, Jennifer Parker-Starbuck, David Z. Saltz, eds. *Performance and Media: Taxonomies for a Changing Field*. Ann Arbor: University of Michigan Press, 2015.

Behrndt, Synne, and Cathy Turner, eds. *Dramaturgy and Performance*. New York: Palgrave Macmillan, 2008.

Bell, John, ed. *Puppet, Masks, and Performing Objects*. Cambridge, MA: MIT Press, 1999.

Benford, Steven, and Gabriella Giannachi, eds. *Performing Mixed Reality*. Cambridge, MA: MIT Press, 2011.

Benjamin, Walter. *Illuminations: Essays and Reflections*. New York: Schocken Books, 1968.

Bennett, Susan. *Theatre and Museums*. New York: Palgrave Macmillan, 2013.

———. *Theatre Audiences: A Theory of Production and Reception*. London: Routledge, 1997.

Birch, Anna, ed. "Special Issue: Site-Specificity and Mobility." *Contemporary Theatre Review* 22, no. 2 (2012).

Birch, Anna, and Joanna Tompkins, eds. *Performing Site-Specific Theatre: Politics, Place, Practice*. New York: Palgrave Macmillan, 2012.

Birringer, Johannes. *Performance, Technology, and Science*. New York: PAJ Publications, 2008.

Bishop, Claire. *Artificial Hells: Participatory Art and the Politics of Spectatorship*. New York: Verso Books, 2012.

———. *Installation Art: A Critical History*. London: Tate Publishing, 2005.

———. "The Perils and Possibilities of Dance in the Museum: Tate, MoMA, and Whitney." *Dance Research Journal* 46, no. 3 (2014): 63–76.

———. *Radical Museology: Or What's Contemporary in Museums of Contemporary Art?* London: Walther König, Köln, 2014.

———. "Unhappy Days in the Art World? De-skilling Theatre, Re-skilling Performance." *Brooklyn Rail*, December 10, 2011.

Boal, Augusto. *Theatre of the Oppressed*. Translated by Maria Jolas and Maria McBride. New York: Theatre Communications Group, 1985.

Bolton, Matt. "Is Art to Blame for Gentrification?" *Guardian*, August 30, 2013.

Bourriaud, Nicolas. *Relational Aesthetics*. Dijon, France: Presses du Réel, 2002.

Breitwieser, Sabine. *Carolee Schneemann: Kinetic Painting*. Munich: Prestel, 2016.

Brenner, Neil, and Roger Keil, eds. *The Global Cities Reader*. New York: Routledge, 2006.

Brook, Peter. *The Empty Space*. New York: Atheneum, 1970.

Brownell, Pamela. "Proyecto Archivos: El Teatro Documental según Vivi Tellas." *E-misférica* 9.1–9.2, "Sujetos de/al Archivo," edited by Diana Taylor and Marianne Hirsch, 2012.

Burgin, Victor. "Situational Aesthetics." *Studio International* 178.915 (October 1969).

Calle, Sophie. *L'hotel*. Paris: Editions de l'Etoile, 1984.

Canning, Charlotte, and Thomas Postlewait, eds. *Representing the Past: Essays in Performance and Historiography*. Iowa City: Iowa University Press, 2010.

Carlson, Marla. "Looking, Listening, and Remembering: Ways to Walk New York after 9/11." *Theatre Journal* 58, no. 3 (2006): 395–416.

Carlson, Marvin. "David Levine's *Bauerntheater*: The Return of the Matrix." *TDR* 52, no. 3 (2008): 34–43.

———. *Places of Performance: The Semiotics of Theatre Architecture*. Ithaca: Cornell University Press, 1993.

Caro, Robert. *The Power Broker: Robert Moses and the Fall of New York*. New York: Knopf, 1974.

Carr, C. *On Edge: Performance at the End of the Twentieth Century*. Middletown, CT: Wesleyan University Press, 1994.

Carroll, Jerome, Karen Jürs-Munby, and Steve Giles, eds. *Postdramatic Theatre and the Political: International Perspectives on Contemporary Performance*. London: Bloomsbury Methuen Drama, 2013.

Carter, Huntly. *The Theatre of Max Reinhardt*. New York: Benjamin Blom, 1964.

Cesare Schotzko, Nikki T. *Learning How to Fall: Art and Culture after 9/11*. New York: Routledge, 2015.

———."Message Send Failure: Site-Unspecificity in Plant Theater's *Dreams of Riley's Friends*; or, Why Won't Riley Respond to My Texts?" *TDR* 60, no. 3 (Fall 2016).

Chaudhuri, Una. *Staging Place: The Geography of Modern Drama*. Ann Arbor: University of Michigan Press, 1995.

Chaudhuri, Una, and Elinor Fuchs, eds. *Land/Scape/Theater*. Ann Arbor: University of Michigan Press, 2002.

Coates, Ta-Nehisi. *Between the World and Me*. New York: Spiegel and Grau, 2015.

Cochrane, Bernadette, and Katalin Trencsényi. *New Dramaturgy: International Perspectives on Theory and Practice*. London: Bloomsbury Publishing, 2014.

Cohen-Cruz, Jan, ed. *Radical Street Performance: An International Anthology*. New York: Routledge, 1998.

———. "Time Travel." *RFK in EKY*. Accessed March 2016. http://rfkineky.org/library/documentation/time-travel.htm.

Cole, Helen, interviewed by Bertie Ferdman. "Careful of Fireworks." *Theater* 44, no. 2 (2014): 62–71.

Collins, Glenn. "Street Theater Audience Must Make a Choice." *New York Times*, July 19, 1990.

Crary, Jonathan. *24/7: Late Capitalism and the Ends of Sleep*. New York: Verso Books, 2013.

Crimp, Douglas. *On the Museum's Ruins*. Cambridge: MIT Press, 1993.

Cummings, Lindsay. "Reviving Feeling Performing Robert F. Kennedy in Kentucky." *Performance Research* 16, no. 2 (2011): 83–90.

Cummings, Scott T. *Remaking American Theater: Charles Mee, Anne Bogart, and the SITI Company*. Cambridge: Cambridge University Press, 2006.

Debord, Guy. "Internationale Situationniste #1 (June 1958)." In *Situationist International Anthology*, translated and edited by Ken Knabb. Berkeley, CA: Bureau of Public Secrets, 2007.

———. *The Society of the Spectacle*. Translated by Donald Nicholson-Smith. 1967. New York: Zone Books, 1994.

de Certeau, Michel. *The Practice of Everyday Life*. Translated by Steven Rendall. Berkeley: University of California Press, 1984.

Deutsche, Rosalyn. "Art and Public Space: Questions of Democracy." *Social Text* 33 (1992): 34–53.

———. *Evictions: Art and Spatial Politics.* Cambridge, MA: MIT Press, 1996.

Deutsche, Rosalyn, and Cara Gendel Ryan. "The Fine Art of Gentrification." *Portable Lower East Side* 4, no. 1 (Spring 1987).

Doherty, Claire. *Situation: Documents of Contemporary Art.* London: Whitechapel, 2009.

Eckersall, Peter. "Towards an Expanded Dramaturgical Practice: A Report on 'The Dramaturgy and Cultural Intervention Project.'" *Theatre Research International* 31, no. 3 (2006): 283–97.

Esslin, Martin. "Max Reinhardt: High Priest of Theatricality." *TDR* 21, no. 2 (1977): 3–24.

Etchells, Tim. *Certain Fragments: Contemporary Performance and Forced Entertainment.* London: Routledge, 1999.

Fainstein, Susan. *The City Builders: Property Development in New York and London, 1980–2000.* 2nd ed. Lawrence: University Press Kansas, 2001.

Faivovich, Guillermo, and Nicolás Goldberg, eds. *The Campo del Cielo Meteorites, Vol. 2: El Chaco.* Stuttgart: Documenta 13 and Hatje Cantz, 2014.

———. *El Taco: The Campo del Cielo Meteorites, Vol. 1.* Stuttgart: Documenta 13 and Hatje Cantz, 2010.

Ferdman, Bertie. "From Content to Context: The Emergence of the Performance Curator." *Theater* 44, no. 2 (2014): 4–19.

———. "Trespass Theater: Jeff Stark on *The Dreary Coast.*" *HowlRound,* November 14, 2014.

———. "Urban Dramaturgy: The Global Art Project of JR." *PAJ* (2012): 12–25.

Ferdman, Bertie, Ryan M. Davis, and Anne Erbe. "Works Sited: A Forum." *Theater* 43, no. 2 (2013): 27–43.

Field, Andrew. *The Arcades Project.* http://thearcadesproject.blogspot.com. August 8, 2007.

Filmer, Andrew. "Making Space for Performance." *Studies in Theatre and Performance* 30, no. 3 (2010): 275–87.

Fischer-Lichte, Erika, and Benjamin Wihstutz. *Performance and the Politics of Space: Theatre and Topology.* New York: Routledge, 2013.

Forsyth, Alison, and Chris Megson, eds. *Get Real: Documentary Theatre Past and Present.* New York: Palgrave Macmillan, 2009.

Foster, Hal. *The Anti-aesthetic.* New York: New Press, 2002.

Fracaro, Nick. "Warring Landscapes." *RAT Conference.* Accessed June 2016. http://ratconference.com/thieves/blog/warringlandscapes.html.

Fraser, Andrea. *Museum Highlights.* Cambridge, MA: MIT Press, 2005.

Freedlander, David. "Urban Folk Art: Performance, Politics, and the Right to the City." *Theater* 40, no. 3 (2010): 25–41.

Freshwater, Helen. *Theatre and Audience.* London: Palgrave Macmillan, 2009.

Fried, Michael. *Art and Objecthood: Essays and Reviews.* Chicago: University of Chicago Press, 1998 (reprint of essays originally published from 1962–77).

Frieze, J., ed. *Framing Immersive Theatre and Performance*. London: Palgrave Macmillan, 2016.
Frye Burnham, Linda. "When Kennedy Came to Kentucky." *American Theatre* 21, no. 6 (2004): 32–35.
Fuchs, Elinor. "Book Review: *Postdramatic Theatre* by Hans-Thies Lehmann. Translated by Karen Jürs-Munby. London: Routledge." *TDR* 52, no. 2 (2008): 178–83.
———. *The Death of Character: Perspectives on Theater after Modernism*. Bloomington: Indiana University Press, 1996.
Gallagher-Ross, Jacob. "City of No Illusions." *PAJ* 37, no. 2 (May 2015).
Gatti, Armand. *Armand Gatti, Three Plays*. Translated by Joseph Long. Sheffield: Sheffield Academic Press, 2000.
———. "Time, Place, and the Theatrical Event." Translated by Nancy Oakes. *Modern Drama* 25 (1982): 69–81.
Geyserland. "Geyser Land." Accessed June 2016. http://www.geyserland.org.html.
Ghenoui, Erik. "Post-Industrial Spaces of Production: The New Brooklyn Economy and the Deutsche Werkbund." In *The Architecture of Industry: Changing Paradigms in Industrial Building and Planning*, edited by Matthew Aitchison. New York: Routledge, 2014.
Giannachi, Gabriella, and Nick Kaye. *Performing Presence: Between the Live and the Simulated*. Manchester: Manchester University Press, 2011.
Giannachi, Gabriella, Nick Kaye, and Michael Shanks, eds. *Archaeologies of Presence: Art, Performance, and the Persistence of Being*. London: Routledge, 2012.
Goldberg, Roselee. *Performance Art: From Futurism to the Present*. New York: Thames and Hudson, 2001.
———. *Performance: Live Art since 1960*. New York: Harry N. Abrams Publishers, 1998.
Gorman, Sarah. "Wandering and Wondering: Following Janet Cardiff's Missing Voice." *Performance Research* 8, no. 1 (2003): 83–93.
Grant, Daniel. "Why 'Site-Specific' Isn't so Specific." *Hyperallergic*, November 26, 2014. Accessed June 10, 2016. http://hyperallergic.com/153338/why-site-specific-isnt-so-specific/.
Gronau, Barbara, von Hartz, Matthias, and Carolin Hochleichter. *How to Frame: On the Threshold of Performing and Visual Arts*. Berlin Sternberg Press, 2017.
Grotowski, Jerzy. *Towards a Poor Theatre*. New York: Simon and Schuster, 1968.
Gussow, Mel. "Theater That Uses the City as a Stage." *New York Times*, July 3, 2003.
Habermas, Jürgen. *The Structural Transformation of the Public Sphere: An Inquiry into the Category of Bourgeois Society*. Translated by Thomas Burger and Frederick Lawrence. Cambridge, MA: MIT Press, 1989 (original German version published in 1962).
Haedicke, Susan. *Contemporary Street Arts in Europe: Aesthetics and Politics*. New York: Palgrave Macmillan, 2013.
Hahn, Daniela. "Performing Public Spaces, Staging Collective Memory: *50 Kilometres of Files* by Rimini Protokoll." *TDR* 58, no. 3 (Fall 2014): 27–38.

Halperin, Julia. “Performers Tell Museums to Get Their Act Together on Fees.” *Art Newspaper*, September 22, 2015.
Hansen, Al. *A Primer of Happenings and Time-Space Art*. New York: Something Else Press, 1968.
Hardt, Michael, and Antonio Negri. *Empire*. Cambridge, MA: Harvard University Press, 2001.
———. *Multitude: War and Democracy in the Age of Empire*. New York: Penguin Books, 2004.
Harvey, David. *A Brief History of Neoliberalism*. Oxford: Oxford University Press, 2007.
———. “The Right to the City.” *New Left Review* 53 (September–October 2008). https://newleftreview.org/II/53/david-harvey-the-right-to-the-city.
Harvie, Jen. *Fair Play: Art Performance and Neoliberalism*. New York: Palgrave Macmillan, 2013.
———. *Theatre and the City*. New York: Palgrave Macmillan, 2009.
Heathfield, Adrian. *Live Art and Performance*. London: Routledge, 2004.
Heathfield, Adrian, and Amelia Jones. *Perform, Repeat, Record: Live Art in History*. Bristol, UK: Intellect Ltd., 2012.
Heddon, D., and Cathy Turner. “Walking Women: Interviews with Artists on the Move.” *Performance Research* 15, no. 4 (2010): 14–22.
Heddon, Deirdre, and Klein, Jennie, eds. *Histories and Practices of Live Art*. New York: Palgrave Macmillan, 2012.
Helguera, Pablo. *Education for Socially Engaged Art: A Materials and Techniques Handbook*. New York: Jorge Pinto Books Inc., 2011.
———. “The School of Panamerican Unrest.” *Pablo Helguera Archive*, June 2006. Accessed May 2, 2016. http://pablohelguera.net/2006/06/the-school-of-panamerican-unrest/.
Henri, Adrian. *Environments, Happenings, and Performance*. New York: Oxford University Press, 1974.
Hill, Leslie, and Helen Paris, eds. *Performance and Place*. New York: Palgrave Macmillan, 2006.
Hirsch, Marianne. *The Generation of Postmemory: Writing and Visual Culture after the Holocaust*. New York: Columbia University Press, 2012.
Hodge, S. S., S. Persighetti, P. Smith, C. Turner, and T. Weaver. *An Exeter Misguide*. Exeter, UK: Wrights and Sites, 2003.
Hodge, Stephen, and Cathy Turner. “Site: Between Ground and Groundlessness.” In *Histories and Practices of Live Art*, edited by Deirdre Heddon and Jennie Klein. New York: Palgrave Macmillan, 2012.
Hoffmann, Beth. “Radicalism and the Theatre in Genealogies of Live Art.” *Performance Research* 14, no. 1 (2005).
Holden, Stephen. “A Carnival of Satire and Savagery, with a Karamazov as Ringmaster.” *New York Times*, July 11, 1990.
Holzapfel, Amy. “The Habit of Realism.” *Theater* 42, no. 1 (2012): 95–107.

Hopkins, D. J., Shelley Orr, and Kim Solga, eds. *Performance and the City*. New York: Palgrave Macmillan, 2009.

Hopkins, D. J., and Kim Solga, eds. *Performance and the Global City*. New York: Palgrave Macmillan, 2015.

Horwitz, Andrew. "Visual Art Performance vs. Contemporary Performance." *Culturebot*, November 25, 2011. Accessed December 2016. http://www.culturebot.org/2011/11/11663/visual-art-performance-vs-contemporary-performance/.

Houston, Andrew. *Environmental and Site-Specific Theatre: Critical Perspectives on Canadian Theatre in English*. Vol. 8. Toronto, ON: Playwrights Canada Press, 2007.

Hunter, Victoria. "Embodying the Site: The Here and Now in Site-Specific Dance Performance." *New Theatre Quarterly* 21 (2005): 367–81.

Husserl, Edmund. *The Phenomenology of Internal Time-Consciousness*. Edited by Martin Heidegger. Translated by James S. Churchill. Bloomington: Indiana University Press, 1969.

Irwin, Robert. "Being and Circumstance: Notes towards Confidential Art." In *Being and Circumstance*. Larkspur Landing, CA: Lapis Press, 1985.

Jackson, Shannon. *Professing Performance: Theatre in the Academy from Philology to Performativity*. Cambridge: Cambridge University Press, 2004.

———. *Social Works: Performing Art, Supporting Publics*. New York: Routledge, 2011.

———. "The Way We Perform Now." *Dance Research Journal* 46, no. 3 (December 2014): 55–61.

———. "When 'Everything Counts': Experimental Performance and Performance Historiography." In *Representing the Past: Essays in Performance and Historiography*, edited by Charlotte M. Canning and Thomas Postlewait. Iowa City: Iowa University Press, 2010.

———. "Working Publics." *Performance Research: A Journal of the Performing Arts* 16 (2011): 8–13.

Jacobs, Jane. *The Economy of Cities*. New York: Random House, 1969.

Jakovljevic, Branislav. "Now Then—Performance and Temporality: Not Once, Not Twice . . ." *Performance Research* 19, no. 3 (2014): 1–8.

———. "The Space Specific Theatre: Skewed Visions' *The City Itself*." *TDR* 49, no. 3 (2005): 96–106.

Jones, Amelia. "'The Artist Is Present': Artistic Re-enactments and the Impossibility of Presence." *TDR* 55, no. 1 (2011): 16–45

———. *Body Art: Performing the Subject*. 1st ed. Minneapolis: University of Minnesota Press, 1998.

———, ed. *A Companion to Contemporary Art since 1945*. Hoboken, NJ: Blackwell Publishing Ltd., 2006.

Kantor, Tadeusz. *A Journey through Other Spaces: Essays and Manifestos, 1944–1990*. Edited and translated by Michal Kobialka. Berkeley: University of California Press, 1993.

Kaprow, Allan. *Assemblages, Environments, and Happenings*. New York: Harry N. Abrams, 1966.

———. *Essays on the Blurring of Art and Life*. Edited by Jeff Kelley. Berkeley: University of California Press, 2003.

———. "Extensions in Time and Space." *TDR* 39 (1968): 153–59.

Karp, Michael. "En Garde Arts." *Theatre Crafts Magazine*, May 1991.

Katz, Vincent. *Black Mountain College: Experiment in Art*. Cambridge, MA: MIT Press, 2013.

Kaye, Nick. *Art into Theatre: Performance Interviews and Documents*. Amsterdam: Harwood Academic Publishers, 1996.

———. *Multi-media: Video—Installation—Performance*. London: Routledge, 2007.

———. *Site-Specific Art: Performance, Place, and Documentation*. London: Routledge, 2000.

Kayim, Gülgün, interview by Bertie Ferdman. "Performance and the City." *PAJ* 37, no. 2 (2015): 42–49.

———."Redefining the Limits: Artangel Blur the Boundaries." *Public Art Review* 16, no. 1 (2004): 10–15.

Kester, Grant H. *The One and the Many: Contemporary Collaborative Art in a Global Context*. Durham: Duke University Press, 2011.

Kirby, Michael. *The Art of Time: Essays on the Avant-Garde*. New York: E. P. Dutton, 1969.

———. *Happenings*. New York: E. P. Dutton, 1966.

Kloetzel, Melanie, and Carolyn Pavlik. *Site Dance: Choreographers and the Lure of Alternative Spaces*. Gainesville: University Press of Florida, 2009.

Knabb, Ken, ed. *Situationist International Anthology*. Berkeley, CA: Bureau of Public Secrets, 1981. Revised and expanded ed., 2006.

Knowles, Dorothy. *Armand Gatti in the Theatre: Wild Duck against the Wind*. London: Athlone Press, 1989.

Knowles, Ric. "Editorial Comment: Spectatorship." *Theatre Journal* 66, no. 3 (2014): xi–xiv.

Kolbert, Elizabeth. "Unsafe Climates." *New Yorker*, December 7, 2015. Accessed January 30, 2016. http://www.newyorker.com/magazine/2015/12/07/unsafe-climates.

Kroeber, Gavin. "The Event Landscape: The Contemporary Encounter of Art and the City." *PAJ* 37, no. 2 (2015): 30–41.

Kroeber, Gavin, and Robert Quillen. "Postshow Theatre." *Theater* 44, no. 3 (2014): 19–29.

Kwon, Miwon. *One Place after Another: Site Specific Art and Locational Identity*. Cambridge, MA: MIT Press, 2002.

Lacy, Suzanne, ed. *Mapping the Terrain: New Genre Public Art*. Seattle: Bay Press, 1995.

Landsman, Aaron, and Mallory Catlett. "City Council Meeting." *Theater* 43, no. 3. (2013): 65–99.

Lavender, Andy. *Performance in the Twenty-First Century: Theatres of Engagement*. London: Routledge, 2016.

Lefebvre, Henri. *The Urban Revolution*. Translated by Robert Bonnono. Minneapolis: University of Minnesota Press, 2003.

———. *The Social Production of Space*. Translated by Donald Nicholson-Smith. New York: Blackwell, 1992. French version originally published in 1974 by Anthropos in Paris.

———. *Writings on Cities*. Translated by Eleonore Kofman and Elizabeth Lebas. Cambridge, MA: Blackwell, 1996.

Lehmann, Hans-Thies. "A Future for Tragedy?" In *Postdramatic Theatre and the Political: International Perspectives on Contemporary Performance*, edited by Karen Jürs-Munby, Jerome Carroll, and Steve Giles. London: Bloomsbury Press, 2013.

———. *Postdramatic Theatre*. Translated by Karen Jürs-Munby. New York: Routledge, 2006 (German ed., 1999).

Lehmann, Hans-Thies, Karen Jürs-Munby, and Elinor Fuchs. "Lost in Translation?" *TDR* 52, no. 4 (2008): 13–20.

Levine, David. "Artist Project / Actors at Work." *Cabinet* 25 (2007).

———. "Artist's Journal." *Theater* 38 (2008): 30–51.

———. "Bad Art and Objecthood." *Art/US* Issue 13 (June 2006).

Levin, Laura. *Performing Ground: Space, Camouflage, and the Art of Blending In*. London: Palgrave Macmillan, 2014.

Lippard, Lucy. *Lure of the Local: Senses of Place in a Multicentered Society*. New York: New Press, 1998.

Livingstone, Sonia M., ed. *Audiences and Publics: When Cultural Engagement Matters for the Public Sphere*. Portland, OR: Intellect Books, 2005.

Lowe, Setha. *On the Plaza: The Politics of Public Space and Culture*. Austin: University of Texas Press, 2001.

Lynch, Kevin. *The Image of the City*. Cambridge, MA: MIT Press, 1960.

Machon, Josephine. *Immersive Theatres: Intimacy and Immediacy in Contemporary Performance*. New York: Palgrave Macmillan, 2013.

Mackey, Sally, and Nicolas Whybrow. *On Site and Place*. London: Routledge, 2007.

Magelssen, Scott. *Simming: Participatory Performance and the Making of Meaning*. Ann Arbor: University of Michigan Press, 2014.

Mahmoud, Jasmine. "Brooklyn's Experimental Frontiers: A Performance Geography." *TDR* 58, no. 3 (2014): 97–123.

Malkin, Jeanette R. *Memory-Theater and Postmodern Drama*. Ann Arbor: University of Michigan Press, 1999.

Malpede, John. "Art and Citizenship." Accessed June 2016. http://www.rfkineky.org.html.

Malzacher, Florian. "Empty Stages, Crowded Flats." Sidsel Graffer and Ådne Sekkelsten. Scenekunsten og de unge [Performing Arts and the Young]. Oslo: Vidarforlaget AS (2014): 116–27.

Malzacher, Florian, and Joanna Warsza, eds. *Empty Stages, Crowded Flats: Performativity as Curatorial Strategy*. Berlin: House on Fire, 2017.

Marcuse, Peter. *Searching for the Just City: Debates in Urban Theory and Practice*. London: Routledge, 2009.

Marranca, Bonnie. "Bodies of Action, Bodies of Thought: Performance and Its Critics," *PAJ* 21, no. 1 (1999): 11–23.
———. "Book Review: *Happenings and Other Acts*." *PAJ* 19, no. 2 (1997).
———. *The Theatre of Images*. Baltimore: Johns Hopkins University Press, 1996.
Martin, Carol. "Bodies of Evidence." *TDR* 50, no. 3 (2006): 8–15.
———. *Dramaturgy of the Real on the World Stage*. New York: Palgrave Macmillan, 2010.
———. "Performing the City." *TDR* 58, no. 3 (2014): 10–17.
———. *Theatre of the Real*. New York: Palgrave Macmillan, 2012.
Mason, Bim. *Street Theatre and Other Outdoor Performance*. London: Routledge, 1992.
Massey, Doreen. *For Space*. London: Sage, 2005.
McAuley, Gay. *Space in Performance: Making Meaning in the Theatre*. Ann Arbor: University of Michigan Press, 1999.
———, ed. *Unstable Ground: Performance and the Politics of Place*. Bruxelles, Bern, Berlin, Frankfurt am Main: Peter Lang, 2006.
McConachie, Bruce. *Engaging Audiences: A Cognitive Approach to Spectating in the Theatre*. New York: Palgrave Macmillan, 2008.
McEvoy, William. "Writing, Texts, and Site-Specific Performance in the Recent Work of Deborah Warner." *Textual Practice* 20, no. 4 (2006): 591–614.
McFadden, Jane. *Walter de Maria: Meaningless Work*. London: Reaktion Books, 2016.
McGrane, Sally. "An Actor Outstanding in His Field." *New York Times*, May 20, 2007.
McKinnie, Michael. *City Stages: Theatre and Urban Space in a Global City*. Toronto: University of Toronto Press, 2007.
———. "Rethinking Site-Specificity: Monopoly, Urban Space, and the Cultural Economics of Site-Specific Performance." In *Performing Site-Specific Theatre: Politics, Place, Practice*, edited by Joanna Tompkins and Anna Birch. New York: Palgrave Macmillan, 2012.
McNamara, Brooks, Jerry N. Rojo, and Richard Schechner. *Environmental Theatre Design*. New York: Drama Book Specialists, 1973.
Mee, Erin. "The Audience Is the Message: Blast Theory's App-Drama Karen," *TDR* 60, no. 3 (2016).
Mendelsohn, Meredith. "11 Female Artists Who Were Pioneering Minimalists." *Artsy Editorial*, September 2, 2016. www.artsy.net.
Merrifield, Andy. *Henri Lefebvre: A Critical Introduction*. New York: Routledge, 2006.
Miles, Malcolm. *Art, Space, and the City: Public Art and Urban Futures*. New York: Routledge, 1997.
Miller, Shane. "Dream Field or Pool Nightmare?" *Greenpoint Star*, March 24, 2005.
Mufson, Daniel, ed. *Reza Abdoh*. PAJ Publications. Baltimore: Johns Hopkins University Press, 1999.
Nelson, Steve. "Redecorating the Fourth Wall: Environmental Theatre Today." *TDR* 33, no. 3 (1989): 72–94.

Obrist, Hans Ulrich, and Lionel Bovier. *A Brief History of Curating*. Zurich: JRP/Ringier, 2008.
Oddey, Allison, and Christine White. *Modes of Spectating*. Bristol, UK: Intellect Books, 2009.
Osborne, Peter. *The Politics of Time: Modernity and the Avant-Garde*. New York: Verso Books, 1995.
Page, Philippa J. *Politics and Performance in Post-Dictatorship Argentine Film and Theatre*. Suffolk, UK: Tamesis, 2011.
Parker-Starbuck, Jennifer. *Cyborg Theatre: Corporeal/Technological Intersections in Multimedia Performance*. New York: Palgrave Macmillan, 2011.
Pavis, Patrice. *Dictionary of the Theatre: Terms, Concepts, and Analysis*. Translated by Christine Shantz. Toronto: University of Toronto Press, 1999.
Pearson, Mike. *Site-Specific Performance*. New York: Palgrave Macmillan, 2010.
Pearson, Mike, and Michael Shanks. *Theatre/Archeology*. London: Routledge, 2001.
Perron, Wendy. "Art/Architecture: A Performance Piece Runs through It." *New York Times*, August 10, 2003.
Phelan, Peggy. "On the Difference between Time and History." *Performance Research* 19, no. 3 (2014): 114–19.
———. *Unmarked: The Politics of Performance*. New York: Routledge, 2003.
Phelan, Peggy, and Helena Reckitt. *Art and Feminism*. New York: Phaidon Press, 2012.
Pinder, David. "Arts of Urban Exploration." *Cultural Geographies* 12, no. 4 (2005): 383–411.
Pine, B. Joseph, and James H. Gilmore. *The Experience Economy: Work Is Theatre and Every Business a Stage*. Cambridge, MA: Harvard Business Press, 1999.
Plant, Sadie. *The Most Radical Gesture: Situationist International in a Postmodern Age*. London: Routledge, 1992.
Pogrebin, Robin. "The Lords of Dumbo Make Room for the Arts, at Least for the Moment." *New York Times*, March 6, 2008.
———. "Selling Culture as an Economic Force." *New York Times*, February 15, 2009.
Rancière, Jacques. *Aisthesis: Scenes from the Aesthetic Regime of Art*. New York: Verso Books, 2013.
———. *The Emancipated Spectator*. Translated by Gregory Elliott. New York: Verso Books, 2011.
Raymond, Gerard. "Theater Takes to the Streets." *New York Times*, June 24, 1990.
Read, Alan. *Theatre and Everyday Life: An Ethics of Performance*. London: Routledge, 1993.
———. *Theatre, Intimacy, and Engagement: The Last Human Venue*. New York: Palgrave Macmillan, 2009.
Real Estate and Theatre Space in New York: A Forum—John Collins, Anita Durst, Susan Feldman, Vallejo Gantner, Jean Guy Lecat, Joseph V. Melillo, and Cathy Nanda. *Theater* 35, no. 3 (2005).
Reason, Matthew. *Documentation, Disappearance, and the Representation of Live Performance*. London: Palgrave Macmillan, 2006.

RFKinEKY. "The Project." Accessed May 2016. http://www.rfkineky.org.
Rich, Sarah. "Bauerntheater and Biorama Projekt: Farming, Acting, and Critical Art." *Worldchanging*, May 16, 2008.
Richardson, Brian. "'Time Is out of Joint': Narrative Models and the Temporality of the Drama." *Poetics Today* 8 (1987): 299–309.
Ridout, Nicholas. *Passionate Amateurs: Theatre, Communism, and Love.* Ann Arbor: University of Michigan Press, 2013.
Roach, Joseph. *Cities of the Dead: Circum-Atlantic Performance.* New York: Columbia University Press, 1996.
———. "A Feeling for Risk: Notes on Kinesthetic Empathy and the World Performance Project." *Theater* 42, no. 1 (2012): 7–9.
Rohd, Michael. *Theatre for Community, Conflict, and Dialogue: The Hope Is Vital Training Manual.* Portsmouth, NH: Heinemann, 1998.
Rojo, Jerry. "Interview: Environmental Theatre." *PAJ* 1, no. 1 (Spring 1976): 20–28.
Rojo, Jerry N., Brooks McNamara, and Richard Schechner. *Environmental Theatre Design.* New York: Drama Book Specialists, 1973.
Romanska, Magda, ed. *The Routledge Companion to Dramaturgy.* London: Routledge, 2014.
Ross, Christine. *The Past Is the Present; It's the Future Too: The Temporal Turn in Contemporary Art.* New York: Bloomsbury Academic, 2012.
Roth, Moira, ed. *The Amazing Decade: Women and Performance Art in America, 1970–1980.* Los Angeles: Astro Artz, 1984.
Rufford, Juliet. *Theatre and Architecture.* New York: Palgrave Macmillan, 2014.
Russeth, Andrew. "How Suite It Is: Sophie Calle Makes an Artwork out of a Hotel Room." *Observer*, October 11, 2011.
Ryzik, Melena. "Everyone out of the Pool (Yes, That Means You)." *New York Times*, August 31, 2008.
Sack, Daniel. *After Live: Possibility, Potentiality, and the Future of Performance.* Ann Arbor: University of Michigan Press, 2015.
Sadler, Simon. *The Situationist City.* Cambridge, MA: MIT Press, 1998.
Salima Krisel, Rebecca. "Gentrifying a Superfund Site: Why Gowanus, Brooklyn Is Becoming a Real Estate Hot Spot." *Consilience: The Journal of Sustainable Development* 14, no. 2 (2015): 214–24.
Sanford, Mariellen, ed. *Happenings and Other Acts.* New York: Routledge, 1995.
Sassen, Saskia. *Losing Control? Sovereignty in the Age of Globalization.* New York: Columbia University Press, 2015.
Savran, David. "The Death of the Avantgarde." *TDR* 49, no. 3 (Fall 2005): 10–42.
Sayre, Henry M. *The Object of Performance: The American Avant-Garde since 1970.* Chicago: University of Chicago Press, 1989.
Schechner, Richard. *Between Theatre and Anthropology.* Philadelphia: University of Pennsylvania Press, 1985.
———. *Environmental Performance.* New York: Hawthorn Books, 1973.
———. "Extensions in Time and Space: An Interview with Allan Kaprow." *TDR* 12, no. 3 (1968): 153–59.

———. *Performance Studies: An Introduction*. New York: Routledge, 2013.
———. "6 Axioms for Environmental Theatre." *TDR* 12, no. 3 (1968): 41–64.
Schipper, Imanuel, "City as Performance." *TDR* 58, no. 3 (2014): 18–26.
Schlatter, James F. "En Garde Arts: New York's New Public Theatre." *PAJ* 21, no. 2 (1999): 1–11.
Schneider, Rebecca. *The Explicit Body in Performance*. New York: Routledge, 1997.
———. *Performing Remains: Art and War in Times of Theatrical Reenactment*. New York: Routledge, 2011.
Schulman, Sarah. *The Gentrification of the Mind: Witness to a Lost Imagination*. Berkeley: University of California Press, 2013.
Sellar, Tom, ed. "Special Issue: Participatory Performance." *Theater* 43, no. 3 (2013).
Serra, Richard. "*Tilted Arc* Destroyed." *Art in America* 77, no. 5 (1989): 34–47.
Shank, Theodore. *Beyond the Boundaries: American Alternative Theater*. Ann Arbor: University of Michigan Press, 2002.
Simon, Joan, ed. (with text by Joan Jonas, Douglas Crimp, Johanna Burton, Barbara Clausen, Richard Serra, and Susan Rothenberg). *In the Shadow a Shadow: The Work of Joan Jonas*. New York: Gregory R. Miller, 2015.
Smith, Neil. "New Globalism, New Urbanism: Gentrification as Global Urban Strategy." *Antipode* 34, no. 3 (2002): 427–50.
———. *The Urban Frontier: Gentrification and the Revanchist City*. New York: Routledge, 1996.
Smith, Terry. *What Is Contemporary Art*. Chicago: University of Chicago Press, 2009, 6.
Soch, Adam. *Reza Abdoh: Theatre Visionary*. Documentary film. Released 2016. Produced by Adam Soch and Sandy Cleary.
Soja, Edward W. *Postmodern Geographies: The Reassertion of Space in Critical Social Theory*. London: Verso Books, 1989.
Solga, Kim. "Blasted's Hysteria: Rape, Realism, and the Thresholds of the Visible." *Modern Drama* 50, no. 3 (2007): 346–74.
Soloski, Alexis. "Under the Radar Tries Its Hand at Site Specific Work." *Village Voice*, January 1, 2008.
Sontag, Susan. *Regarding the Pain of Others*. New York: Picador, 2004.
Sosa, Cecilia. "Mi Vida Después: Non-kin Affects in Post Dictatorial Argentina." In "After Truth," edited by Jill Lane and Marcial Godoy-Anativia. *E-misférica* 7, no. 2. http://hemisphericinstitute.org/hemi/en/e-misferica-72/sosa.
Speranza, Gabriela. "El Chaco en Kassel and the Weight of Uncertainty." In *The Campo del Cielo Meteorites, Vol. 2: El Chaco*, edited by Guillermo Faivovich and Nicolás Goldberg. Stuttgart: Documenta 13 and Hatje Cantz, 2014.
Stark, Jeff. "The Dreary Coast." *PAJ* 37, no. 2 (2015): 50–51.
———. *The Dreary Coast*. Unpublished manuscript, 2014.
Stein, Gertrude. *The Autobiography of Alice B. Toklas*. New York: Harcourt, 1933.
Stiglitz, Joseph. *The Price of Inequality*. New York: W. W. Norton, 2013.
Strasberg, Lee. *The Lee Strasberg Notes*. Edited by Lola Cohen. New York: Routledge, 2010.

Strasberg, Lee, and Richard Schechner. "Working with Live Material." *Tulane Drama Review* 9, no. 1 (1964): 117–35.

Taylor, Diana. *The Archive and the Repertoire: Performing Cultural Memory in the Americas*. Durham: Duke University Press, 2003.

———. "Villa Grimaldi." June 2015. Accessed May 29, 2016. http://villagrimaldi.typefold.com/.

Tecklenburg, Nina. "Reality Enchanted, Contact Mediated: A Story of Gob Squad." *TDR* 56, no. 2 (2012): 8–33.

Tellas, Vivi. "Proyecto Archivos." Accessed March 2016. http://www.archivotellas.com.ar/.

Templeton, Fiona, and Steve Nelson. "'YOU-The City' vs. Nelson-The Critic." *TDR* 34, no. 2 (1990): 12–17.

Thompson, Nato. *Living as Form: Socially Engaged Art from 1991 to 2011*. Cambridge: MIT Press, 2012.

Tomlin, Liz. *Acts and Apparitions: Discourses on the Real in Performance Practice and Theory, 1990–2010*. Manchester, UK: Manchester University Press, 2013.

Trezise, B. and Caroline Wake, eds. *Visions and Revisions: Performance, Memory, Trauma*. Copenhagen: Museum Tusculanum Press, 2013.

Turner, Cathy. *Dramaturgy and Architecture: Theatre, Utopia, and the Built Environment*. New York: Palgrave Macmillan, 2015.

———. "Mis-Guidance and Spatial Planning: Dramaturgies of Public Space." *Contemporary Theatre Review* 20, no. 2 (2010): 149–61.

———. "Palimpsest or Potential Space? Finding a Vocabulary for Site-Specific Performance." *New Theatre Quarterly* 20 (2004): 373–90.

———. "Site-Specific Performance." *Contemporary Theatre Review* 22, no. 3 (2012): 425–26.

Van Kerkhoven, Marianne. "European Dramaturgy in the 21st Century: A Constant Movement." *Performance Research* 14, no. 3 (2009): 7–11.

Wagner, Matthew. *Shakespeare, Theater, and Time*. New York: Routledge, 2012.

Wake, Caroline. "Headphone Verbatim Theatre: Methods, Histories, Genres, Theories." *New Theatre Quarterly* 29, no. 4 (2013): 321–35.

Ward, Julie Ann. *Self, Esteemed: Contemporary Auto/biographical Theatre in Latin America*. Dissertation, University of California, Berkeley, 2013.

Werth, Brenda. *Theatre, Performance, and Memory Politics in Argentina*. New York: Palgrave Macmillan, 2010.

Weyergraf-Serra, Clara, and Martha Buskirk, eds. *The Destruction of Tilted Arc: Documents*. Cambridge, MA: MIT Press, 1991.

White, Gareth. *Audience Participation in the Theatre: Aesthetics of the Invitation*. London: Palgrave Macmillan, 2013.

Whybrow, Nicolas, ed. *Performance and the Contemporary City*. New York: Palgrave Macmillan, 2010.

Wickstrom, Maurya. *Fiery Temporalities in Theatre and Performance: The Initiation of History*. London: Methuen Engage Series at Bloomsbury Methuen, 2017.

———. "Thinking about Temporality and Theatre." *JADT* 28, no. 1 (Winter 2016).

Wiles, David. *A Short History of Western Performance Space*. Cambridge: Cambridge University Press, 2003.
———. *Theatre and Time*. London: Palgrave Macmillan, 2014.
Wilkie, Fiona. "Mapping the Terrain: A Survey of Site-Specific Performance in Britain." *New Theater Quarterly* 18, no. 2 (2002): 140–60.
———. *Performance, Transport, and Mobility: Making Passage*. New York: Palgrave Macmillan, 2015.
———. "The Production of 'Site' Site-Specific Theatre." In *Contemporary British and Irish Drama*, edited by N. Holdsworth and M. Luckhurt. 100–101. Oxford: Blackwell, 2008.
———. "Site-Specific Performance and the Mobility Turn." *Contemporary Theatre Review* 22, no. 2 (2012).
———. "Wri(gh)ting Walking." *PAJ* 29, no. 2 (2007). Wrights and Sites. http://: www.mis-guide.com.
Young, Paul David. *NewARTtheatre: Evolutions of the Performance Aesthetic*. New York: PAJ Publications, 2014.
Zukin, Sharon. "Naked City: The Death and Life of Authentic Urban Places." New York: Oxford University Press, 2010.

Index

Italicized page numbers indicate figures.

Bertie Ferdman is a contemporary performance scholar whose essays have appeared in *TDR*, *Theater*, *PAJ*, *Theatre Journal*, *Theatre Survey*, *Performance Research*, HowlRound, and TCG. She is also an associate professor at the Borough of Manhattan Community College at the City University of New York.

Theater in the Americas

The goal of the series is to publish a wide range of scholarship on theater and performance, defining theater in its broadest terms and including subjects that encompass all of the Americas.

The series focuses on the performance and production of theater and theater artists and practitioners but welcomes studies of dramatic literature as well. Meant to be inclusive, the series invites studies of traditional, experimental, and ethnic forms of theater; celebrations, festivals, and rituals that perform culture; and acts of civil disobedience that are performative in nature. We publish studies of theater and performance activities of all cultural groups within the Americas, including biographies of individuals, histories of theater companies, studies of cultural traditions, and collections of plays.

Queries and Submissions
Scott Magelssen, Editor
magelss@uw.edu

Founder and Editor, Robert A. Schanke, 2000–2014

Other Books in the Theater in the Americas Series

Shadowed Cocktails: The Plays of Philip Barry from "Paris Bound" to "The Philadelphia Story"
Donald R. Anderson

Adapturgy: The Dramaturg's Art and Theatrical Adaptation
Jane Barnette

A Gambler's Instinct: The Story of Broadway Producer Cheryl Crawford
Milly S. Barranger

Unfriendly Witnesses: Gender, Theater, and Film in the McCarthy Era
Milly S. Barranger

The Theatre of Sabina Berman: "The Agony of Ecstasy" and Other Plays
Translated by Adam Versényi
With an Essay by Jacqueline E. Bixler

Experiments in Democracy: Interracial and Cross-Cultural Exchange in American Theatre, 1912–1945
Edited by Cheryl Black and Jonathan Shandell

Staging Social Justice: Collaborating to Create Activist Theatre
Edited by Norma Bowles and Daniel-Raymond Nadon

Messiah of the New Technique: John Howard Lawson, Communism, and American Theatre, 1923–1937
Jonathan L. Chambers

Composing Ourselves: The Little Theatre Movement and the American Audience
Dorothy Chansky

Ghost Light: An Introductory Handbook for Dramaturgy
Michael Mark Chemers

The Hanlon Brothers: From Daredevil Acrobatics to Spectacle Pantomime, 1833–1931
Mark Cosdon

Richard Barr: The Playwright's Producer
David A. Crespy

Stage for Action: U.S. Social Activist Theatre in the 1940s
Chrystyna Dail

Women in Turmoil: Six Plays by Mercedes de Acosta
Edited and with an Introduction by Robert A. Schanke

Rediscovering Mordecai Gorelik: Scene Design and the American Theatre
Anne Fletcher

Californios, Anglos, and the Performance of Oligarchy in the U.S. West
Andrew Gibb

A Spectacle of Suffering: Clara Morris on the American Stage
Barbara Wallace Grossman

American Political Plays after 9/11
Edited by Allan Havis

Performing Loss: Rebuilding Community through Theater and Writing
Jodi Kanter

Presidential Libraries as Performance: Curating American Character from Herbert Hoover to George W. Bush
Jodi Kanter

Unfinished Show Business: Broadway Musicals as Works-in-Process
Bruce Kirle

Swim Pretty: Aquatic Spectacles and the Performance of Race, Gender, and Nature
Jennifer A. Kokai

Staging America: Cornerstone and Community-Based Theater
Sonja Kuftinec

Words at Play: Creative Writing and Dramaturgy
Felicia Hardison Londré

Entertaining the Nation: American Drama in the Eighteenth and Nineteenth Centuries
Tice L. Miller

Memory, Transitional Justice, and Theatre in Postdictatorship Argentina
Noe Montez

Theatre and Cartographies of Power: Repositioning the Latina/o Americas
Edited by Jimmy A. Noriega and Analola Santana

Documentary Trial Plays in Contemporary American Theater
Jacqueline O'Connor

Working in the Wings: New Perspectives on Theatre History and Labor
Edited by Elizabeth A. Osborne and Christine Woodworth

Cuba Inside Out: Revolution and Contemporary Theatre
Yael Prizant

Stage, Page, Scandals, and Vandals: William E. Burton and Nineteenth-Century American Theatre
David L. Rinear

Contemporary Latina/o Theater: Wrighting Ethnicity
Jon D. Rossini

Angels in the American Theater: Patrons, Patronage, and Philanthropy
Edited and with an Introduction by Robert A. Schanke

"That Furious Lesbian": The Story of Mercedes de Acosta
Robert A. Schanke

Caffe Cino: The Birthplace of Off-Off-Broadway
Wendell C. Stone

Teaching Performance Studies
Edited by Nathan Stucky and Cynthia Wimmer

Broadway's Bravest Woman: Selected Writings of Sophie Treadwell
Edited and with Introductions by Jerry Dickey and Miriam López-Rodríguez

The Humana Festival: The History of New Plays at Actors Theatre of Louisville
Jeffrey Ullom

Childhood and Nineteenth-Century American Theatre: The Work of the Marsh Troupe of Juvenile Actors
Shauna Vey

Our Land Is Made of Courage and Glory: Nationalist Performance of Nicaragua and Guatemala
E. J. Westlake